D1091176

"All Power to the Imagination!"

FLORIDA STATE
UNIVERSITY LIBRARIES

APR 16 1997

TALLAHASSEE, FLORIDA

Modern German Culture and Literature
General Editor: Peter Hohendahl, Cornell University
Editorial Board: Russell Berman, Stanford
University; Jane Caplan, Bryn Mawr College; Ute Frevert,
Freie Universität, Berlin; Martin Jay, University of
California, Berkeley; Sara Lennox, University
of Massachusetts, Amherst; Klaus Peter, University of
Massachusetts, Amherst; Klaus R. Scherpe,
Freie Universität, Berlin

"ALL POWER TO THE IMAGINATION!"

The West German Counterculture
from the Student Movement
to the Greens

SABINE VON DIRKE

University of Nebraska Press

Lincoln and London

HQ
799
.G5
V66
1997

© 1997 by the University of
Nebraska Press. All rights reserved
Manufactured in the United
States of America. ∞ The paper in
this book meets the minimum
requirements of American Nation-
al Standard for Information
Sciences–Permanence of Paper for
Printed Library Materials,
ANSI Z39.48-1984. Typeset in Adobe
Minion and Fontek Isis.
Book designed by R. Eckersley

Library of Congress
Cataloging-in-Publication Data
Von Dirke, Sabine, 1960–
All power to the imagination! :
the West German counterculture
from the student movement
to the Greens / Sabine von Dirke.
p. cm. – (Modern German
literature and culture). Includes
bibliographical references
and index. ISBN 0-8032-4663-3
(cl: alk paper) 1. Subculture –
Germany. 2. Social movements –
Germany – History – 20th
century. 3. Youth movement
– Germany – History –
20th century. I. Title. II. Series.
HQ799.G5V66 1997
306'.1'0943—dc20 96-19044
CIP

CONTENTS

ACKNOWLEDGMENTS

I would like to take this opportunity to express my gratitude to a few of those who have helped to shape this project. I want to thank Russell Berman, who has taught me about the Frankfurt School and encouraged me to work in the field of cultural studies. I am also highly indebted to David Wellbery and Sabine Wilke for my intellectual development. I am very grateful to my friend and colleague Michelle Mattson for the many stimulating discussions we had about my work. On the more material side of life, I owe much to my mother, whose generosity allowed me to conduct research in Germany for extended periods of time. Above all, I am deeply indebted to my husband for his manifold support, encouragement, and untiring confidence in me and my project.

INTRODUCTION: Culture and Hegemony

Postwar West Germany is often described as a stable democracy characterized by a homogenous rather than conflictual political culture. Closer inspection of the political, social, and cultural developments challenges this perception and reveals numerous instances of political discontent and protest early on in the history of the Federal Republic. The immediate postwar period and the 1950s, for example, saw their share of political protest crystallizing around armament issues. These early peace movements and other subcultural expressions of dissent were, however, successfully contained by the dominant culture. A decade later, the student movement was the first sociopolitical and cultural upheaval that thoroughly disrupted the harmony of the Adenauer era and had lasting impact on the further development of West German society. The advent of the student movement marks the beginning of the West German counterculture, which has grown over the years into a significant political force, as the success of the ecology movement and of the first alternative daily newspaper, *die tageszeitung,* attests. We cannot understand today's Germany without knowing the historical and conceptual developments of this counterculture. This study therefore examines the sub- and countercultural history of West Germany from the 1950s through the mid-1980s.

The counterculture received much attention right from the beginning, particularly from social scientists, who coined the term "new social movements" as a summarizing identifier for a variety of oppositional movements such as the citizens' initiatives, the women's movement, the ecology movement, the peace movement, the squatters' movement, and the alternative movement. Since each of these practiced an alternative politics as well as lifestyle, the term *alternative movement* is often used as a synonym for the new social movements as a whole, stressing the commonalities of the variety of oppositional and countercultural groups. Some studies blur the historical specificity of the new social movements by subsuming all postwar protest to a notion of social movement. This study uses the terms *new social movements* and *alternative movement* exclusively with respect to the countercultural groups from the mid-1970s to the mid-1980s. It is also different from much social science research, which focuses on the counterculture's origins and structure, its alternative concept of politics, and its effect on established political and social institutions.[1] Instead, it analyzes the correlation between the counterculture's alternative politics and its aesthetic concepts and artistic practices.

As the term *counterculture* already indicates, its politics, artistic practices, and aesthetic concepts emerged in opposition to those of mainstream society. At first, then, we need to clarify the key terms — *culture, counterculture, subculture,* and finally *hegemony* — that represent the conceptual framework for our analysis. Especially the two terms *counterculture* and *subculture* are often employed indiscriminately, and even the notion of culture suffers from conceptual imprecision. The latter is often used as if there were a consensus as to its definition, where in fact culture means different things for different people and social groups.

According to Raymond Williams, two noncongruent definitions of culture have become most common. The term *culture* is frequently employed in a narrow manner to refer only to the manifestations of the "cultivation of the mind," as in "arts and human intellectual work."[2] This understanding of culture brings it close to the notion of aesthetics, that is, the science of beauty and art, and is therefore preeminent in traditional literary and cultural criticism. The other notion of culture is much broader in scope and originated from anthropology and sociology. It defines culture as "the peculiar and distinctive 'way of life' of a group or class, the meanings, values and ideas embodied in institutions, in social relations, in systems of beliefs, in mores and customs, in the uses of objects and material life. Culture is the distinctive shapes in which this material and social organisation of life expresses itself. . . . Culture is the way the social relations of a group are structured and shaped: but it is also the way those shapes are experienced, understood and interpreted."[3] This all-encompassing definition conceptualizes culture both as material manifestation—for instance, works of art—and as institutions and processes, while emphasizing the latter. Second, it views society not as a homogenous entity but as a collection of various social groups, which develop distinct cultures and struggle with each other for dominance, or in other words, for cultural hegemony.

The concept of hegemony stems from Antonio Gramsci's *Prison Notebooks*,[4] which he wrote during his incarceration under the Fascist regime in Italy from 1929 to 1935. Gramsci's concept found widespread interest among Western Marxists after World War II, since it theorizes why the working class has failed as the historical revolutionary subject in Western industrialized societies and has instead become more and more integrated into the existing economic and social order. The notion of integration lies at the center of the Gramscian idea of hegemony. In contrast to coercive domination, hegemony represents rule through consent. The ruling class or configuration of ruling social groups succeeds in establishing a framework of ideas, beliefs, and values, which it disseminates through the various institutions of civil society, such as the educational system, the church, and the media. Thus the ruling elites mold the majority's worldviews, interests, and desires according to their own. The ruling classes appear more as leaders than as oppressors because they have convinced the majority to follow them. For Gramsci, hegemony was characteristic of postfeudal, particularly bourgeois societies and was the latter's secret of success.

The scholars at the Birmingham Center for Contemporary Cultural Studies adopted Gramsci's theory of hegemony and applied it to postwar Great Britain. Comparing the prewar to the postwar period, they argue that the 1950s represent a "period of true 'hegemonic domination.'"[5] They stress the ideological role of affluence for dismantling working-class resistance and for generating the "spontaneous consent" to the authority of the dominant classes. The functioning of hegemonic domination has become increasingly problematic since the 1960s owing to a polarization of society. As a result, conflict has appeared more and more on all levels of society, and while "the dominant classes retain power, . . . their 'repertoire' of control is progressively challenged, weakened, exhausted."[6] This description holds true for postwar West Germany as well, which experienced a period of class consent and social harmony under the auspices of the "economic miracle," the period of exuberant economic growth from the 1950s to the late 1960s.

If, however, rule by hegemony requires consent, then the hegemonic powers have to generate it through persuasion rather than force. Yet this implies that there is always the potential for dissent. Hence hegemony "is a matter of the nature of the balance struck between contending classes: the compromises made to sustain it; the relations of force; the solutions adopted. . . . The idea of 'permanent class hegemony' or of 'permanent incorporation' must be ditched."[7] Cultural hegemony is thus stable but always contested, not only by various classes but especially from within the hegemonic class by sub- and countercultures.

Countercultures position themselves explicitly and fundamentally against their dominant counterpart and try to develop an alternative way of life. They challenge the hegemonic culture with a holistic approach, negating all of its values and traditions and struggling for radical and comprehensive change. In contrast, subcultures can coexist more easily with the hegemonic culture, since they do not stand in fundamental opposition to it. Members of subcultures relate to the hegemonic culture differently, particularly regarding work and leisure time. They accept the standards of the hegemonic culture with respect to their work time, but not with respect to their leisure time. Subcultures do not call for or work toward a transformation of society as long as they can carve out a niche for themselves during their leisure time.

Although subcultures can develop in all social strata, the research of the Birmingham Center suggests that subcultures are mostly working-class phenomena. While subcultures comply with the hegemonic culture regarding the workplace and articulate their dissent only during their leisure time and mostly through a particular style of clothing and behavior, countercultures do not make this distinction but challenge the hegemonic culture on all fronts. Countercultures often receive therefore much more public attention than subcultures, since their challenge to the established culture is not only fundamental but also comes from within the hegemonic culture.[8] Countercultures are primarily middle-class phenomena. Following these definitions, I understand the student movement and the subsequent oppositional movements as countercultures and not as subcultures, since they too strove for fundamental political and social transformations.

Finally, although I prefer the all-encompassing definition of culture as a social group's articulation of its whole way of life, this study has a more narrow scope. It focuses on those aspects of the counterculture that express its perception of the work of art and the status and function of artistic production and reception within society. In order to distinguish this specific part of culture from culture as a whole way of life, the term *aesthetic culture* is used throughout this study. The term should not be taken to imply a narrow definition of culture as a separate sphere autonomous from other spheres of life such as economics and politics. Quite to the contrary, this study of the West German counterculture examines precisely how alternative political ideas and theories were translated into alternative notions of art and cultural politics that challenged those of the hegemonic culture.

In order to gain a better understanding of the cultural caesura that the student movement from the mid-1960s to the early 1970s still represents for West Germany today, chapter 1 maps out the social and political atmosphere of the 1950s, in which the generation of the student activists grew up. It discusses the first youth subcultures—the working-class Halbstarken phenomenon and the middle-class existentialists—which boomed only for a short period of time during the middle and late 1950s. In comparison to the countercultural developments a decade later, which grew into a lasting social force, the hegemonic parent culture was still successful in reintegrating the dissident voices in the 1950s. In addition, this chapter functions as a further elaboration of the theoretical underpinnings of this study regarding the distinction between sub- and countercultures.

Chapter 2 is devoted to the first genuine counterculture, which originated in the university and was thus called the student movement. It traces the student movement's adaptation of the work of the Frankfurt school—mainly the theories of Herbert Marcuse, Theodor W. Adorno, and Walter Benjamin—for its attack on the "bourgeois" ideology of the autonomy of art and culture. It concludes by juxtaposing one of the alternative aesthetic practices of the student movement, the agitprop street theater, with the debate about the "death of literature" in 1968–69 that the students' rejection of a "bourgeois" aesthetic had ignited.

Chapter 3 examines the continuation of this literary critical debate in the mid-1970s, centering on the debate about New Subjectivity, and the implications of the Red Army Faction's terrorism on the political climate in the Federal Republic of Germany. The debate on New Subjectivity carried a heavy ideological charge. Many critics hailed it as the return of the West German writers to belles-lettres and true literary themes such as individual subjectivity after the politicization of culture and the preference for operative and documentary genres during the 1960s. The comparison of a paradigmatic literary text of New Subjectivity, Peter Handke's *A Moment of True Feeling*, and a nonliterary text originating in the counterculture and addressing the issue of terrorist violence, the famous Buback Obituary, demonstrates that the discourse of New Subjectivity reached beyond the confines of literature. Far from representing a total break with the student movement of the 1960s, it in fact made a significant contribution to the formation of the post-1968 counterculture. Since New Subjectivity was, however, only perceived as a literary discourse, the Buback Obituary, which used a new subjectivist approach to discuss terrorist violence, was misunderstood and created a public uproar. Close examination of the discourse on terrorism is necessary to comprehend the development of the counterculture in the wake of the student movement, since the hegemonic culture accused the entire counterculture of having a strong affinity to terrorism — an accusation that in turn led to further estrangement of the counterculture from mainstream West Germany.

The following two chapters examine the new social movements of the 1970s and 1980s. The broad range of the new social movements, as well as the fact that many of them retreated from the established public sphere, raises methodological problems that need to be addressed first. Instead of performing a variety of local analyses of individual new social movements, my study is guided by the observation that there were a number of common constituents to the fundamental opposition that the multitude of new social movements articulated. Consequently, they shared a matrix of intersecting and overlapping concepts, attitudes, and cultural practices that take them beyond their diversity and unify them as one cultural phenomenon. I refer to this shared way of life, or in other words, attempts to develop alternative social structures,[9] as the alternative culture (*Alternativkultur*) instead of alternative movement, a term that highlights the dimension of political activism.

In the case of the alternative culture it is extraordinarily difficult to find written manifestations (texts), because the alternative culture opposed the privileging of the written word traditionally characteristic of mainstream "high" culture. Writing therefore was not necessarily meant to be published but became a therapeutic mode of self-expression and self-actualization with strong autobiographical features, and it was often distributed solely within a small circle of friends. For this concept of writing—referred to as the "Writing Movement" (*Schreibbewegung*)—literary categories were irrelevant and replaced with the category of authenticity.[10] For instance, Fritz Zorn's *Mars*, the story of his bourgeois socialization or rather alienation, and Verena Stefan's *Shedding*, the story of her feminist liberation, are on the one hand, strongly indebted to the idea of authenticity, since they clearly mark that the author and narrator or protagonist are one and the same person. On the other hand, these two books are exceptions to this trend because they were published. In addition, the alternative culture took a strong antitheoretical stance in response to the student movement's proliferating, highly theoretical discourse, which could be summarized in analogy to many other alternative slogans: "Theory? No, Thank You!" (*Theorie?—Nein Danke!*).

The alternative culture was not mute but successfully established its own channels of publication, which played an important role for its self-perception. This study examines such nonliterary materials as fliers, political platforms, and above all articles from the first West German alternative daily newspaper—*die tageszeitung* (the daily times). Chapter 4 is therefore devoted to *die tageszeitung*, generally referred to as *die taz*, which represents to date one of the most successful attempts of establishing an alternative public sphere.

Chapter 4 not only summarizes the historical development of *die taz* but also shows how the return to the category of subjectivity was played out in terms of the public sphere by analyzing the *taz*'s journalistic concept and practices in comparison to those of the established press.

Chapter 5 discusses the alternative culture's aesthetic concepts and practices based on close scrutiny of the cultural section from the first publication of the *taz* in 1979 to 1983. This chapter analyzes how the alternative concept of a participatory, grassroots politics was translated into the notion of a participatory culture. An embrace of elements of folk culture because of its perceived participatory and collective nature and a rejection of a highly intellectual literary culture in favor of an aesthetic of the body and the image characterize the alternative culture during the late 1970s and early 1980s.

Chapter 6 focuses on the ecology movement and the West German party of the Greens. The ecology movement has had the most lasting influence on West German society precisely because it developed into a viable political party. Furthermore, the Greens incorporated most of the demands of the various new social movements and can therefore legitimately be perceived as a mouthpiece of the alternative culture up to the mid-1980s. The stance of this green-alternative culture was charged to be not only antitheoretical but also antiaesthetic. Ecological discourse and the party of the Greens function as perfect examples for an analysis of the Greens' failure to develop a coherent aesthetic theory.

Finally, by way of comparison, the conclusion summarizes the transformations of aesthetic paradigms from the student movement to the green alternative culture. The trajectory of this development can be summarized as follows: The alternative culture moved away from the prescriptive aesthetics of the late student movement's orthodox Marxism, which was based on a rigidly defined class subject, and toward a reintegration of a variety of aesthetic positions based on the plurality of subject positions and the cultural diversity of contemporary West Germany. Whether the constant changes that the West German counterculture underwent since its beginnings in the 1960s represent indeed a sellout is the last question that this study addresses.

CHAPTER 1: Cultural Hegemony and Youth Subcultures in the 1950s

*Ja dann wird wieder in die hände gespuckt
wir steigern das bruttosozialprodukt.*

*Yeah, now we roll up our sleeves again
We're raising the gross national product.*

Geier Sturzflug, "Bruttosozialprodukt"
(Gross national product), 1977

The rock band Geier Sturzflug's "Bruttosozialprodukt," with lyrics set to a happy melody reminiscent of 1950s popular music, became a big hit in the early 1980s in the context of the country's political turn — the *Wende*, as it was called in German. After thirteen years with the Social Democratic–Liberal (SPD-FDP) coalition, the party credited with the postwar "economic miracle," at the helm, the Christian Democratic Union (CDU) and its Bavarian twin the Christian Social Union (CSU) took over and promised change. Geier Sturzflug's New Wave song captures in ironic fashion the spirit of mainstream West German society at both times — the 1950s and the 1980s — when the country, led by the center-right parties, focused all its energy on the economy. The song satirizes German *Fleiß* (industriousness), to which popular opinion ascribes the quick postwar recovery. The song tells the tale of elderly and disabled people secretly hurrying to the factory when the whistle blows early in the morning and turning into workaholics who sing in unison with the work rhythm. As the manager of Geier Sturzflug points out, the band had no intention of praising capitalism and the economic boom that materialized in the 1980s but instead wanted to ridicule the workaholism and consumerism of contemporary West German society.[1] But even satire is not immune to reappropriation by mainstream culture and on the hegemonic forces' own terms.

Another song by Geier Sturzflug, "Besuchen sie Europa, solange es noch steht" (Visit Europe while it's still there), which thematizes the arms race between the two superpowers and the potential of Europe's going up in the flames of a nuclear war, points up to more parallels between the two decades. The introduction of a new weapon system—the neutron bomb—by the Carter administration in 1978 and Ronald Reagan's anti-Soviet rhetoric in the 1980s were direct descendants of the arms race and Cold War mentality of the 1950s. As a result, both periods gave rise to anticommunism and arms protests.

In light of these parallels, the popular 1950s revival occurring from the late 1970s to the mid-1980s did not come as a surprise. The mass media disseminated a picture of the 1950s as a happy time of swinging petticoats, asymmetrical design, and sentimental Tin Pan Alley music. Though research on all aspects of life in the 1950s was published in the early 1980s, detailed or critical assessments were ignored in favor of a mythical reconstruction of this era—the "falsche Fünfziger" as a *Spiegel* article commented with a critical pun.[2] "Falsche Fünfziger" literally means counterfeited fifty-mark bills and figuratively refers to a deceitful person. From a 1980s perspective the "economic miracle" looked like a "fake fifty" in this double sense. On the one hand, West Germany experienced tremendous economic growth during the 1950s, which slowly but surely put more money into working people's pockets. On the other hand, the revival's mythical image of the 1950s as a happy-go-lucky time was as insubstantial as counterfeit money. The prosperity was bought at the expense of the future: the safe and sound promises of the 1950s had turned into potential ecological and nuclear disaster by the 1980s.

The song "Gross National Product" points precisely to this deceptive image of the 1950s in their 1980s revival. It expresses the 1980s conservative political agenda—the appeal to the 1950s virtues of industriousness and a high work ethic—but in a highly ironic fashion, adopting the happy-go-lucky music of the most popular genre of the 1950s—the *Schlager* (Tin Pan Alley music). Its lyrics, however, are a far cry from those of the *Schlager*, whose world consisted of white marriage carriages and romantic nights in Florence and Paris.[3] The *Schlager*'s lyrics portrayed a world of fantasies and not realities such as work. They were affirmative and uncritical, reflecting the carefree attitude of the majority, which did not think of questioning society's materialism as Geier Sturzflug's lyrics do twenty years later. Geier Sturzflug's deliberate juxtaposition of a sentimental 1950s popular music form with modern social reality—work, the economy, and consumerism—imbues the whole song with an ironic and subversive effect. The song thereby criticizes the attempt to anachronistically revive the culture of the past and points to the sore spot in both the CDU/CSU's invocation of the 1950s and the decade's mythical reconstruction by the entertainment industry. The material basis of life in the 1980s, when the CDU/CSU took over government, was quite different from that of the 1950s. In the 1950s the majority of West Germans gained in material wealth, and hardly anybody was left behind in the long run. This no longer held true for the 1980s, when the Federal Republic moved toward the "two-thirds" society, where a third of society is left to fall through the widening cracks of the welfare state while the other two thirds enjoy a higher and higher standard of living—a trend aggravated by unification.

Apart from its revival in the 1980s, the decade of the 1950s merits closer inspection because it was the formative period for the hegemonic culture of West Germany and for the generation that became the first carrier of a lasting counterculture a decade later, namely, the student movement. The members of the student movement generation were socialized during the 1950s primarily through the university track of *Gymnasium* (high school), which they attended in preparation for their future status as the professional and cultural elite. Their protest was a rebellion against the "fake fifties," which Margarete von Trotta referred to as "times of lead" in *Die Bleierne Zeit*, her film exploring the biographies of two members of this generation, Gudrun Ensslin, whose middle-class life ended in terrorism, and her sister, who became an activist in the women's movement.[4]

Studying the material conditions and the hegemonic aesthetic culture under which these young West Germans were socialized is necessary in order to understand the criticism they raised a decade later. This chapter first examines the most important aspects of 1950s culture, particularly the correlation between the "economic miracle," political consciousness (or perhaps the lack thereof), and dominant aesthetic paradigms. Finally, we turn to instances of rebellion against the secure world of the 1950s, namely, the first youth subcultures in postwar West Germany: the existentialist youth and the Halbstarken.

The "Economic Miracle"

The "economic miracle" was made possible only by focusing all human resources on reconstruction and industrial productivity, quite as the song *Gross National Product* describes. This project indeed paid off by transforming the Allied start-up capital, the money provided by the Marshall Plan, into an economic success story. In 1952 the West German economy already had a trade surplus, and only two years later West Germany occupied the third position in world trade behind the United States and Great Britain. This economic boom was part of a larger global constellation, mainly shaped by the growing tensions between the two superpowers, whose confrontation the Federal Republic felt so harshly again in the 1980s. The first violent eruption of this tension, the Korean War (1950–54), gave the West German economy a hefty boost, leading to tremendous growth rates and virtually full employment by 1960, both unthinkable today. The "economic miracle" allowed all West Germans to get their piece of the pie, which amounted to an average increase in wages of 76 percent.[5]

The controversy surrounding the currency reform of 1948 masterminded by Ludwig Erhard is forgotten in today's celebration of the "economic miracle." Since the Soviet zone did not participate, the currency reform indicated that a unified Germany might not emerge from the ashes of the Second World War. Lifting price controls and abandoning food stamps created at first more hardship than immediate benefit for the general population. Still, the hard new currency brought back plenty of goods previously available only on the black market. But at the same time, it produced price hikes, which put the merchandise in the shop windows beyond the means of most Germans, many of whom had been unemployed or had earned only low wages in 1948 and 1949. For all of these reasons, the reform initially generated resentment and strikes.[6] But as soon as the majority of West Germans had the wherewithal to stuff themselves to match the portly physique of their economic leader, they embraced Ludwig Erhard's concept of the social market economy wholeheartedly. Erhard's economic program allowed the West Germans to find a positive moment of identification with their country after the Holocaust and World War II had made it difficult to develop a German national identity. The phrase "Made in Germany" filled the West Germans with pride and their wallets with hard DM currency.

The "economic miracle" had mobilized the good old German virtues of discipline and industriousness and turned society quickly into one big consumer club. "Wealth for Everyone!" became its slogan, which aimed at eroding class identifications.[7] The hegemonic discourse no longer conceptualized West Germany as a class society but as a leveled-out or well-adjusted middle-class society.[8] This ideological articulation of the "economic miracle" proclaimed the end of class distinctions and the beginning of a new era in which the performance principle would allow all citizens to rise as high as their talents and industriousness would take them. Most income went into consumption, starting with food as a top priority after the years of undernourishment and deprivation. A tremendous feeding frenzy, the *Freß-Welle*, washed over the country in the 1950s. As productivity rose and vacation time increased, the West German travel mania took the place of this preoccupation with food. Since the mid-1950s larger and larger numbers of vacationers flocked to the *Hunnen-Grill*, the Mediterranean beaches, for the sun, still unencumbered by worries about skin cancer or polluted beaches.

While the West Germans performed well in the economic arena, their progress toward the development of a democratic culture was less clear. The historically high turnout on election days should not deceive us about political interest in the 1950s. "Politics? No, thank you!" was the most commonly held stance among the West Germans well into the 1960s. Like burned children, the majority turned their backs on active political engagement after their stint with National Socialism. Instead of confronting the "most recent past," as the twelve years of Nazi rule were commonly referred to, the Federal Republic was happy to settle into a general amnesia about this time and especially about the Holocaust. Those who went to school during the 1950s and 1960s were drilled on history from Greek and Roman antiquity to the glory days of the Holy Roman Empire. One short period of German history remained, however, conspicuously absent—that from 1933 to 1945.[9] Lack of information meant lack of knowledge and the danger of the subtle continuation of long-cherished myths and mentalities. Numerous opinion polls conducted during the 1950s show West German society still strongly influenced by authoritarian structures and thinking.[10]

A retreat from politics altogether was the response of the majority of the younger West Germans to their experience with National Socialism and the hardship of the war and immediate postwar years. Particularly those who had fully participated in the Nazis' youth organizations saw their youthful idealism abused and betrayed. As a result, they had grown weary of political ideas and were prone to view politics only as propaganda and ideology.[11] Moreover, for most of them no active political education took place—neither at home nor in school. In his groundbreaking study of German youth from 1945 to 1955, Helmut Schelsky, one of the dominant empirical sociologists in postwar West Germany, called this generation the skeptical one and hailed it for its dispassionate and pragmatic attitude toward life. He was not concerned about the depoliticization of youth and life in West Germany, but viewed it as a necessary development. According to his research, these young Germans were more interested in their professional career, material wealth, and private happiness than in the larger sociopolitical context. He finds the roots of this pragmatism in the immediate postwar situation, which required this generation to perform like adults in order to insure the subsistence of their often fatherless families.[12]

Nevertheless, the 1950s youth accepted the Federal Republic's representative democracy. It approached the state, however, with a consumerist attitude, viewing it first and foremost as the guarantor of economic and social stability. It would be wrong to blame solely the young for this attitude. After all, they did as expected and emulated their parents, who had been focused on the material aspects of life since the end of the war.[13] At the same time, a minority of this very same youth was the first to show signs of discomfort with the

Republic of the "economic miracle" and dissent from mainstream culture.

Hegemonic Culture: Between Restoration and Innovation

Economic growth meant more spending money and leisure time, generating a tremendous expansion of the sphere of culture during the 1950s. Like the school system, aesthetic culture showed most clearly the differentiation of society, which the ideology of affluence and of the middle-class society tried to diffuse. An overarching binary structure of institutionalized culture developed from the very beginning of the Federal Republic, namely, the split into a minority culture of the educated elites and a majority culture of the less-educated masses. One feature was and until today remains absent: no genuine proletarian culture emerged in postwar West Germany. This was due not only to the new ideology of the satisfied middle-class society but to the Nazis' successful destruction of the thriving working-class consciousness and culture of the Weimar Republic.

Many of the left-wing intellectuals and artists who survived in exile did not return to the West but settled in the East. The result was a dearth of leftist intellectuals and artists in the Federal Republic, who could have helped to recreate a genuine proletarian culture. In addition, the GDR offered no convincing alternative cultural model. Quite to the contrary, the intensity with which state authorities shaped and controlled the sphere of East German culture was too reminiscent of the totalitarian Nazi regime for the taste of the West Germans and their allies. The anticommunism characteristic of Cold War rhetoric in the 1950s foreclosed an open discussion of a socialist aesthetic or any alternative, comprehensive cultural politics. Finally, the Social Democratic Party (SPD) and the unions had embarked on an integrationist course, realizing that the economic success of the Federal Republic was more and more eroding the remnants of working-class consciousness and culture. In a strategic move, the SPD shed the last socialist planks from its party platform in 1957 in order to position itself better for being elected to govern the country.

Even though only a small proportion of the entire West German population shared the aesthetic paradigms of the educated elites, those paradigms remain central to this study for two reasons. First of all, this elite culture was hegemonic; in other words, these institutionally sanctioned artistic expressions represented the standards against which all other cultural expressions were measured. Schools and universities helped to establish the hegemony of these aesthetic paradigms by teaching them to the next generation of the elite, which in many instances happened to be the future student activists who attended *Gymnasium* during the 1950s and early 1960s. But schools were not the only source of aesthetic education. The parents' cultural preferences also played a significant role, as well as the debates carried out in the public sphere, primarily in the cultural sections of newspapers or specific cultural journals to which the children of the educated elites had access.

The hegemonic culture was not, however, totally homogeneous. Two dominant cultural paradigms emerged in close correlation to the agenda of the political parties, as Jost Hermand points out. He has labeled them the conservative Adenauer agenda and the liberal Erhard agenda, after the two leaders most prominent in shaping the Federal Republic during the 1950s.[14] These two approaches to aesthetic culture differed in many ways, but they were not mutually exclusive. They rather formed the "historical bloc," "an alliance of ruling-class factions" that is necessary for establishing cultural hegemony, which is based, after all, on the consent of the subordinate social strata.[15]

According to Hermand, the liberal spectrum was divided on the issue of the mass media and the entertainment industry into a populist group and an elitist-modernist group. For the populist liberals, the freedom of choice that the individual exercises in the sphere of economics applied also to the sphere of culture. They did not argue for a unified culture but saw its differentiation into a variety of cultural options as an expression of an open, pluralist society. But even those who embraced a pluralist culture made a qualitative distinction between "low" mass culture and the "high" culture of the elite. A characteristic of the liberal spectrum was its preference for innovation in aesthetic culture rather than preservation. Innovation meant finding new and different artistic forms. Though its proponents did not dismiss the classics or the heritage of Western culture in general, they rejected any form of a realist aesthetic, that is, content-oriented and referential works of art, as historically obsolete. In its most radical articulation, these liberal critics embraced a formalist aesthetic and viewed abstract art, serial music, and experimental literature as superior forms of art.

Historical and political forces molded this new formalist aesthetic. Because of the Nazis, Germany had been cut off from all international cultural developments between 1933 and 1945. As a result, there was a strong desire to bridge this gap and catch up. Furthermore, the overt political instrumentalization of art and the emergence of socialist realism as the prescribed aesthetic in the Eastern Bloc rendered realist models impossible in the West for political reasons. Liberal critics saw any kind of engaged art—whether politically, religiously, or commercially inspired—as an aesthetic regression.[16] They adhered instead to the Kantian paradigm of the autonomy of art—a theory they shared with the conservative culture critics. On the other hand, the definition of autonomy by this liberal agenda differed from that of the conservatives. Hermand summarizes the elitist-modernist aesthetic as a drive for autonomy from ideological implications by reducing art to its so-called material basis, be it form, color, sound, or words, as in the aestheticism of the turn of the century.[17] He points out that the antirealist postulate was much more difficult to uphold in literary production because of the nature of literature, which is more content bound than the fine arts or music. The field of literature therefore represents the most diverse and contested among the arts. The elitist modernist critics hailed poetry, and especially "concrete poetry" (*Konkrete Poesie*),[18] as the most modern and innovative literary genre and proclaimed the novel to be in a deep crisis if not obsolete. Other authors such as Heinrich Böll continued to write novels in a realist tradition.

The literature written during a specific period does not necessarily help in comprehending the hegemonic aesthetic paradigm because of the diversity of styles that can be found in any period. Literary criticism in journals and the literary scholarship at German universities give us a much clearer picture. Academic literary criticism plays an important role in forming the canon and validating an analytic-interpretive approach to literature. Academic literary scholarship is of special interest for us, because all German teachers for the schools were trained at the university. The teachers not only carried the analytic-interpretive methods they had learned there into the schools but also combined them with a specific pedagogical objective by and large in accordance with the conservative Adenauer agenda. The elitist-modernist aesthetic outlined above developed instead outside the academy in the cultural sections of the newspapers and in art and literature journals. If it entered the university at all, it was in the margins.

Not innovation but preservation, the cultivation of the literary heritage, was central to the Adenauer agenda and its accompanying academic literary scholarship. The canonic works (*Klassiker*) of German literature constituted the almost exclusive reading at the universities and the high schools, since those works appeared to be safely distant from the collaboration of the academic discipline of German literary studies (*Germanistik*) with the Nazi regime. The discipline as a whole reacted like most Germans; it retreated from politics and settled into a comfortable amnesia about its role from 1933 to 1945. An attempt to come to terms with the discipline's past of complicity with Nazism did not take place until the infamous annual conference of the German Literary Studies Association (*Germanisten-Tag*) in 1966.[19] The past had its effect on the literary scholarship nonetheless.

A good case in point is the reception of exile literature (*Exilliteratur*). Aside from the classics, literary anthologies used in West German schools contained authors of the inner emigration (*Innere Emigration*) such as Werner Bergengruen, Hans Carossa, and Ernst Jünger, as well Ernst Wiechert and even some writers who had been supportive of Nazism. These authors outnumbered by far representatives of contemporary literature and the Weimar Republic.[20] The Nazis had been successful after all with their denunciation of literary modernism as "degenerate" and "un-German" (*undeutsch*). The books that were burned in May 1933 and their authors did not return to the classrooms in the 1950s. The reception of exile literature took place outside the schools and academia much later, during the 1960s and 1970s. As a result, modern urban life, which was a strong thematic focus of literary modernism during the Weimar Republic, was absent from the schools' literary anthologies. Instead, the school-books presented an image of Germany as an idyllic agrarian culture.[21] It is, however, questionable whether this image promoted the proclaimed pedagogical objectives of the German literature classes, which defined literature as advice for life (*Lebenshilfe*) and aimed beyond the aesthetic at the ethical education of its students through literature. If this literary canon did not even present the life world of the students, the question arises how it could have functioned as an "interpretation of life" (*Seinsdeutung*) and "illumination of the world" (*Daseineserhellung*),[22] to cite only two of the most frequent terms used at the time in defining the function of the German literature class.

As already mentioned, the school curricula have to be seen in close correlation with the literary scholarship practiced at the universities. The leading West German scholars despised extratextual aspects of literary analysis as ideologically tainted and hailed New Criticism under the German label *Werkimmanenz*. Not sociohistorical categories or an Enlightenment epistemology, but sympathetic understanding, spiritual consubstantiality, and literature as an inner experience were the key words for the interpretive project—best exemplified by Emil Staiger's *Die Kunst der Interpretation*, which drew strongly on Martin Heidegger's ontological definition of art. Like the liberal, avant-gardist criticism, the conservative literary scholarship defined literature as an autonomous totality. The German literature class became therefore an exercise in high idealism that responded to "the needs of the suffering and isolated individual with universal humanism, to physical misery with beauty of the soul, to external slavery with inner freedom, to brutal egotism with duty and virtue. The spiritual and intellectual world was separated out from civilization and elevated as a value in itself. . . . The reception of cultural activities and objects gained a dignity that placed it far above daily life, becoming an hour of worship and edification."[23] With their traditional canon and their New Criticism approach, the German literature classes of the 1950s were not a hotbed of critical thinking but an exercise in restoration in the service of the hegemonic classes.

Youth Subcultures in the 1950s: Existentialists and Halbstarke

While the majority of the students, if they did not embrace this aesthetic, at least endured it with indifference, a minority of the 1950s youth started to challenge it, indicating that not all was well in the young Federal Republic. This minority recognized the discrepancy between the conservative worldview passed on in German literature classes and their real life experiences. The conservative literary canon had no meaning for them, and they turned instead to contemporary foreign literature shunned by the high school. French existentialism and the American beat poets became strong influences on some high school and university students. These students started to call the hegemonic aesthetic into question, as the recollections of a member of this 1950s youth demonstrates:

> The literature we were taught in school was pretty and vacuous, but in a kitschy way. Hesse was still bearable, but Carossa, Binding, Wiechert, that hurt. We had to discuss these blowhards in school. It was like we were being trained in hypocrisy. And we wanted to distance ourselves from this kind of literature. We had some teachers in school with whom we could talk, but in the end, even they always asked, What about the Good? Really fake junk. We were fascinated by Sartre. . . . Through existentialism, I got access to another way of thinking. I no longer asked myself about the Good, the True and the Beautiful—but I am my freedom. So I found my own way of thinking, and no longer thought or behaved as expected.[24]

Such self-reflective statements were not typical for the 1950s. As a matter of fact, the 1950s youth rarely articulated its dissent in an oral or written form. Instead, it realized its challenge to the hegemonic culture rather "obliquely, in style."[25] Students expressed their opposition not in programs and political demands but in their aesthetic preferences, most visibly in their style of clothing and their choice of music. Although their opposition was restricted to their leisure time and they therefore represented subcultures that did not grow into a lasting counterculture, dissent through style should not be reduced to the meaningless cycle of fashions that come and go.

As Dick Hebdige has convincingly argued in his study of punks in the United Kingdom, "style in subculture is . . . pregnant with significance. Its transformations go 'against nature,' interrupting the process of normalization. As such they are gestures, movements toward a speech which offends the silent majority, which challenges the principle of unity and cohesion, which contradicts the myth of consensus."[26]

The two 1950s subcultures which we will subsequently discuss—the existentialists and the Halbstarken—did precisely this: their emergence belied the ideology of the satisfied middle-class society and represented a prelude to the coming cultural disaffiliation of larger and larger parts of the younger generation. They resented and offended the parent culture but did not yet aim at a radical change of society. These two subcultures were quite distinct from each other, reflecting the social stratification of postwar West Germany. The Halbstarken phenomenon consisted mostly of working-class youth, whereas high school and university students constituted the existentialist bohemia.[27]

Hans-Hermann Krüger, who has researched the existentialist subculture most thoroughly, titled one of his articles on this subject "I didn't see any Exis: Searching for a youth counterculture in the 1950s."[28] His title highlights the minority status of this group, which was so small that it did not dominate the visual landscape of the 1950s as the punks would two decades later. The existentialists were indeed less colorful than the punks, but they shared black as their favorite color. This is no coincidence. The youth of both decades saw "No Future" written on the horizon. As the color defining sadness and sorrow in Western culture, black was dominant for both men's and women's styles. Blue jeans and black parkas were main components of the male existentialist outfit, while black turtleneck sweaters could be worn by both sexes. The existentialist young women looked quite different from the nice girl next door in a white blouse and pleated skirt. Aside from their black clothes, the women sported either supershort haircuts like Jean Seberg's in the film *Breathless* or high hairdos dyed blond like Brigitte Bardot's. Men's clothing items were not off-limits for women either, as the recollection of a female "Exi" shows: "It started with black turtlenecks, then hair dyed white, black slacks, black coat, black head scarf, black shoes, black socks, and a long black woman's pipe."[29]

Unisex clothing was not an issue for the predominantly male subculture of the Halbstarken, whose perception of the female gender role did not differ from those of their parents. The Halbstarken subculture was novel, however, in appropriating elements of American mass culture denounced by conservative cultural critics. Rock and roll was the music of the Halbstarken. Buddy Holly and Elvis Presley were their idols. The rebel images of James Dean and Marlon Brando were their inspiration. They not only dressed like their film and music heroes—tight jeans, leather jackets, small ties, greasy hair—but also imitated their provocative behavior. This style violated the dress and behavioral code of the dominant culture as much as the existentialists' black outfits. The tight jeans showed off the body. The long and carefully styled hair ridiculed the 1950s clean-cut image of masculinity.

We might smile today at the public outrage that alternative dress codes ignited in the Federal Republic, but we should not forget about the historicity of cultural developments. For one, fashion had not yet reached the postmodern stage of anything goes, but functioned as a social signifier and element of control back then more so than in today's society. Secondly, West Germans still adhered to more rigid and stifling social norms during the 1950s than did Americans. Not only did the existentialists' and Halbstarken's break with the prescribed dress code of the time aim at distinguishing them from the nondescript majority culture, but their particular styles represented a symbolic articulation of dissent and resistance as well. Although as Hebdige suggests, it is more useful to regard subcultural styles as "mutations and extensions of existing codes rather than as the 'pure' expression of creative drives,"[30] the Halbstarken style was not simply an unimaginative imitation of American mass media imagery, as it was often branded by conservative critics. Using Claude Lévi-Strauss's concept of homology, Hebdige argues that style represents a "meaningful mutation," since the subculture picks from the existing cultural codes only those objects in which it recognizes its central values held and reflected. The unisex attire worn by many existentialists functioned as a symbolic rejection of traditional gender roles.

At a time when a woman's life was measured by her marital success, rejecting the publicly endorsed image of femininity required courage perhaps equal to political protest.

The reception of the French existentialist bohemia went, however, beyond attire. Sartre's existentialism, with its nihilistic tendencies and emphasis on individual choices, stood in striking opposition to the conservative and often clerical worldview imposed on the students in school. The same held true for the American beat poets such as Kerouac, Ginsberg, and Corso. Yet the West German existentialist youth was far less radical than their American role models. Though they admired it, hardly any member of this generation realized the beat generation's radical break with society. Dissent was still restricted to leisure time activities while one pursued an acceptable career. Drugs were not part of this rebellion against the parents either, and only a few dared to practice the free sex propounded by their role models. The exploration of sex and drugs was left to the next decade.

Existentialist philosophy, however, provided an intellectual framework for articulating the deeply felt resentment of the double standards that West German middle-class youth encountered everywhere in mainstream culture. At the center of the existentialist youth's alienation and resentment was their parents' material orientation, philistine lifestyles, and voluntary subjugation to stifling social norms. The existentialist youth opposed them with an emphatic embrace of personal freedom and individuality.[31] Krüger argues that the existentialist subculture represented varying degrees of identification with its French and American predecessors rather than a unified group.[32] This also distinguishes the existentialists from their working-class counterpart, the Halbstarken, with their strong group identity and hierarchical structures.

Not until the late 1960s did middle-class youth protest gain the kind of public attention attained by the Halbstarken in the 1950s. The Halbstarken were discussed everywhere — in the media, in academic circles, and even in the federal parliament.[33] Why did the Halbstarken elicit an almost panicked response from the hegemonic culture? The worried attention could not have been due to the numbers of youth engaged in this mode of dissent. A sociological study of the 1950s that asked the question "How strong are the Halbstarken?" pointed out their minority status and reminded the adult world to keep things in perspective: "Those who see today's youth only from the narrow perspective of the *Halbstarken-Problem* run the danger of a one-sided judgment, focusing only on those excesses that have and will always exist, and overlooking the normal and healthy aspects of today's youth."[34]

The Halbstarken were a minority phenomenon as much as the existentialists, though they were probably less of a threat than the latter because they lacked a broader ideological vision of rebellion.[35] But in comparison to the existentialists, who retreated from the public eye into their smoky enclaves, the jazz clubs, the Halbstarken appeared in public. These fifteen- to twenty-year-old males gathered in groups on streets, public squares, and parks. They literally occupied these spaces with their vandalism, harassment of passersby, conscious violation of traffic rules, contempt for authority, and noise. The main source of noise was the small motorcycles that many Halbstarken could afford because they already had their own income from work. From 1956 to 1958 mass brawls and vandalism took place after many rock 'n' roll concerts or films such as *Rock around the Clock* and *Jailhouse Rock*. These disturbances ended in confrontations with the police.

The violence and the public display of disrespect for the authorities—parents as well as the state authorities—scared the public, as a 1950s study on the Halbstarken shows. "These youths do not recognize the authority either of the state or of adults. This is especially true with regard to the authority of the police, their parents, and their teachers; they are particularly provocative and cunning, without respect and obstinate in dealing with these adults. On the other hand, they tend to recognize the authority of their friends and peers."[36] This contemporary voice expresses precisely what Stuart Hall and others have pointed out in their seminal study on postwar youth subcultures in Britain. Both subcultures—working-class Halbstarke and middle-class existentialists—"were seen, by moral guardians and the control culture, as marking a crisis of authority. . . . This is a break in, if not a breakdown of, the reproduction

{24}

of cultural-class relations and identities, as well as a loss of deference to betters and elders."[37]

Public opinion was split on the issue of the Halbstarken between a more liberal and a law-and-order position.[38] Nobody disputed that the aggressive and violent behavior of the Halbstarken expressed a deeper crisis of West German society, but the two positions differed in their explanatory models and the countermeasures they suggested. The liberal line of reasoning saw the Halbstarken protest not as criminal behavior but as a result of the changing social situation, particularly the stronger social control of youth in the 1950s in comparison to the immediate postwar years, and the double standards of West German society. The revolt against the authorities represented for the proponents of this position an expression of the youth's new desire for democratic freedom, which could not tolerate illegitimate authoritarian demands of parents and the government. The liberal line of argument asked for understanding of and tolerance for these young people, suggesting increased funding for youth centers based on their belief in pedagogy's ability to reform and rechannel "deviant" behavior.[39]

The conservative or law-and-order faction perceived the Halbstarken phenomenon as criminal behavior and blamed sociocultural changes for it. The conservative critics identified as the chief culprit the erosion of the traditional family structures resulting from the materialist orientation of the majority of the West Germans. In this argument, they came down hard on working mothers for neglecting their children. Secondly, they criticized the liberalization of school education, and some loudly decried the abolition of physical punishment in school. Finally, they made the mass media responsible for the decline of the West German youth. While the liberals argued for understanding and discussion, the conservative position saw an authoritarian response on the part of parents and social institutions as the only adequate measure to control the rebellious youth. This was only grist for the mills of some policemen. According to recollections of Halbstarke, the police matched the youth's aggressive behavior with uncalled-for brutality, though moderate and conciliatory responses on the part of the police also existed and usually showed more positive results.[40]

The hegemonic parent culture was most obsessed with controlling the youth's fascination with boogie-woogie and rock 'n' roll. The strong physical and sexual elements of rock 'n' roll represented the most radical provocation to the 1950s prudish hostility to the body. From the perspective of the parents there was in this case reason to worry, as Rolf Lindner points out with respect to the parent culture's perception of these modern dances:

> The opposition between boogie-woogie and ballroom dancing was not only a clash of two different dance styles but also of two normative systems: just as ballroom dancing was not only an expression of good breeding but also displayed the well-bred person at his or her best (tactful, tasteful, and with a sense for limits), boogie-woogie contained a message that went beyond the violation of formal dance rules. The "eccentric groove" and "lackadaisical casualness" was a violation of "one doesn't do that" conformism, which understood dance rules as a way of disciplining the body. No wonder that the grown-up guardians of morality at that time believed that culture would collapse if this discipline were to break down.[41]

The body and its sexuality were central to both youth cultures. In comparison with the existentialist youth, which mainly theorized about sexual liberation, the Halbstarken did not theorize but practiced it. They did not believe in the postponement of sexual gratification as preached by the dominant parent culture and lived out their sexuality. Sexual encounters were common and necessary to gain status in the hierarchy of the in group. Whether it was a very fulfilling sexuality for the women who engaged in it is questionable, because of the machismo that dominated this subculture and the lack of knowledge about sex.[42] Although sexually more active than the majority of the German youth, they did not ignite a sexual revolution in West Germany. The 1960s and its middle-class counterculture had to come about for that.

As the Halbstarken subculture had been a novelty in terms of its appropriation of products and images of American mass media, it was also the first instance of the pattern of innovation and reintegration into mainstream culture that subcultures consistently face.

Since this predominantly working-class youth group had money at its disposal, industry discovered its value as a consumer. As soon as industry started to market the styles and to a certain extent the contents of the youth protest, the Halbstarken culture changed. The liberals' relaxed approach to the social phenomenon of youth dissent paid off. Capitalism was the force and the market was the place were the youth dissent became reintegrated into mainstream society.

Socializing the working-class youth into a well-adjusted labor force was absolutely necessary for the success of the "economic miracle." Hence fears of an "epidemic" spread of the Halbstarken subculture were also based on the social makeup of the Federal Republic. The majority of the West German youth went to vocational schools, and only a tiny minority was university bound. Since West Germany experienced a severe labor shortage during this time period, however, a mass rebellion of working-class youth was threatening for the "economic miracle." This explains in part why the dominant parent culture focused its attention on containing the dissent of the Halbstarken instead of that of the existentialist youth.

Also, the middle-class youth's subculture was not as far from the hegemonic parent culture as the existentialists themselves might have thought. Their aesthetic preferences overlapped with the liberal avant-garde's elitist-modernist paradigm, even if they opposed the conservative cultural paradigm. Jean-Paul Sartre was no stranger to the West German stages of the 1950s, the theater of the absurd became a model for many German playwrights, and Albert Camus's work was readily available in German translation. As long as the middle-class existentialists confined their radicalism to the realm of art and culture, the parent culture had no great reason to be worried. Consequently, the existentialist subculture could run its course more unencumbered by parental or public intervention than its working-class counterpart, the Halbstarken.

CHAPTER 2: "All Power to the Imagination!" The Student Movement of the 1960s

In the 1960s West Germany, like many other industrialized countries, experienced a wave of protest, carried mainly by its youth, that came to be known under a variety of names: "the '68 revolt" (referring to its high point of mobilization), "the student movement" or "rebellion" because the universities were at its center, or "the New Left" in order to highlight its political agenda and at the same time distinguish it from the old, working-class left. Similar to the 1950s Halbstarken phenomenon, the dominant parent culture responded with panic to this "cultural disaffiliation" of the younger generation,[1] since it sensed that this protest movement emerging from its own center—the middle class—was more dangerous to its cultural hegemony than previous youth dissent.

In comparison to the 1950s, the 1960s social and cultural upheavals went beyond subcultural confines. It combined a revolution of lifestyles with new cultural and aesthetic paradigms as well as with political demands. The 1960s protesters refused to accept the political marginalization of the youth. Instead, they demanded a political mandate for themselves and challenged mainstream society on all grounds in the most radical manner. In other words, this generation did not just want to "drop out of circulation"[2] temporarily like the existentialist youth or the Halbstarken did, but demanded change, which it tried to implement by developing its own counterculture. As a result, mainstream culture viewed even explicitly nonpolitical aspects of this middle-class counterculture—for example, a hippie lifestyle—as political and potentially dangerous for its hegemony.

The hegemonic culture had reason to be concerned because of the strategic location of middle-class youth as the future economic, political, and intellectual elites. In the case of the existentialist youth, the self-recruitment process of middle-class elites had still functioned. They were granted space and time for dissent, but were reintegrated into mainstream society as soon as they entered into their professional careers and accepted the elite status they were offered by the hegemonic culture. In the case of the 1960s counterculture this self-recruitment process was disrupted, and the equilibrium of coercion and consent necessary for hegemony was tipped off balance without immediate prospect for adjustment.

In addition, the 1960s upheavals took place precisely at the point in time when West Germany suffered its own "Sputnik crisis" and started to evaluate critically the merits and success of its educational system. Georg Picht's assessment of the postwar school system as an educational catastrophe had triggered this scrutiny and subsequent reforms of the school system. Picht argued from the perspective of the economy's demand for a highly qualified labor force, which the current educational system did not produce. For one, Picht attracted attention to the insufficient funding for all levels of schooling and the devastating effects it would soon have on the general educational level of the work force. Secondly, he pointed out that many young scientists left West Germany to go abroad, where they found better employment and research opportunities. Both problems of the educational sector would rather sooner than later lead to a major setback in technological development and the Federal Republic's competitiveness in the world market.

The expansion of educational opportunities were initially not driven by the idea of equal opportunity (*Chancengleichheit*), but by mere economic interests.[3] At a time when economic necessity forced the ruling elites to expand higher education, that is, to allow more children from nonacademic families to go on to the university, the hitherto valid equation of upward mobility with a high degree of conformity and loyalty to the hegemonic culture broke down. Instead, critical thinking had penetrated the universities, where Marxism experienced a renaissance and called the entire value system of the hegemonic parent culture into question. A highly sophisticated theoretical discourse on all issues characterized the student movement and differentiated it from previous subcultural movements.

{30}

The student movement's elaborate analysis of contemporary society and politics also contributed to the hegemonic culture's taking this protest much more seriously than its youthful predecessors. Furthermore, unlike many other European countries that experienced similar upheavals during this time period, the generation gap was much more pronounced in West Germany due to the legacy of the Nazi past.[4] The parents' silence about their past had eroded trust among their children, and the images of the Holocaust overshadowed the democratic-humanitarian rhetoric of mainstream West Germany with which the youth had grown up.

Whether it is nostalgically hailed or angrily denounced, nobody can dispute the strong and enduring impact of the student movement on politics and culture in postwar West Germany. It broke with the Adenauer era's culture of conformity and instead developed a culture appreciative of criticism and protest from which the first citizens' initiatives could rise in the 1970s and grow into strong new social movements. In short, the student movement represented a politics of fundamental opposition interested, not in the redistribution of political power within the parameters of the established system, but in reshaping social consciousness for a lasting political and cultural revolution. It is therefore not surprising that the student movement has gained commemorative status in the Federal Republic. Taking the years 1967–68 as their cue, newspapers, magazines, and publishing houses regularly generate many pages on the anniversary of the student movement.[5]

Because of its lasting impact, the 1960s counterculture has already been studied, and we can keep general remarks about its focal points of criticism and it subcultural components brief. Although an alternative aesthetic articulated itself in the very lifestyle of this protest movement, the present study does not examine the subcultural elements such as the hippies and *Gammler*—the two main groups of dropouts during the 1960s. Instead, it focuses on the correlation between the political and cultural concepts that the student movement developed, since it is elaborate theoretical discourse that distinguishes the student movement from other subcultural youth protest and accounts for its lasting influence. As Richard McCormick points out, "aesthetic theory had a very great influence, especially as formulated by Herbert Marcuse, Theodor W. Adorno, and Walter Benjamin, who infused art with political, indeed utopian, significance" and viewed it as a "nonalienated praxis in the midst of, and in resistance to, reified industrial society."[6]

The 1960s protest rediscovered a theoretical tradition—psychoanalysis and Marxism—partially lost due to Nazism and partially repressed by the sociopolitical restoration and anticommunism of the 1950s. At first, the students' reception of Marxism took place through the theories of the Frankfurt school, particularly through the abovementioned theorists. We therefore need to trace, on the one hand, the student movement's adaptation and criticism of the Frankfurt school, and concentrate, on the other hand, on the specific function the students ascribed to art and culture for their revolutionary project. To put it in a nutshell: What is the correlation between the students' political and cultural-critical claims?

Since the student movement understood itself as a counterculture, it deliberately positioned itself against the hegemonic culture, which it referred to as the "Establishment" or, with respect to aesthetic issues, as "bourgeois" culture. Though the latter is by no means a new term, the student movement pushed the notion of bourgeois culture into the limelight of contemporary debate and gave it a negative connotation. Furthermore, it challenged the Establishment's—that is, in our terminology, the hegemonic culture's—theory of the autonomy of art and culture by pointing to culture's foundation in social class. The students argued for a politically committed art, and they promoted new genres that used an operative aesthetic. In the case of literature, for instance, this transformation of the aesthetic paradigm resulted in the famous debate about the "Death of Literature," which had larger repercussions throughout the 1970s, although literature did not expire as announced.

This description of the 1960s counterculture suffers so far from the inevitable flaw of generalization, presenting it as the homogenous movement it never was. Though the protest crystallized around a common sentiment of opposition to the hegemonic parent culture and a set of focal issues and canonic texts, it exhibited at the same time a polyphony of theoretical approaches and ideological camps. Within this polyphony we can distinguish two major tendencies: a traditionalist socialist one, which competed with an antiauthoritarian one.[7] As the term *traditionalist* implies, these student groups exhibited a stronger orientation toward the political and theoretical paradigms of the Old Left, embodied in the traditional socialism of the worker's movement. The antiauthoritarian wing was critical of these traditions and embraced instead the critical theory of the Frankfurt school, since it was interested in both material and psychological repression in contemporary society.

As with all social movements, the student protest followed a trajectory that started long before it gained public attention. Determining the exact beginning and end of a social movement represents, therefore, a challenge because of its dynamic nature. Still, we can distinguish several phases of the student movement, which will help to structure our approach to it. The reconstruction of the repressed traditions of Marxism and psychoanalysis through the theoreticians of the Frankfurt school was at its beginnings, and the movement was most true to the epithet "antiauthoritarian" at this early point in time, when Herbert Marcuse's work enjoyed wide popularity among the students. His theories never eliminated the individual subject but tried to locate space within the reified society, which the individual could use to overcome its alienation. He defined this strategy as the "Great Refusal," to which we shall return later. Antiauthoritarianism, then, meant both the questioning of authority, particularly the established authorities of the Adenauer era, and the emancipation of the repressed individual in order to realize its genuine subjectivity. "Personal emancipation," as McCormick characterizes this initial phase—included "sexual liberation, and the enjoyment of pop culture, from rock music to Louis Malle's film *Viva Maria*" and "was not considered separate from political struggle. The personal and the subjective were an integral part of the movement" at this point in time.[8]

As the student movement ran its course, the focus shifted away from the category of individual subjectivity to that of social class and collective agency. By 1968–69 a rigid materialist approach started to win over the antiauthoritarian tendencies, conceptualizing everything only in terms of class and objectivity. Personal problems and questions of the individual constitution of subjectivity were tossed out the window as irrelevant to the international class struggle. By the early 1970s the student movement reached its final stage, dissolving into numerous orthodox political groups of a Marxist, Marxist-Leninist, or Maoist derivation. Since they had been trained in an elaborate theoretical discourse and in political activism, they appear to have dominated the university landscape into the mid-1970s. They were, however, quickly challenged by the so-called Spontis, one of the first articulations of a new era of countercultural criticism and practice, which referred back to the antiauthoritarian beginnings of the student protest. Before jumping to the end of the story, let us first take a brief look at the student movement's focal points of criticism, which will also help to delineate the similarities and differences between it and its followers in protest—the new social movements.

Domestic and International Issues of Critique and Opposition

There is no doubt that the new social movements (i.e., the countercultural activities thriving since the mid-1970s) are as unthinkable without the 1960s as the student movement itself would be without the broader context of the extraparliamentary opposition (*außerparlamentarische Opposition* or APO). Andrei Markovits and Philip Gorski note that "the term APO never designated a single organization or tendency. Rather, APO was a loosely constituted negative alliance between a diffuse array of groups united against a shared opponent."[9] This opponent was the Establishment, that is, the traditional party system and the parents' hegemonic culture. The SPD's ambiguous position on rearmament, and especially the nuclear armament, of West Germany during the 1950s and early 1960s, had alienated many of its younger supporters. The Grand Coalition of CDU/CSU and SPD, formed in 1966, epitomized for many citizens, including the students, the dysfunctionality of representative democracy in the Federal Republic. The Grand Coalition had finalized a disenchantment with the SPD as a genuine alternative within the parliamentary system.

The reason was that the Grand Coalition allowed for passing of the Emergency Laws, for which a two-thirds majority in the federal legislature was necessary. These constitutional amendments enabled the government to suspend most civil rights, such as the right of free assembly, freedom of speech (including the press), and the right to go on strike in the case of a national emergency. The government's bill did not specify what constituted a national emergency and also called for legislation simplifying the recruitment of citizens for national service in such a situation.[10] The Emergency Laws generated a public outcry because of their similarity to the Emergency Laws of the Weimar Republic, which had been the legal avenue for Hitler's smooth alignment (*Gleichschaltung*) of all spheres of social and political life and the elimination of his opponents. Raised if not in the spirit but at least with the rhetoric of democratic rule, the students resented the Grand Coalition and the Emergency Laws as antidemocratic and viewed an extraparliamentary opposition as the call of the day, not least because of their country's Nazi past.

Aside from the Emergency Laws, two other events of the 1960s heightened the students' sensitivity to the double standards of the democracy they inherited and became controversial issues between them and the parent culture. Internationally, the Vietnam War became the focal point for the 1960s youth-based protest. Even before the heyday of the student movement, student associations had supported the antiarmament protests of the Easter Marchers and other disarmament advocates. The brutal warfare against the Vietnamese people, however, defied the humanitarian rhetoric of the United States—the model democracy for West Germany in the postwar period. Initially, the students hoped to generate opposition to the war by simply informing the public about its nature and the true motives behind it. In other words, they believed that the general public would join the protest against the war as soon as the curtain of deception was torn from their eyes. Yet the students' emphatic call for an end to the Vietnam War fell on deaf ears. The majority of the West German population remained indifferent to the plight of the Vietnamese people, and the coalition government of CDU/CSU and SPD continued its support for the U.S. government. This only heightened the students' distrust of representative democracy because "in the case of Vietnam, the social and political representatives again proved themselves not to be the honest democrats whose authority would have sufficed to soothe the emerging distrust of the official version of democracy in the FRG."[11]

Distrust is indeed the key word describing the younger generation's relationship to their elders who ran the Federal Republic. How could they believe those who had withheld from them the horrifying truth of the Holocaust? The Frankfurt Auschwitz Trial in 1965 against former guards of death camps introduced the majority of the German youth for the first time to the horrors of the Holocaust and heightened their sensibility for the question of historical failure and guilt, which was carried back into the families. The studies of the Frankfurt school on fascism, particularly the concept of the authoritarian personality, left a strong impression on this generation of young West Germans. Inquiry into the Holocaust and its historical and sociopsychological origins became a preoccupation for the student movement, and the students rigorously challenged their grandparents' and parents' amnesia about this part of German history. That a successor to Hitler's NSDAP, the NPD, emerged again in the 1960s, was not declared unconstitutional, and was voted into several state legislatures—most notably so in Baden-Württemberg in 1968 with 10 percent of the popular vote—added to the younger generation's anxieties that fascist mentalities had survived beyond 1945. It is therefore no surprise that students began to challenge the authoritarian structures with their probing social analysis and sweeping demands for democratization.

The university system was one of the prime targets of the students' agitation. The analysis and criticism of the status and function of the university as an educational and social institution was central to the students' discussion of the reorganization of social structures and values. The Frankfurt school's critical understanding of technology, with its analysis of the dialectics of technology and domination, shaped the students' thinking on these matters.[12] With respect to the university system, the students fought on two fronts. They demanded the democratization of the old, hierarchically structured university (*Ordinarienuniversität*), which did not allow for any student participation in defining the academic curriculum and gave the individual professor almost absolute power over his subordinates. At the same time they fought the growing subjugation of the university

to the needs of business and industry. Although the students attacked technological rationality as supporting structures of domination, they did not denounce technology in itself, as a statement
by Bernd Rabehl, one of the leading theorists among the students,
shows: "Technology is essential to the bourgeois vision of the future;
it means everything. Technology is part of the bureaucracy and a
wasteful expense; it permanently reproduces power. It aims at the
perpetuation of capitalist domination. Therefore this technology as
it now exists must be destroyed, eliminated. . . . Not the knowledge
that it contains, not its domination of nature, but its current structure and goals must be eliminated."[13]

The 1960s had not yet developed an awareness for the destructive
potential of technology, but followed Marcuse's lead, who viewed
technology favorably as a potential means of liberation.[14] In contrast
to one of the main concerns of the new social movements — preservation of nature in the face of a pending ecological disaster — the students of the late 1960s believed in the Western paradigm of progress
and "that technology, under truly democratic control, . . . could be
liberating."[15] The 1968 revolt was the last revolution that did not yet
know about the depletion of the ozone layer, as Daniel Cohn-Bendit
and Reinhard Mohr, both former student activists, subtitled their
historical account of the student movement twenty years later. As
they point out in their introduction, contrary to their successors, the
generation of 1968 exhibited no traces of an apocalyptic mood, but
still believed that they could shape a brighter future.[16] All it took was
a little imagination. Consequently, "All Power to the Imagination!"
(*Phantasie an die Macht!*) became their battle cry.

Imagination As a Productive Force

Behind this popular slogan lurked a much more complex and, from
the perspective of the parent culture, threatening concept. "All Power
to the Imagination!" was not solely an insult implicitly referring
to the older generation of Germans as boring, but it did signal
the student movement's attack on the stifling authoritarian structures of the Adenauer era. The initial antiauthoritarian impetus of
the student movement was strongly influenced by the discovery

of Freudian psychoanalysis, which analyzes the complex structure of the individual in terms of consciousness and subconsciousness, dream and pleasure, and imagination and reality. The reconstruction of a genuine subjectivity leading to human solidarity and the unity of personal and political commitment was the big antiauthoritarian dream, which in the end lost out against Marxian concepts of class and the class struggle.

While reading Marx himself soon became a must for every politically engaged student, the reception of Freud took place almost entirely through the work of Wilhelm Reich and Herbert Marcuse and not by reading the original,[17] since Freud's oeuvre did not offer itself easily to the analysis of social class. The students used Freud's model of the Oedipus complex, but his cultural theory that all of civilization was founded on repression, or, to be more precise, on the postponement of immediate gratification of instinctual needs and desires, remained suspect.[18] For the antiauthoritarian students, shaking off the shackles of internal repression and external oppression in all its contemporary forms was the preeminent goal. From their perspective, Freud's cultural theory simply justified the repressive character of contemporary society. They were no longer willing, however, to accept renunciation as an anthropological given but insisted on the realization of their dreams, and thus, in Freudian terms, on the pleasure principle.

The openly propagated sexual revolution was only one aspect of the actualization of the pleasure principle. Thanks to the now readily available oral contraceptives and Reichian sexual theories, the generation of 1968 was the first in postwar West Germany to freely practice what their predecessors—the existentialist youth—only theoretically discussed, namely, sex. Up to this point in time, control over its progeny's sexuality represented an expression of parental authority. Now a significant element of social control had slipped out of the parents' hands and raised worries that the youth's predilection for the pleasure principle would lead to an unabashed hedonism threatening the Protestant work ethic on which not only the "economic miracle" but all of the parent culture's hegemony rested.

For our focus on cultural politics and aesthetic concepts, not Reich but Marcuse's adaptation of Freud is more significant. In his study *Eros and Civilization*,[19] Marcuse attempted to reverse the Freudian theorem of "an irreversible and unavoidable interdependency between progress in the evolution of society and unhappiness in the repressed psyche of individual man, between individual self-denial and the diversion of psychic energy for collective purposes."[20] Marcuse inquired into the psychological foundations of a nonrepressive culture that at the same time does not fall prey to repressive desublimation. Picking up on Freud's metapsychology, which constructed imagination as a mental process not totally subjected to the reality principle, Marcuse describes the fate of the psychic economy in late capitalism as one in which "reason prevails: it becomes unpleasant but useful and correct; phantasy remains pleasant but becomes useless, untrue—a mere play, daydreaming. As such, it continues to speak the language of the pleasure principle, of freedom from repression, of uninhibited desire and gratification, but reality proceeds according to the laws of reason, no longer committed to the dream language."[21] In other words, imagination had not totally vanished from late capitalism, but had lost its power to the reality principle.

According to Freud, the gratification that is necessary for the functioning of the psychic economy can take three different forms: dream, fantasy or imagination, and neurosis. Whereas Freud claimed that all three modes of gratification are regressive, Marcuse defined imagination as the only one of these three that has a progressive and therefore liberating potential. He derives from Freud, and at the same time places in opposition to Freud, the statement that fantasy "has a truth value of its own, which corresponds to an experience of its own—namely, the surmounting of the antagonistic human reality."[22] Fantasy or imagination articulates itself beyond the individual's dreams collectively in art. Art does not succumb to the contemporary reality principle—instrumental rationality—because it follows a different logic, namely, that of the pleasure principle.

Marcuse therefore criticized the bourgeois approach to aesthetic culture, which led to the loss of the unity of cognitive processes and aesthetic-sensuous experience. Using the transformation of the notion of aesthetic in the history of philosophy to demonstrate "the repressive treatment of the sensuous (and thereby corporeal) cognitive processes,"[23] he sharply criticized bourgeois ideology, which has transformed the original concept of art as a philosophical discipline of sensuous cognition into a separate science of art. He viewed Kant's aesthetic theory as an attempt to save the genuine content of the notion of aesthetic as pertaining to the senses exactly at that point in time when the reductive bourgeois understanding of aesthetic as pertaining to beauty and art became dominant. Marcuse claimed that aesthetic experience represents for Kant the mediator between the intellect and the senses, thereby reinstituting human sensuousness in its cognitive function. He picks up on the Kantian theorem and deduces an emancipatory claim from it: "The philosophical effort to mediate, in the aesthetic dimension, between sensuousness and reason thus appears as an attempt to reconcile the two spheres of the human existence which were torn asunder by a repressive reality principle. The mediating function is performed by the aesthetic faculty, which is akin to sensuousness, pertaining to the senses. Consequently, the aesthetic reconciliation implies strengthening sensuousness as against the tyranny of reason, and, ultimately, even calls for the liberation of sensuousness from the repressive domination of reason."[24]

It was precisely this aspect of Marcuse's redefinition of Freud that made him attractive for the student movement's own conceptualizations. Marcuse's theory held the promise to overcome alienation and create a human society through the integration of sensuous experience, imagination, and abstract thought. While Marcuse's emphasis on the cognitive function of sensuousness found practical expression in the hippie subculture, it did not enter the student movement's theoretical plan. As the student movement ran its course, an abstract theoretical language deprived of any sensuous and concrete aspects won the upper hand, as many former student activists sadly acknowledge in retrospect.[25]

The narrow focus on the revolution and the primacy of the Marxist concept of class struggle obstructed a more comprehensive adaptation of Marcusian theorems. This became clear in a seminal article written by Peter Schneider on imagination in late capitalism, emphasizing Freud's understanding of imagination as the substitute of unconscious desires on the level of consciousness.[26] Schneider argues that in contrast to dream or neurosis, imagination can indeed overcome the censorship that controls and ultimately represses the unconscious desires. Going beyond Marcuse, Schneider maintains that imagination has therefore a revolutionary potential and can pave the way to action. "Unlike dreams, once the imagination has overcome censorship, . . . the wishes contained in the imagination can acquire, with the support of the conscious mind, material to satisfy themselves in reality and to develop further. In contrast to dreams, the wishes of the imagination can separate themselves from their infantile objects and establish a historical relationship to reality."[27] For Schneider, emancipation from capitalist repression represents only a question of turning imagination into a productive force against the repressive reality principle. The student movement's emphasis on imagination, which Schneider's essay articulates, reflects its demand for the transformation of society through the liberation of the creative faculties and the libidinal energies of the human being. The slogan "All Power to the Imagination!" calls for the transformation of imagination into revolutionary energy and aims at overcoming the repressive reality principle on the individual as well as on the collective level.

Both Freud and Marcuse saw in art the social space where imagination found refuge because of its autonomy from other spheres of society. For Freud, art represented the only possible escape from neurosis, that is, from the inevitable result of a repressive social reality. It has this potential because of its autonomous status vis-à-vis the reality principle. Marcuse follows Freud, maintaining that only art has been able to resist capitalism's reality principle — instrumental rationality. He views aesthetic form as the essential category that prevents art from falling prey to this dominant reality principle, since "behind the sublimated aesthetic form, the unsublimated content shows forth: the commitment of art to the pleasure principle."[28] In other words, art preserves the unfulfilled humanitarian ideals. It is therefore through aesthetic form that autonomous art represents the "Great Refusal," the "protest against the unnecessary repression"[29] imposed on the individual by late capitalism.

Marcuse argues that "form is the negation, the mastery of disorder, violence, suffering, even when it presents disorder, violence, suffering. This triumph of art is achieved by subjecting the content to the aesthetic order, which is autonomous in its exigencies. The work of art sets its own limits and ends, it is *sinngebend* [creates meaning] in relating the elements to each other according to its own law: . . . The content is thereby transformed: it obtains a meaning (sense) which transcends the elements of the content, and this transcending order is the appearance of the beautiful as the truth of art."[30] Marcuse was, however, fully aware of the ambivalence of form. Since it at the same time criticizes and reconciles social reality, form has an affirmative moment as well. The positive examples of form he cites as his models of an authentic and emancipatory art — surrealism, Brecht's theater of estrangement and serial music — demonstrate that it is not form in itself but only the most advanced aesthetic form that transcends the reality principle in his eyes.[31]

Marcuse's defense of the autonomy of art and privileging of most avant-garde art (i.e., of abstract modernism — typical also of Adorno's aesthetic) caused his aesthetic theory to fall out of favor with the students. They saw him in this regard as a representative of the bourgeois aesthetic that they so vigorously resented. The students were no longer content with art's function as a sanctuary for desires and ideals repressed by the hegemonic bourgeois culture. Instead of aesthetic ersatz, they demanded the fulfillment of the utopian images. Schneider, for example, criticized bourgeois art for preaching denial and renunciation, since it presents utopian images of freedom and happiness only in the separate sphere of aesthetic culture without reference to their realization. Hence bourgeois art directly feeds into the capitalist order. It shows the masses their suffering solely for the purpose of adjusting them to it. For the students, even the most avant-garde forms of bourgeois art no longer represented an alternative, as Schneider's criticism of serial music — one of Marcuse's positive examples — demonstrates. Schneider perceived serial music as an expression of capitalism that reinforces class structures with its elitist attitudes.[32]

This kind of antielitism was characteristic of the student movement and inspired much of its aesthetic theory and cultural politics. In contrast to the cultural politics and organizations of the traditional labor movement such as the SPD, which cultivated bourgeois culture and strove to educate the working class to appreciate it, the students argued for an art genuine to the working masses. Schneider's article cites the concert of Moscow's factory sirens that a worker conducted the day after the revolution as an example and opposes it to a showpiece of bourgeois culture, the "Ode to Joy" from Beethoven's Ninth Symphony. Schneider argues that the music of the factory sirens represents, not merely a substitute for "the impossible desires of the isolated individual, but the expression of their social gratification and the hope for such future gratification."[33] Using instruments of their own life world, the masses can develop their own authentic art and realize its liberating potential. Schneider saw this kind of mass art as emancipatory mainly for two reasons. It does not require specialized knowledge, because it is produced by the workers themselves and with means genuine to them. Second, this art is no longer simply an aesthetic illusion but articulates the reality of the working class.

Hence pushing art from the pedestal on which bourgeois aesthetic had placed it was one of the main concerns of the students. They wanted to reintegrate art as an emancipatory practice into the life world of the working masses. Because of their extensive study of Marx, the students knew at the same time that their emancipatory project would fail without a social revolution. They challenged, however, the traditional Marxian notion that the revolution needs to be based on the socioeconomic situation and the working class. They developed their own theory of what the revolution should look like in a Western industrialized country like the Federal Republic and called it the cultural revolution.

The Concept of the Cultural Revolution and Its Revolutionary Subjects

The student movement derived its notion of the cultural revolution from Mao, as many implicit and explicit references to the leader of the Chinese Revolution show, though they did not copy Mao step by step.[34] Historically, the term denotes a specific time period—September 1965 to April 1969—and a specific event in the long process of the Chinese Revolution: the concerted effort of the Chinese Red

Army to purge the culture of revolutionary China of all bourgeois elements. Mao developed and applied the concept of cultural revolution in order to affirm his power against opposing groups within the political leadership of the People's Republic.

The Chinese revolutionary project was of particular interest to the students for several reasons. First, it represented an existing counterexample to the orthodox Marxist revolutionary theory, which the student movement rejected. Mao's revolution took place in a country without a class-conscious proletariat and was nevertheless successful. Second, China functioned as an alternative model to the existing socialism in Eastern Europe. Despite the myth spread about the student movement, that it was a devotee of Moscow, the students criticized the Soviet Union and its satellite states' political and social policies as not truly socialist.[35] Finally, Mao's concept of the cultural revolution was antibourgeois, aiming at the remnants of a bourgeois ideology after the socioeconomic revolution had taken place. This antibourgeois tendency was attractive for the students, since they saw the hegemonic bourgeois culture at the root of all alienation and oppression.

The notion of cultural revolution means therefore a radical attack on all of the hegemonic culture's norms and values, a revolution that goes far beyond the material expropriation of the dominant social classes. At its foundation lies a comprehensive concept of culture in contrast to the traditional notion that reduces culture to the intellectual and artistic expression of a people. Schneider's article on imagination in late capitalism contains the most widely accepted definition of the students' concept of the cultural revolution:

> The cultural revolution is therefore not an aesthetic substitute for the revolution, a revolt in the museum, an assault in the park, an outrage in the theater. Such a definition would leave culture in the ghetto where capitalism has imprisoned it. The cultural revolution in late capitalism is more impatient, more generous, less easily satisfied than the economic-political revolution. It includes not only a sublation [*Aufhebung*] of all capitalist relationships but also a revolution of all relationships in which the human being becomes a commodity and

the commodity becomes a subject: the relationship between the sexes, between parents and children, between neighbor and neighbor, between the car and its owner. It asks, for example, whether we can still tolerate cars. The cultural revolution leaves nothing untouched.[36]

The advocates of the cultural revolution did not argue that it can indeed replace the political and economic one, but rather that it is its absolutely necessary complement. Schneider, for instance, explicates the dialectics of the socioeconomic and cultural revolution with respect to the May events of 1968 in Paris. He maintains that the tanks that de Gaulle had sent to the rebellious working-class neighborhoods show the insufficiency of the merely cultural revolution. The cultural revolution alone cannot succeed without the revolutionary transformation of the material conditions, that is, the social and political structures of society. The socioeconomic revolution is necessary in order to seize power from the repressive state apparatus.[37] But the socioeconomic revolution alone cannot generate the revolutionary consciousness necessary for a successful completion of the revolutionary process. The political and economic revolution needs to start with a cultural revolution and needs to be transformed back into a cultural revolution. In this model, the cultural revolution represents either a continuation of socioeconomic changes or their anticipation, depending on the historical moment and the particular social context.[38]

The adaptation of a Maoist notion of a cultural revolution indicates that not all was well with traditional Marxism and that the students had a clear understanding of the specific socioeconomic conditions in postwar West Germany. Marx's theory of pauperization (*Verelendundgstheorie*), which predicted that the impoverished proletariat would rise up against its bourgeois oppressors, had no bearing on postwar reality. The Federal Republic of the "economic miracle" showed no signs of an increasing material misery of its working class, the revolutionary subject according to Marx, but rather of a growing embourgeoisement of the revolutionary subject. This posed the question, Who was supposed to carry out the cultural revolution the students envisioned?

That the Frankfurt school presented a Marxism rethought from the perspective of advanced capitalism accounts for its attraction among the students. It indeed offered theoretical help in explaining why the working class could no longer function as the revolutionary subject and who might take its place today. Marcuse's cultural theory in particular exhibits a strong belief in the possibility of change in spite of the apparent solidity of late capitalist society. It locates moments of resistance and change within society by dismantling the myth of the broad and content middle class and the liberal argument that a pluralist society represents a maximization of individual freedom. Instead, Marcuse demonstrates how the consumer is trapped in a web of commercial manipulation that has only one goal: to pacify the individual and thereby safeguard the status quo. Moreover, his *One-Dimensional Man* explains why Marx's revolutionary subject, the proletariat, failed, while at the same time exonerating it. Hence Marcuse does not have to give up the idea of revolutionary change but shifts the focus of the struggle.

Based on the deception theory of the Frankfurt school, his *One-Dimensional Man* analyzes in detail how the various channels of consumer culture manipulate human desire. For Marcuse, capitalism's force of commodification has less to do with its appetite for goods than with the reproduction of cultural hegemony. "The means of mass transportation and communication, the commodities of lodging, food, and clothing, the irresistible output of the entertainment industry carry with them prescribed attitudes and habits, certain intellectual and emotional reactions which bind the consumers more or less pleasantly to the producers, and, through the latter, to the whole. The products indoctrinate and manipulate; they promote false consciousness which is immune against its falsehood."[39] Marcuse explains the failure of the working class as the revolutionary subject with the inescapability of the vicious cycle of manipulation and deception in late capitalism. Hence the working class "no longer appears to be the living contradiction to society."[40] It is rather as integrated and therefore as unable to break through the universal system of deception as any other social class.

In spite of this devastating analysis of contemporary society, Marcuse's work offered hope. In his article "Repressive Tolerance" he points to contemporary social forces that represent a new revolutionary potential.[41] Influenced by the civil rights movement in the United States, he argues that marginalized social groups are the only ones that could possibly ignite revolutionary transformation, provided they are able to achieve unity for the political struggle. Marcuse's "theory of marginalized groups" (*Randgruppentheorie*) became the steppingstone for the students' reconceptualization of the revolutionary subject.

The students, however, did not apply Marcuse's theory to the social conditions and the political situation in West Germany in a simplistic manner. Bernd Rabehl, Christian Semler, and Rudi Dutschke, leading activists of the student movement, show in a discussion published in the *Kursbuch*—the main public forum for the student movement—that they were aware of the differences between the United States and the Federal Republic.[42] They refrain from identifying themselves as a marginalized group. Instead, they identify suddenly unemployed workers—a reality during the recession of 1967—as a potentially militant force, since these workers have been unexpectedly pushed to the margins from a central and secure position within society. Rabehl, Semler, and Dutschke argue that these unemployed workers cannot bring about the revolution by themselves. Even if they were to be radicalized by the threat to their immediate material existence and become militant, they lack recognition of the social totality; in other words, they are crippled by the false consciousness that the one-dimensional society imposes on them.

Here the students saw themselves and the academic intelligentsia come into play. Since the students have already developed a consciousness for the repressive and exploitive character of late capitalism, they are in an avant-garde position. The student movement has therefore the role to revitalize the emancipation of the crippled con- sciousness among the workers in order to develop a countercultural environment from which the revolution can finally arise. Marcuse's exoneration of the working class allowed the students to think about a new revolutionary subject as the alliance of the working class and themselves, or even the entire intelligentsia. While the working class still functions as the mass basis necessary for the revolution, the intelligentsia (i.e., the student movement) functions as a kind of midwife for the revolutionary consciousness among the proletariat.

On a more practical level, the question arose as to how the students could reach out to and unite with the working class. In response, student activists left the university and sought employment as assembly line workers in order to agitate the proletariat at its workplace. They set up socialist cells (*Basisgruppen*), small groups consisting of workers and students, which read and discussed Marxist theories together in order to develop a revolutionary consciousness and strategy. While the pragmatists among the student activists got their hands dirty in the factories, the theorists of the student movement focused on the strategic location of the intelligentsia in order to analyze where structural changes could be implemented most effectively. For the latter, art and the entire sphere of culture gained significance for the student movement's cultural-revolutionary theory, since art participates in the production and circulation of images, values, and public opinion, or, in other words, in the production of consciousness.

The student movement's concept of cultural revolution did not advocate the abolition of artistic production or deny the emancipatory and utopian images contained in older works of arts. Its concept of art differed from that of the hegemonic culture in its insistence on an art that leads to the realization of these utopian images, that is, an art that leads to practice. The student movement developed a concept of a politically engaged or committed art that negates the bourgeois paradigm of aesthetic culture as a separate sphere from that of politics and economics. This concept was not original to the student movement, but had been debated since the 1920s by Walter Benjamin and Bertolt Brecht, to name only the most prominent German proponents.

The students' concept of an engaged art ascribed to aesthetic culture two particular functions: agitation and propaganda for the revolution.[43] *Agitation* means the mobilization of the desires and imagination against the repressive reality of late capitalism. The art of agitation needs to represent, on the one hand, the desires of humankind and, on the other hand, the actual conditions of life in late capitalism. It requires that art compare images of real life to those that show new and better conditions of life.[44] This comparison dispenses, however, with artistic form, since it was with form that a bourgeois aesthetics trapped imagination in the ghetto of art. In its propagandistic function, art revitalizes human desires that in the past had been neutralized in the work of art. Schneider, for example, writes: "Art as propaganda would select utopian images from the written history of human desire and liberate them from the formal distortions imposed upon them by the conditions of material life, and it would finally show these desires the path to their realization that has now opened up. It is clear that art as propaganda needs to be subjected to stronger formal requirements than art as agitation. In contrast to all previous art, these new forms must keep the demand for realization alive; this aesthetic must be a strategy for the realization of the desires."[45]

As Barbara Büscher and Andreas Huyssen correctly point out, the student movement's concept of aesthetic culture has much in common with the aesthetic of the historical avant-garde as well as with pop art and the art happenings of the 1960s, since both of these movements strove for a reintegration of life world and art.[46] The concert of the factory sirens, which Schneider cites, functions as an example of a collective aesthetic practice that explodes the bourgeois concept of aesthetic culture by integrating the life world into art. The same holds true for Schneider's citation of Bosch's, Breughel's, and Goya's paintings as blueprints for a human urban environment as well as his understanding of Brecht's and Majakowski's poems as guidelines for political theory. The student movement's concept of aesthetic culture aimed at a sublation of bourgeois art as an individualized and consumptive social practice in favor of a collective, creative cultural practice. In this sense the cultural revolution incorporated the erasure of the border between producer and recipient, between culture and life world.[47]

Adorno, Benjamin, and the Culture Industry

The Frankfurt school supplied most of the key concepts for the student movement's analysis of cultural hegemony. Perhaps the most significant and at the same time most controversial one was Adorno's notion of the culture industry, which defines all mass culture as a mode of deception. Adorno's negative stance regarding mass entertainment dates back to the 1930s and his controversy with Walter Benjamin, to whose positive evaluation of mechanically reproduced art Adorno responded with his essay "On the Fetish Character in Music and the Regression of Listening." The fact that Horkheimer and Adorno devoted a whole chapter of the *Dialectic of Enlightenment* to the culture industry, and that the latter reissued these thoughts during the 1960s in his essay "Culture Industry Reconsidered," demonstrates the significance of this concept for the Frankfurt school.[48] Adorno argues that in contrast to authentic art, which maintains an autonomous status, the economic principles of capitalism permeate all mass culture production. In the culture industry, as in the marketplace in general, the use value is not of interest but only the exchange value, since the market is driven by one goal only—the maximization of profit. Commodification is the central category for all mass culture products, Adorno concludes, and "cultural entities typical of the culture industry are no longer also commodities, they are commodities through and through."[49]

The culture industry's marketing efforts do not, however, stop here. The culture industry sells more than entertainment for a high profit margin. It sells first and foremost premanufactured models of identification, thereby confirming and reinforcing submissive attitudes. The totalitarian character of the culture industry does not leave any space for the development of a genuine subjectivity, but constructs the individual as a consumer not only for its material products but for its ideology. For Adorno, the culture industry is nothing but a surreptitious sales pitch for the adjustment of the individual to the powers that be. "In contrast to the Kantian, the categorical imperative of the culture industry no longer has anything in common with freedom. It proclaims: you shall conform, without instruction as to what; conform to that which exists anyway, and to that which everyone thinks anyway as a reflex of its power and omnipresence. The power of the culture industry's ideology is such that conformity has replaced consciousness."[50]

For Adorno, like Marcuse, aesthetic form represents the central category for the production of authentic art. Only by developing a distinct aesthetic form, by becoming more and more hermetic, can art withstand penetration by the culture industry.[51] Adorno therefore justifies hermetic art—the most avant-garde articulations of aesthetic culture—as the only "successful model of enlightenment"[52] in a society dominated by the deceptive practices of the culture industry. He emphatically rejects any aesthetic concept that prescribes for art a didactic or other instrumental function, such as the students' understanding of art as agitation and propaganda. From Adorno's perspective, art ceases to exist and deteriorates into the culture industry as soon as it gives up its autonomy in order to become politically engaged, or, negatively phrased, tendentious.

The student movement followed Adorno's analysis of the culture industry closely, as a programmatic article by members of the Sozialistischer Deutscher Studentenbund (SDS, or Socialist German Student Association) demonstrates. The article, "Art As a Commodity of the Mind Industry," was published in the West German weekly *Die Zeit* in the fall of 1968.[53] The SDS followed Adorno's basic tenets of the total commodification of products of the culture industry and their deceptive power, but it disapproved of his distinction between authentic art and the products of the culture industry as elitist. At the core of the students' problem with the later Frankfurt school and especially Adorno was the latter's rejection of any immediate political application of his theoretical insights. As Peter Uwe Hohendahl points out, this refusal to move from theory to praxis was the logical consequence of Adorno's social theory.[54] Adorno saw no possibility for change in the reified social reality of late capitalism, and he therefore could not appreciate the student movement's call for a cultural revolution. Permanent critical reflection and authentic art represented for Adorno the only effective modes of resistance to late capitalism. As was the case with Marcuse, the students clashed with Adorno's aesthetic theory because it was grounded in the dichotomy of "high" and "low" culture, which the student movement wanted to overcome.

Disgruntled by Adorno's refusal to move from theory to praxis, the students pushed Adorno's approach a step further by combining it "with a version of Marcuse's thesis of the affirmative character of high art—a reductionist version, in which high art, viewed as nothing but a means of domination, is deprived of its utopian and anticipatory element," as Huyssen critically comments.[55] Collapsing the binary model of "high" versus "low" culture—that is, treating "high" and "low" culture alike—the students claimed that late capitalism does not offer any escape from the universal system of deception, not even for products of "high" culture. The SDS article therefore incited passionate responses by numerous well-known critics and writers of all political views precisely for subsuming the elite, avant-garde culture sanctioned by these very critics to the concept of the culture industry.[56]

In addition, the students' claim that "high" culture serves as a means to intimidate the masses was scandalous because it contradicted the ideology of bourgeois art's emancipatory function. The SDS maintained that the majority of the people are excluded from genuine participation in "high" culture because of the expert knowledge it requires. "High" culture consolidates class distinctions and functions as a means to demonstrate and safeguard the hegemony of the ruling elites. "The production of art becomes an instrument of domination, which has been accepted as legitimate in the public sphere. This domination—intellectual domination—is the precondition for domination in all other areas. It produces a general willingness on the part of the dominated to acknowledge the competence of the dominant class. By stripping rationality from the experience of art, art becomes intimidating and thus consolidates the consciousness of subordination."[57]

For the SDS, elite culture represents the true culprit because its principles—originality, virtuosity, and spontaneity—are the foundation of the repressive nature of bourgeois art. It is not surprising that the student movement denounced originality and virtuosity, because their valuation ran counter to its antielitism. More interesting is the students' negative response to the category of spontaneity, which gained in value only a few years later as one of the fundamental elements of the post-1968 counterculture. The shift toward privileging the collective over the individual made spontaneity suspect. The SDS, for example, equated it with the cult of the genius (*Geniekult*), which since the eighteenth-century Sturm und Drang movement had put the individual on a pedestal and scorned the collective.

Peter Zadek, whom the hegemonic culture highly praised in the 1960s as a progressive theater director, represented for the SDS a perfect example of this oppressive bourgeois aesthetic.[58] The students charged him with replacing realistic details of the plays, which are necessary for a communicative reception, with his subjective whims. In other words, the students accused Zadek of stripping the theater of its concreteness, which points beyond itself to a larger social reality. Instead, his theatrical productions are absorbed in self-referentiality. Since they smooth over the antagonism between material and social reality, the theater remains nothing but theater and, from the perspective of the SDS, represents just another branch of the entertainment industry. The students criticized Zadek's production aesthetic primarily for remaining on the level of mere beautiful illusion (*schöner Schein*), instead of revealing the alienation and contradictions of the present day. "The theater does not allow for any inference back to reality, but pretends that it is a part of reality. It suggests that the problem is solved by concentrating on oneself and retreating from a disappointing daily existence."[59] The student movement was at the same time concerned about the response that this kind of art promotes, namely, an individualized reception that demanded the suspension of rationality. The SDS argued that spontaneity withdraws from the sphere of rational discourse, thereby undermining a critical assessment of the aesthetic product. It turns the recipient into a passive consumer exposed to an onslaught of the artist's subjective and spontaneous ideas, which are left to be affirmed as strokes of genius.[60]

The SDS article still bears witness to the strong influence of Adorno on the students and their difficulty in developing an alternative aesthetic. It does not, however, provide suggestions that go beyond the Frankfurt school–styled critique of ideology, although the article calls for a "progressive" art. The article implicitly alludes to a few categories for a new aesthetic in its critique of Zadek. These categories are not new but based on bourgeois realism and reminiscent of the aesthetic paradigm of socialist realism in the Eastern Bloc.

Whether these categories are useful in forging a progressive or even revolutionary aesthetic out of the existing one is highly questionable. Huyssen, in particular, points out the contradiction between the "gloomy picture" of contemporary art that the article paints and the call "for the creation of a progressive art."[61]

As the students' antiauthoritarian ideals receded into the background and concrete political activism and the desire for a revolutionary alliance with the working class became the dominant paradigm, the student movement's positive attitude to the Frankfurt school of Adorno began to change. As already mentioned, Adorno's analysis of the interdependence of technology, oppression, and alienation in capitalism precluded developing a concrete strategy for change. Instead, Adorno's generally bleak outlook seemed to shut off all hope that the hegemonic culture could be overthrown. The students recognized the position of impotence into which they had maneuvered themselves with these concepts both practically and theoretically. They did not completely abandon Adornian critical theory but instead turned to the early Frankfurt school of the 1930s, especially Walter Benjamin's work.

The students' discussion of Adorno and Benjamin continued a debate these two Frankfurt school theorists carried on in the 1930s. At stake then and in the 1960s were the status and function of the culture industry. The debate pitted an Adornian perspective, which viewed all modern technology from photography and radio to film and television as nothing but cogs in capitalism's deception machinery, against a Benjaminian position that technology has a liberating potential as well. The evaluation of modern technology represented an important issue for the student movement in many ways. On a personal level, popular culture, especially rock 'n' roll, film, and television, played a significant role in the life of West German youth in the postwar period. The 1968ers were children of the electronic media and grew up with the offerings of the culture industry. To simply dismiss it was unthinkable. In terms of the students' antielitism, it was equally problematic simply to ignore those leisure activities favored by the masses. Benjamin's work provided a new critical framework because of his belief in the liberating potential of mechanical reproduction techniques. The students' almost verbatim adoption of

Benjamin's theorems was motivated by their desire to get out of the dead end that Adorno's concept of the culture industry represented.

As Ansgar Hillach points out, Benjamin's theory prophesied that an alliance of the working class and the new technologies is possible, even if the culture industry applies those technologies for its own ends, and that the intelligentsia would play a significant role in this revolutionary process.[62] In particular, two of Benjamin's essays published in the 1930s caught the eye of the students: "The Author As Producer" and "The Work of Art in the Age of Mechanical Reproduction." In these essays, Benjamin took an overtly materialist turn in order to derive from the historical changes of art those progressive moments that could become the foundation for a materialist aesthetic.[63] He based his theory on the Marxian concept of the conditions of production (*Produktionsbedingungen*) and Marx's claim that capitalism breeds the contradictions that will lead to its own demise. Benjamin, like Marcuse, whom many see as Benjamin's successor, generated hope that revolutionary change is after all possible and that the modern technologies of mechanical reproduction could play a vital role in this process.

Mechanical reproduction represents for Benjamin a chance to explode the hegemony of an affirmative bourgeois aesthetic in two ways. First, the new technology alters already existing works of high culture by destroying their aura of uniqueness through their mass reproduction. When integrated into the production of art itself, the technology thus breaks with "the referential mimetic aesthetic and its notion of the autonomous and organic work of art."[64] Second, technology generates a different mode of reception. Cultural production that is based on mechanical reproduction—film, for example—replaces the bourgeois individual and contemplative reception with a collective and distracted reception, which Benjamin believed to have instructional and organizational power. In contrast to bourgeois modes of reception, which function as ersatz for the unfulfilled desires of the masses and so protects the status quo, collective reception has the potential to lead to a social praxis that realizes change.

Overcoming the status quo was the student movement's goal, and its initial emphatic embrace of Benjamin's aesthetic theory is best expressed in Helmut Lethen's contribution to the debate in 1967: "The dignity of this 'materialist theory of art' consists precisely in its refusal to accept the social impotence of bourgeois art and in its insistence that the promise of art be materially realized. The violence contained in his ideal of collective reception is not just Benjamin's irritated reaction to the cynicism of those who maintain that only a private-elitist reception of art is adequate even during the class struggle. This is also the decisive difference from the aesthetic theory of Adorno, who feared the eruption of aesthetic barbarism if all privileged aesthetic education were to be abandoned."[65]

While some student movement theorists, such as Lethen, followed Benjamin very closely and sometimes got swept up in a polemic against Adorno, others developed a more critical approach. Michael Scharang, for instance, accounts for the historical difference between the 1930s and postwar West Germany and problematizes Benjamin's basic Marxist assumption that capitalism creates the contradictions that lead to its own demise. He maintains that late capitalism is more or less shielded from revolutionary change despite recurring economic recession. Because of capitalism's hegemony, everything can be reintegrated into the existing order through the process of rationalization. He argues that "the dominant want to remain dominant. All changes within systems of domination take place under this law. That which is changed is nothing but the rationalized old."[66] Hence there is no guarantee that technology inevitably functions as a progressive force, certainly not as long as it is at the disposal of the hegemonic powers.

Even for Scharang's critical approach to Benjamin, technology remains a central category, and he agrees with Benjamin that the relationship between art and technology poses not only new political but aesthetic issues as well. It has superseded the nineteenth-century aesthetic paradigm, which denied the sociohistorical foundation of its artifacts and identified the aesthetic as "the eternally functioning harmony, the essence of which appears in that which manifests itself as beautiful beyond social reality."[67] For the "Adornian" Scharang, both art and social reality appear as second nature. While Benjamin saw this alliance broken thanks to mechanical reproduction, which emancipated art from ritual, Scharang views contemporary art still as trapped in its illusionary character. Not surprising for a student movement theorist, Scharang rejects a return to traditional forms of "high art" as an alternative. He insists on art's shedding its illusionary character, that is, its ideology of autonomy, in favor of an art of praxis.

As Scharang points out, art can no longer adhere to a pretechnological concept of production because of the historical development of the forces of its production. Instead, he attempts to salvage modern reproduction techniques by introducing a subtle but significant distinction. He argues that two modes, or rather two uses, of mechanical reproduction exist. One is indeed Adorno's understanding of technology as a means of domination. The repressive use of contemporary technology generates a mode of reproduction that "forces on the affected society the character of being a reproduction, a linear reproduction, which creates the eternal return of the same and a retrograde consciousness that is denied the prospect that it could be otherwise."[68] The culture industry operates on this principle. Scharang calls the other option "technical reproduction" or "the technique of reproduction," which is distinct from the previous form with respect to the application of new technologies and the receptive attitude it promotes. This new type of aesthetic production articulates the historical position of the forces of production, but it reflects at the same time the repressive moments of contemporary technology. Hence art reflects upon its own status, thereby transcending itself, and thus can no longer function as a sublimation of unfulfilled desires in a realm beyond reality. "With regard to art, the meaning of mechanical reproduction could instead be seen in the destruction of a pure sphere of art by the desublimation of the aesthetic dimension. Progressive desublimation means the making available of a repressed dimension of reality for a truly liberated society."[69]

We have previously seen that art had a significant role to play in the emancipatory and revolutionary project of the student movement. Benjamin's thesis of the politicization of art in response to fascism's aestheticization of politics represents the key concept for the students and their attempts to develop a new materialist aesthetic.[70] For many student movement theorists, the materialist approach exhausted itself in this aspect of Benjamin's theory — the politicization of the work of art. The focus was on the similar situation of the working class and the intellectuals, namely, that neither has control over the means of production because they do not own them. Interpreted as a natural affinity between these two social groups, the students foresaw a new alliance between workers and intellectuals that was destined to bring about the revolution. Benjamin did not go far enough for Scharang, however, and he disagrees with Benjamin's basic theorem that mechanical reproducibility has emancipated art from the realm of ritual. He argues that as long as art cannot liberate itself from its illusionary character, it remains tied to ritual, even if a secularized one. That art sheds its illusory nature can therefore no longer be discussed in terms of the emancipation of art, but in terms of its end.

Scharang's article reflects an important aspect of the 1960s aesthetic discussion—the debate about the death of literature. On the other hand, and quite similar to the contradictory nature of the SDS article on art as commodity, Scharang still tries to develop a strategy that aims at transforming art into an emancipatory and revolutionary instrument. Following Benjamin, Scharang expects the artist to take an engaged position. Artistic means or techniques that reflect the difference between that which is and that which ought to be should be developed in order to restore art's rational quality. Second, Scharang calls upon the artists to seize ownership of their means of production in order to control them.

Postulating revolutionary solidarity between workers and students because of their analogous position vis-à-vis the means of production did not solve the problems confronting the student movement's revolutionary theory. The question remains, What is precisely the relationship between these two social groups? We have previously discussed the students' self-understanding as a kind of midwife for the revolutionary consciousness that the West German working class lacked. The concept of the culture industry rendered the function of the intelligentsia even more complicated. The Benjaminian turn of the student movement was a response to this dilemma, not only because of his call for partisanship in artistic and cultural production, but also because of the materialist dialectic that his reception reintroduced.

This turn and the student movement's ambivalent approach to Adorno is also reflected in the SDS article. The article does not use the Adornian term "culture industry" but rather Hans Magnus Enzensberger's term "mind" or "consciousness industry" (*Bewußtseins-industrie*). Enzensberger developed this term in his 1962 essay "Industrialization of the Mind," following in parts Adorno's line of argument. He criticizes, however, the Adornian term "culture industry" as deceptive because it still veils the fact that the consciousness industry is immediately and purposefully entwined with the economic and political makeup of society.[71] The main difference between these two theorists consists, however, in Enzensberger's basic assumption that capitalism creates the contradictions that will lead to its own demise. His affinity to Benjamin's cultural theory made Enzensberger attractive for the SDS group. Enzensberger presupposes an inherent dialectic of the mind industry, which simultaneously generates moments of affirmation and negation of the existing social order. He argues that the mind industry needs to grant certain liberties at least on a theoretical level in order to be effective. For instance, the consciousness industry needs to pay lip service to basic human rights, particularly freedom and equality. According to Enzensberger, people's belief in the fiction that they freely determine their own fate and that of their community is cultivated because it in fact makes them susceptible to domination. The consciousness industry cannot function successfully without propagating false consciousness. Hence it is in a permanent flux, producing and multiplying its own contradictions, since it can never truly grant that which it promises.

For Enzensberger, hope for change rests precisely in this dialectic inherent to the mind industry. While deceiving the masses, it at the same time cracks open its own smooth surface and exposes its immanent contradictions. Thus Enzensberger locates a moment of resistance in the space that opens up between these contradictions. He maintains that although the means of production of the consciousness industry are not in the hands of the intelligentsia, this intelligentsia still represents the productive force on which the culture industry has to rely.[72] If the intelligentsia refuses to work for the culture industry, it ultimately breaks down. This is precisely the point where the intelligentsia gains power to shape at least part of the culture industry, even if they do not own the means of production. Like Benjamin, Enzensberger calls on the artists and intellectuals to make use of the space of resistance that is inherent to the consciousness industry.

Art Is Dead! Long Live the Street Theater!

By 1968 Enzensberger seemed to have changed his optimistic tune and was accused of sounding the death knell for literature in the journal *Kursbuch*, which he edited. This charge stemmed from a profound misreading of his position. *Kursbuch* simply spelled out the crisis of literature in contemporary society in two contributions to its November 1968 issue by Karl Markus Michel and Enzensberger himself. Michel's article "Ein Kranz für die Literatur" (A wreath for literature) focused on the French student movement, but its analysis also applied to West Germany, while Enzensberger's article "Commonplaces on the Newest Literature" discussed specifically West German literary culture. Both essays raised much controversy for three reasons. First, their evaluation of postwar literary culture in West Germany was extremely negative and was subsequently mistaken as a pronouncement of literature's death. Second, they viewed the student movement as a positive influence on German culture. In comparison to the students, the left-liberal literary establishment came out badly in Michel's and Enzensberger's essays. Finally, the metaphor of the death of literature, which these articles used, challenged the self-understanding of the West German literary intelligentsia as an oppositional force within society.

Michel, for instance, harshly criticized experimental literature à la Heissenbüttel, which had been cherished by the cultural elites as the most avant-garde mode of literary writing. Michel argued that this so-called avant-garde literature was progressive only with respect to form. Its content was, however, far removed from social reality, and he concluded that "the regions into which [this literature] advanced cannot be found on any utopian atlas and much less so on any atlas of society."[73] West German literature in the postwar period thus functioned only as a "social clue like magic, myth, religion in the past," even when it tried to strike a critical pose.[74]

While the socioeconomic and political restoration ran its full course, literature began to compensate for a number of historical, political, and social shortcomings, which Enzensberger poignantly summarized as "the wish to compensate, at least intellectually, for the complete bankruptcy of the German Reich; the evidently urgent need, regardless of the great collective crime, to once again be regarded as a cultured people"; and finally as "a form of anti-fascism, that satisfied itself with having better taste than the Nazis and that manifested its democratic mentality by buying what the former called 'degenerate': pictures on which nothing can be recognized and poems with nothing in them."[75]

To put it in a nutshell: literature and its authors became institutionalized as the social conscience of the German nation, but at the same time neutralized as a political force. Still, neither Michel nor Enzensberger had suggested that literature was dead. Instead, they claimed, it was simply useless: "Literary works cannot be accorded an essential social function under present conditions."[76]

The French student movement had originally disseminated the slogan "L'art est mort, ne consommez pas son cadavre," which was quickly picked up by the West German students and was also at the heart of the misunderstanding about the death of literature. Both Enzensberger and Michel emphasized that this slogan was nothing new, but represented an old metaphor deeply rooted in the Western tradition. Michel points out that the students draw in their slogans and graffiti on such canonic names as Heraclitus, Nietzsche, Camus, and Rimbaud, and not solely on such heroes of the proletarian revolution as Mao and Che Guevara. He argues that "this is all Occident, and even the line about the death of art has belonged for at least 150 years to the sacred inventory of the very culture against which it is now played; it is part of a beautiful ritual of melancholic lament or prophetic promise—lament for a world that has no more dreams, and a promise of another world that will no longer need any."[77]

Unraveling the cultural heritage of the student movement's protest was not an attempt to belittle the students as lacking originality.

On the contrary, for both Michel and Enzensberger, the student movement's use of these traditions for their graffiti had a much larger import than they ever had when published in more customary places such as books. The space in or on which the graffiti were written—walls of houses and other public edifices—was itself meaningful. The strength of the graffiti does not arise from the bourgeois category of originality, but from its omnipresence. The message itself is not novel either; it is a call for the political realization of the always promised but never fulfilled gratification of social and individual desires.[78] Michel, viewing the developments of the student movement and the changes it initiated with great hope, maintained that the decay of literature was not initiated by the students' criticism. He argued that the student movement's protest against and criticism of established literary culture had a positive effect on it, even if it exposed literature's impotence.[79]

Enzensberger too endorsed the student movement's turn away from literature (i.e., from belles lettres) in favor of operative genres.[80] He nevertheless took an equally critical look at the West German literary elite and the student movement. He criticized the latter for taking aim at the wrong target—the older generation of West German authors. He suggested instead that the students focus their attention and revolutionary energies on cultural institutions, since it was not literary writing in itself that Enzensberger viewed as the problem but its incorporation into the culture industry.[81] Enzensberger attracted attention to the institutionalized structures of domination and called on the students for a revolutionary transformation of the cultural institutions. His criticism of the student movement's attack on various authors was not a defense of the literary status quo. Instead, he appealed to members of the West German intelligentsia to support the student movement with their literary efforts. They should participate in what Enzensberger called a political literacy program for Germany. They should begin to use so-called operative genres, that is, politically committed texts stripped of any fictionality, along the lines of Günter Walraff's reports about factory work, Ulrike Meinhof's political commentaries, or Bahman Nirumand's book on Persia.[82] For Enzensberger, not all literature was dead, but only that which claimed fictionality and autonomy. He too argued for a committed literature and supported the students' call for documentary genres with his own works.

The student movement's preference for documentary literature did not, however, come out of nowhere. The reemergence of a documentary literature expressed the crisis of literary writing in postwar West Germany even before the students' attack on bourgeois culture articulated it most radically.[83] The discussion about operative genres had dominated the literary discourse since the early 1960s, primarily based on the success of the documentary theater. Documentary theater historically precedes the student movement and anticipated some of the issues that became pertinent for the latter as well. As early as 1962 Rolf Hochhut's documentary drama *The Deputy* posed the question of the responsibility for the Nazi past and the Holocaust, which preoccupied the students. The student movement's protest could reciprocate by stimulating documentary theater. The best examples are perhaps author Peter Weiss's play on the Vietnam War as well as Enzensberger's documentary play on the revolution in Cuba and his documentary novel on the Spanish revolutionary Durruti.[84]

In spite of their radical slogan about the death of art, the students did not abandon it altogether. They used aesthetic means to articulate their demands. Their protest marches were colorful, and they used satire and parody to ridicule the authorities. They wanted to endow art again with a social function: no longer beautiful illusion but partisan witness to the real world and its injustices. This function required art to leave its ghetto, which the hegemonic culture had ideologically cloaked as the autonomy of art. The student movement therefore tried to develop its own artistic expressions as an alternative to the hegemonic bourgeois culture. Street theater is a good case in point for illustrating the student movement's struggle for an alternative aesthetic praxis.[85]

At the heart of the street theater was its emergence from a specific political situation — the extraparliamentary opposition in the 1960s, of which the student movement was a significant part — and its foundation on an operative aesthetic. It is related to the documentary theater in that it also uses authentic documents and the principle of montage and has a similar didactic impetus. Like the documentary theater, street theater aimed to inform its audience about sociopolitical issues and to encourage critical assessment of them. Street theater was, however, more radical than the documentary theater. For one, it abandoned the entire institution of the theater instead of trying to work within its parameters, as the documentary playwrights did. Second, it aimed at eventually transforming the audience from passive spectators to actors in the political arena. Since the street theater started as a mode of political activism, it had little to do with the crisis of the established and publicly financed theaters, the *Staatstheater*, in the Federal Republic. Still, these public theaters' immediate response to street theater demonstrates that the hegemonic culture felt threatened by the students' experiments in alternative artistic practices.[86]

As with many aspects of the student movement, the street theater is a complicated phenomenon. The borders between street theater in the narrow sense of the word—theater groups that performed only on the street—and independent theater groups, the number of which increased dramatically in the 1970s, are fuzzy.[87] The motivation, aesthetic strategies, and goals of street theater and other independent theater groups were very similar if not identical. They developed out of the same political milieu, and in some cases street theater groups turned into permanent independent groups, addressing a more specific audience such as apprentices or prison inmates.

This retreat from the streets, which provides the most general audience, had several reasons. Many street theater groups had sprung up in the struggle against the Emergency Laws.[88] Once those laws had been passed by the federal legislature, these street theater groups were faced with the bitter recognition that their mode of protest had had little impact on parliamentary decisions. In addition, many street theater groups experienced a high degree of hostility from the men and women on the streets they tried to address. For instance, one such organization, the Socialist Street Theater Berlin (West), reports that their theatrical events were successful only with already politicized high school and university students, but failed miserably with the depoliticized larger public, particularly with workers: "Our early morning attempts to perform our plays in front of factories in Berlin failed miserably, not only because anticommunist and antistudent prejudices were particularly stubborn in Berlin, but also because the workers did not have any desire—for understandable reasons—to watch our plays at six o'clock in the morning. We were lucky if we got away without being beaten up."[89]

Within the street theater movement we can distinguish two main tendencies: the action-oriented street theater (*aktionistisches Straßentheater*) strongly inspired by antiauthoritarian ideals, and agitprop theater in the tradition of workers' theaters during the Weimar Republic. The action-oriented street theater did not use any theatrical codes that might have marked the event as theater, since it wanted to prevent the passersby from easily slipping into a passive spectator role. The goal was to eliminate the separation of spectators and actors and to turn the spectators into actors in order to channel the audience's energy into direct political actions. The action-oriented theater was controversial within the student movement. While some groups saw the transformation of the audience from spectators to actors as the essential role of street theater and as an element of the overall cultural revolution,[90] others were more critical. The latter, more attuned to the fact that no class-conscious proletariat existed in West Germany, cautioned against premature attempts at agitation.[91] Since action-oriented theater groups were met with lack of understanding and therefore with much hostility on the part of the audience, it proved to be short-lived.

Agitprop theater groups were much more positively received on the streets. Their success had to do with their reliance on the same theatrical means as those of their predecessors in the 1920s and 1930s; that is, they drew on already established, recognizable, and accepted aesthetic codes.[92] Descriptions of the agitprop theaters emphasize the stereotypical presentation of the dramatis personae by the use of props and masks—the workers in hard hats and overalls, the capitalist with a potbelly, cigar, and top hat—exaggerated acting, and visual aids such as photographs and posters articulating the political message of the performance.[93] These plays or revues were always based on a topical issue and used the technique of montage, interrupting the flow of the plot with songs and spoken texts, thereby feeding quotations and other informational material into the play, often by means of a chorus. This kind of theatrical presentation aimed at preventing an individualized and psychological identification with the characters of the performance, in which the political content could be lost.

One of the most difficult problems for most street theaters was the dialectic of form and content. They were either carried away by the artistic component, resulting in the reception of the performance as an entertaining spectacle, or by the political content, in which case the performance became a mere oral recitation (*Sprechstück*) with no aesthetic appeal and thus often unable to attract the attention of passersby. Though most street theater groups came to understand the significance of the dialectical relationship of aesthetic form and political content by way of trial and error, they insisted on the primacy of the political. The aesthetic means had no value in themselves but were first and foremost a vehicle for the political end; as one group phrased it, "to promote changing our society absolutely must be the focal point of each and every performance."[94] For this and other groups, street theater should remain on the level of agitation and propaganda.

Not every street theater group was so ambitious. Some were critical of such a sweeping endorsement of agitation and saw themselves more in an Enlightenment tradition. They rejected pure agitation and propaganda as tantamount to the manipulative strategies of the culture industry. For them, the educational impetus of their theater had to prevail by providing the audience with an opportunity to take an informed position. They took to the street because they saw the streets as the last censorship-free environment and street theater as the only possible space for developing an alternative public sphere.[95] The biggest problem, which led to much frustration, was the inability of most groups to reach beyond the community of the already converted. Street theater ran the danger of quickly deteriorating into a politically ineffective, mere "culinary pleasure at political events of the left," as one street theater group critically assessed their own work.[96] Whether the efforts of the street theater and other aesthetic practices of the student movement restored a genuine social function to art is questionable. Aesthetic issues played, however, a significant role for the conceptual framework of the student movement and its goal of cultural revolution.

CHAPTER 3: Post-1968 Blues:
Spontis, Violence, and
New Subjectivity

By the mid-1970s it was clear: not art, but the student movement, had died. Still, the upheavals the students' protest had
generated did not allow for a return to business as usual. The
conceptual vacuum that the student movement left behind set the
stage for a protracted struggle among various social and political
groups attempting to fill it. The reasons for the student movement's
decline were manifold. For one, life cycles played an important role.
Many student activists concluded their studies and left the university.
A fair number embarked on "the long march through the institutions," which means they reentered mainstream society by taking
jobs within the hegemonic culture. Their goal, however, was to reform society from within. Others went mainstream without carrying
any cultural revolutionary ambitions over into their new middle-
class lifestyle. Second, the hegemonic culture proved itself to be more
adaptable to change than expected. It managed to integrate part
of the student movement's demands into its own agenda and thus
partially contained the challenge. Finally, the students had failed to
resolve one of the most burning questions of their antiauthoritarian
beginnings, namely, the split between the personal/subjective and
the political/objective dimensions.

As the student movement ran its course, collective political identifications had gained the upper hand to the extent that personal issues
or matters of subjectivity were denounced as counterrevolutionary.
With the movement's orthodox Marxist turn, the individual and
his or her needs were totally subsumed to the concept of class. The
international class struggle was everything, the individual nothing.
As a result, those aspects of life that had traditionally been relegated
to the private sphere, such as subjectivity and personal needs, had

{67}

little place in the student movement's universe, even though many student activists suffered under these conditions, as they admit in retrospect. The shortcomings were apparent already in 1968, when women started to protest the omission and often belittling of their concerns as "personal," that is, secondary to the political struggle and therefore insignificant. Helke Sander's infamous speech in that year, where she harshly criticized the male student activists' sexist behavior and asserted that the private sphere is political, put the personal back on the agenda of countercultural politics.[1]

This protest of female students marked only the beginning of a time in which subjectivity and the self became ever more prominent. The notion of a "politics of the self," as Richard McCormick so aptly translated the German phrase *Politik in der ersten Person*, signifies a new perception of political commitment and activism that is oriented toward the immediate and personal concerns of its practitioners: "Theoretical and global perspectives were renounced in favor of attention to local and personal issues, to immediate and concrete problems, to concern with direct physical and sensual experience—and to sexual politics."[2]

The 1970s witnessed the emergence of not only a strong and lasting women's movement but also numerous other countercultural groups, often subsumed under the term *new social movements.* Although these new social movements were extremely critical of the student movement, their alternative concept of politics of the self has its precursor in the antiauthoritarian phase of the student movement. Initially, the students' view of the process of politicization did not abstract from the personal-affective dimension of life, but rather aimed at overcoming the separation of the private and the public sphere within bourgeois culture by emphasizing the personal and subjective dimension of experience. At the same time, we cannot obliterate the significant differences between the student movement and the new social movement, or, in other words, of the post-1968 counterculture. The alternative culture aggressively developed its own projects (bookstores, printing and crafts shops, farm co-ops, and so forth) in an attempt to create a countereconomy and a whole alternative lifestyle, instead of striving to change mainstream society itself as the former activists of the student movement still tried to do. As a result, the new social movements approached the question of the political struggle no longer within the framework of social class, but instead primarily with respect to personal experience and the concrete problems of everyday life.[3] All of this amounted to a retreat from mainstream culture, which was often criticized as a self-ghettoization of the post-1968 counterculture.

Those "bourgeois" critics against whom the student movement had directed its attacks became hopeful that the tide had finally turned. They were interested in resurrecting their aesthetic as the hegemonic paradigm and hailed the new interest in the self, personal relationships, self-expression, and subjectivity, particularly in literature. In this context they made use of the debate on the death of literature, which we have previously discussed, "as an anticipatory cliché, preparing the entrance of the new as the saviour of a much assailed literary tradition."[4] Literary critics coined the label New Subjectivity, which is today often used to designate the 1970s as a coherent literary epoch. It implicitly defines the literature of this time in opposition to the literature of the 1960s, equating the period of the student movement with a politicization of literature that eliminated subjectivity from literary representation. New Subjectivity is therefore meant to mark the 1970s as the break with the cultural politics of the late 1960s and herald the beginning of a new literary era characterized by depoliticization and a return to the bourgeois aesthetic traditions the student movement had challenged.[5]

This kind of literary-historical generalization is problematic, for literary-historical periodization has the tendency to obliterate the complexity of literary developments and reduce them to a mono-causal model that reads each literary development merely as a reaction to the previous one.[6] Literary-historical approaches are also questionable if they fail to problematize the correlation as well as the discrepancy between actual literary production—narrative, dramatic and poetic texts—and its discussion in literary criticism. In the Federal Republic, where academic literary criticism has separated itself from journalistic criticism, the latter strongly influences the identification, naming, and promotion of literary trends.[7] It is first and foremost journalistic literary criticism that develops dominant literary paradigms. Its criticism is based on ideal types of "good" literature, so to speak, against which it judges the current literary production. Most importantly, the literary critics rarely make their implied model of "good literature" explicit—a practice that had drawn harsh criticism from the student movement.

It is therefore often more fruitful to analyze transformations of the literary critical paradigms than of the literature itself, since this analysis highlights the significance of literary critical discourse in shaping the perception of literature. At the same time, it captures the discrepancy between the proclamations of literary criticism and actual literary production. Hence the conceptualization of a literary period in terms of transformations of the literary paradigm not only helps to avoid the reductive pitfalls of periodization but underscores as well the ideological implications of literary criticism and literary historiography.[8]

Although a single epithet such as New Subjectivity does not suffice to capture the complexity of the literature of the time, it nevertheless articulates the dominant paradigm. Karen Kramer convincingly illuminates the intricacies of the term New Subjectivity in the 1970s literary critical discourse. She argues that the term New Subjectivity functioned as a "free floating signifier" that "named less a delineated content than a conceptual free space—an ideological, open space—over which widely differing intellectual and political tendencies struggled to dispose."[9] My examination of the dominant cultural and political discourse during the 1970s follows Kramer's conceptual lead but with special emphasis on how the discourse on New Subjectivity and terrorism intersected and rendered the counterculture's position even more difficult.

Still Opting for the Revolution: The Significance of the RAF

The confrontation of the post-1968 counterculture with its predecessor, the student movement (or, in other words, left-wing oppositional politics) was further complicated by a radical minority of student activists who started to use violence to pursue their project of revolutionary change. The terrorism of the Red Army Faction (RAF, also known as the Baader-Meinhof Group) overshadowed all of West German society and politics during the 1970s.[10] In its attempts to come to grips with terrorism, especially to discover its origins, the public discussion circled around the correlation between imagination and violence. The equation was simple for the political right. The right blamed critical social scientific and philosophical analyses of capitalist society for having fueled RAF terrorism. Especially Marcuse—perhaps the most significant intellectual figure for the student movement—was used as a scapegoat to support this argument.[11]

Pushed to the limits by the increasing frequency and ruthlessness of the RAF's violence, the SPD government finally caved in to the pressure of the opposition and approved far-reaching legal measures against terrorism, quite in contradiction to the SPD's campaign slogan of 1969: "Dare More Democracy!" (*Mehr Demokratie wagen!*). The *Radikalenerlaß*—also known as *Berufsverbote*—was one of the most significant legal changes and had a powerful effect on the generation of the student movement. Passed in 1972 under the SPD administration, the *Radikalenerlaß* or *Berufsverbote* required a thorough background check for all government and state employees, including their political beliefs and history of activism. Membership in a communist or other left-wing student group could lead to exclusion from employment in the public sector. This law was threatening for those young people whose professional skills were in demand almost exclusively in the public sector, for instance, the entire educational sector, where the government had a monopoly on job distribution.

Changes in criminal law and judicial procedure, which were designed to combat terrorism as well as the expansion of the Federal Agency for the Protection of the Constitution (*Verfassungsschutz*), exemplify only one aspect of the transformation of political culture in West Germany during the 1970s.[12] In a desperate attempt to put an end to terrorist violence, the government authorities tried to control the entire public discourse. This meant that aesthetic culture was as affected by new legislation as the criminal justice system itself. Terrorism achieved that which the student movement had been striving for: the breakdown of the boundaries between art and politics. In 1976 amendments were passed in parliament to the already existing legislation on the distribution of written or visual products glorifying and promoting violence. This newly drafted legislation referred specifically to politically motivated violence (*Gewaltparagraphen* 88a, 130a). Hence the television and film industries did not have to fear liability for their portrayal of acts of everyday violence. The absurd extent to which these laws could be taken quickly became apparent. Since the laws were designed to be retroactive, they had the potential to apply to Kant and Hegel as well, because of their defense of the French Revolution.[13] While most great names of Western culture were not touched by the new laws and the accompanying debate, the paranoid witch-hunt against the intellectual fellow travelers of terrorism (*Sympathisanten*) nevertheless produced censorship, self-censorship, and denunciation within the sphere of cultural production. In his essay on the 1970s, Michael Rutschky gives an excellent assessment of terrorism's less tangible effects. He argues that terrorism deeply affected all aspects of the "universe of speech" and essentially "restructured the representation of individual and social life."[14] His analysis is based on the Habermasian ideal of a societal discourse free of fear in order to form a consensus through rational reasoning without recourse to violence or the threat thereof.

The film *Deutschland im Herbst* (*Germany in Autumn*) captures perhaps best "the mood of hysteria, fear and despair that befell all sections of West German society in the autumn of 1977" because of terrorism.[15] It is an episodic film shot as a coproduction among the most prominent West German directors at the time and edited by Alexander Kluge. The title has a double meaning: It refers to the historical high-water mark terrorism reached in the fall of 1977 with the kidnapping of Hanns-Martin Schleyer (president of the two most important employers' associations), the hijacking of a Lufthansa plane, and the death of the RAF's leaders, Andreas Baader, Gudrun Ensslin, and Jan Carl Raspe, in the maximum security prison in Stuttgart-Stammheim. It also metaphorically describes the 1970s as a period in which a frosty wind cooled down the heated hopes of the student movement and gave rise to a new conservatism in the Federal Republic.[16] One episode—a satirical sketch written by Heinrich Böll and directed by Volker Schlöndorff—illustrates Rutschky's point that terrorism significantly altered the universe of cultural production in West Germany. The sketch shows members of a television program board debating whether a production of Sophocles' *Antigone* for a program called "Youth and Classic Literature" can still be broadcast.

The link between the classical play and the contemporary political situation is quite obvious throughout the film, which opens with footage of the state funeral of Hanns-Martin Schleyer, the victim of RAF terrorists, and closes with scenes from the funeral of the RAF leaders mentioned above. As in Sophocles' play, one person receives a state funeral whereas the others were first denied the right to be buried according to social and religious customs. Like Creon, the ruler of Thebes, whose hatred expresses itself in denying Antigone the right to bury her brother's body, the West German public exhibited a strong desire for revenge and vehemently protested the burial of the terrorists at a public cemetery. In the *Antigone* sketch, the director is required to open his production with a preface in which he clearly distances himself from any connection between his adaptation of Sophocles' play and the current terrorism. The director presents to the board three possible prefaces, but finally the board decides to put the play with the "terrorist women" on ice until the political situation itself cools down.[17] Böll and Schlöndorff reveal how the general hysteria and political climate influenced artistic freedom and demonstrate that art is after all not autonomous but deeply entrenched in politics.

Both the New Subjectivity and the discourse on the RAF are crucial for understanding the development of the West German counterculture in the 1970s. We therefore need to analyze these two aspects, which shaped the political and cultural atmosphere as nothing else did during this time. As we shall see, the concept of subjectivity was not confined to the sphere of literature, but permeated a variety of discourses, albeit under different labels such as New Sensibility, New Introspection, New Narcissism, and New Mode of Socialization [*Neuer Sozialisationstyp*]. Still, whether used by the left or the right, these terms were not employed in a neutral fashion but functioned as combative concepts. Hence they often assumed a derogatory connotation that conceals the fact that a radically subjective approach dominated literature and politics alike, or, in other words, that the literature of New Subjectivity shared much with the post-1968 countercultural development. The terrorism of the RAF also clouded these connections, because whenever terrorist violence was the issue, only a crude rhetoric of distancing was permissible. Consequently, radically subjective statements about the RAF were not recognized as a part of this paradigm of New Subjectivity and were thus doomed to be misunderstood.

The intersection of New Subjectivity and RAF terrorism surfaced most blatantly in the infamous Buback Obituary, which ignited a public outcry and a perception of the post-1968 counterculture as fellow travelers of terrorism.[18] We will analyze this countercultural text in comparison to one of the paradigmatic texts of literary New Subjectivity, Peter Handke's novel *The Moment of True Feeling*, in order to demonstrate how both literature and the new countercultural movements participated in the same discursive transformations, although they were evaluated quite differently by the hegemonic culture. The Buback Obituary also helps clarify why such an insurmountable rift between mainstream culture and the counterculture opened up during the 1970s, a rift that amounted to a breakdown of the cultural consensus and a further differentiation of postwar West German culture.

New Subjectivity: A Necessary Return to Belles Lettres?

Since the Frankfurt Book Fair of 1975, traditional literary critics had been on the forefront in defending what Barbara Kosta calls the "reorientation from a politically engaged literature based on documentary formats . . . to a self-reflective format with the reintroduction of narrative writing."[19] An October 1975 review by Marcel Reich-Ranicki, the chief reviewer of the conservative daily *Frankfurter Allgemeine Zeitung*, praises the literary production in the middle of the 1970s as a necessary "return to belles lettres" and equates it with a heightened appreciation of literary quality. Reich-Ranicki sharply attacks the generation of the student movement: "With respect to literature, nothing came of the student movement, whose leaders and activists were certainly not taciturn. Was the revolt of 1968 perhaps the deed of a loquacious yet speechless generation?" He goes on to answer his rhetorical question with a clear yes. Whereas older writers remained productive and relevant in the mid-1970s, those of the student movement had already begun to fade. Reich-Ranicki devalues the literary works of the latter as insignificant, commenting, not without malicious glee, "The return to literature, despised and denounced six or seven years ago, appears to be difficult."[20]

Reich-Ranicki sees a literary future for the 1968 generation of writers, provided they recognize that they went too far astray with their materialist aesthetic and operative genres. In his opinion, they only need to return to the bourgeois literary tradition, that is, the modern novel originating with Flaubert and modern poetry in the wake of Baudelaire. He names, for example, Max Frisch, Siegfried Lenz (whom he praises for his return to the literary tradition of the novella), Erich Nossack, and Thomas Bernhard as positive contemporary literary models. He holds them in high esteem because these authors are above literary fashions; their writing did not succumb to the politicization of literature the student movement demanded. Instead, they adhered to the true function of literature, which Reich-Ranicki defines as the representation of the individual's suffering in the contemporary world.[21] The advocates of this position denied that this suffering could be thematized politically in terms of "great topoi and anonymous correlations like History, Late Capitalism, and the Bourgeois Subject."[22] Instead, literature can articulate this theme only in individual, existential terms.

The proponents of this position tried to distinguish themselves from those "of yesteryear, who at any occasion explain to us that the novels of Fontane and Thomas Mann are better than today's."[23] Looking at the literary models that these critics cite—Flaubert's or Fontane's realism, Thomas Mann's modernism, Tucholsky's poignant irony—one must acknowledge that Reich-Ranicki and his colleagues did not call for an uncritical, socially blind literature. The majority argued against literature's retreat from the challenges that contemporary society poses and even criticized the regressive tendency of some contemporary literature.[24] They still upheld the idea that literature has to take a critical stance toward society, but within the confines prescribed by the category of the individual. Literature has to speak in the name of the individual against those institutions and powers that try to use or abuse it.[25]

As was typical for the advocates of this position, Reich-Ranicki spoke in very general terms of these "institutions and power," ignoring any deeper social analysis that might allow for a clearer delineation of structures of domination. His argument is, however, purposefully crafted to portray literature beyond ideology and tendentiousness, while maintaining at least on the surface a critical edge. The traditional literary critics argued against an operative aesthetic, instead aiming to resurrect the ideology of literature's autonomy, which relegates literature to the status of a "social conscience" —admonishing but always impartial.

Taken to its extreme, as in the case of Peter M. Stephan's contribution to the debate, even the role of literature as a social conscience could be rejected. He rigorously denounces any politically engaged art because politics is intrinsically connected with the struggle for power. Consequently, he views politics as being in opposition to poetics, which represents for him "the impotence of language" and the "utopia of that which has not yet come into being." For Stephan, the utopian dimension of poetry deteriorates if it is applied to daily life or used for political ends. Operating with the old stereotype of "dirty" politics versus "pure" poetry, he retreats to a 1950s position that grants literature a lasting influence by reducing it to an eternal existential entity that is above social and political life. Literature can therefore only develop a humane counterimage to inhuman politics, but it must refrain from political commitment in order to be "in a higher sense moral."[26] Stephan hailed the poetry of New Subjectivity for having precisely this transcendental quality.

Stephan's definition of New Subjectivity contradicts Reich-Ranicki's. The latter took pains to differentiate his positive understanding of subjectivity from a self-indulgent, regressive introspection (*Innerlichkeit*) or narcissism, thereby insisting on a socially critical but impartial literature—a literature above the fray of day-to-day politics: "We do indeed need the New Subjectivity much and happily discussed nowadays. We do not need a new regressive introspection. If the renewed consciousness of literature equals a retreat from the public sphere, if it is a reaction to politicization, if 'the inward path'—to cite a title by Hermann Hesse—were to become fashionable, this would mean that the German writers still like to go from one extreme to the other and that the baby is thrown out with the bathwater."[27]

The proponents of this position stressed the necessity of objectifying the subjective experience on which aesthetic representation has to be based. Objectification had been one of the most significant categories in the student movement's discourse and its attempts to develop a materialist aesthetic. Objectification meant to overcome the hegemonic bourgeois perspective focusing on the individual in favor of a collective, proletarian one. The students' understanding of objectification was therefore a far cry from that of traditional literary critics. The latter sought refuge in a turn toward the natural sciences because of their reputed objectivity. Emphasizing the subjective moments of research in the natural sciences, this approach established a connection between natural sciences and literature. It argued that subjectivity functions as the common denominator for aesthetic culture and science, which differ only in the thematic scope and the mode of representation.[28] Only if literary representation strikes the balance between subjectivity and objectivity does it gain validity.

Like Reich-Ranicki, another critic, Dieter Zimmermann, returns to an author who neither belongs to the generation of the student movement nor literary New Subjectivity for exemplifying his thesis, namely, Uwe Johnson. Zimmermann praises Johnson for the variety of material he collected and integrated into his work in order to go beyond his personal experience and to transcend his limited subjective horizon. He compares one of the paradigmatic texts of New Subjectivity, Nicolas Born's novel *Die erdabgewandte Seite der Geschichte* (The dark side of history), with Johnson's work and criticizes Born's text for lacking a second narrative perspective. In short, Zimmermann mainly argues for multiperspectivity in literature.

These two categories—wealth of material and multiperspectivity —are strongly indebted to a positivistic scientific paradigm that believes in amassing data in order to achieve representational objectivity and underscore the argument that the aesthetic of traditional literary critics was founded on nineteenth-century paradigms. The self-reflexive attitude of traditional literary criticism, which distinguished a positive concept of New Subjectivity from a negative one of regressive introspection, should not deflect from the fact that

New Subjectivity represented indeed ammunition for reestablishing "the separation of literature and politics—a very German tradition which had been challenged during the 1960s."[29] At the same time, the concept of New Subjectivity articulated within the hegemonic discourse one of the key concepts of the 1970s: the self and his or her voice, which no longer had to sing in unison with the international class struggle.

The Left on New Subjectivity/New Sensibility

For the left, and particularly for the student activists, the situation was much more complicated than for the hegemonic culture. For one, the student movement had splintered into numerous left-wing circles, which were constantly combating each other. In addition, the left as a whole was facing a radically subjective approach to politics and culture, which articulated itself in a generational rift within the counterculture. The women's movement's credo that the personal is the political had continuously gained in support, first and foremost among the post-1968 activists—the carriers of the emerging new countercultural movements. The West German left was divided on this issue into two major camps, roughly speaking: On the one hand were those hostile to the new countercultural developments then crystallizing around the notion of subjectivity; this group took a negative view of New Subjectivity as a revitalization of bourgeois thinking. On the other hand were those who sided with the new movements, praising them as progressive in comparison to the rigid left-wing culture of the later student movement; members of this group were consequently more accepting of the paradigm of New Subjectivity.

Though aware of the problematic revival of subjectivity, particularly its susceptibility to exploitation for conservative ends, the latter position perceived symbolic systems such as literature as a privileged space in which to overcome such past sins as the reduction of the entire life world to the political in a traditional, narrow sense. One of the leftist defenders of this new approach to politics and culture, Hazel E. Hazel, argued with great caution for understanding the progressive nature of New Subjectivity: "The new interest in literature and the poetic, the individual, and sensitivity could nevertheless be seen as political progress once the term 'left' had almost become a synonym for 'limited' and 'narrow-minded' and 'disorganized.' "[30] From this perspective, New Subjectivist literature such as Karin Struck's *Klassenliebe* and Peter Schneider's *Lenz* represent a step in the right direction, since these texts try to mediate subjective experience and search for a new identity after the failure of the student movement. The category of subjectivity takes on a positive meaning in opposition to the student movement's category of class as the predominant identifying code.

These left advocates of New Subjectivity maintained that processes of identification cannot be based only on theoretical and political ideas that abstract from the individual's sensuous needs and desires. They perceived this abstraction, which expressed itself in the rejection of bourgeois aesthetic culture as a faulty response to the students' demand "to sublate the separation of politics and the personal."[31] This position in defense of subjectivity as the ground for processes of identification and therefore against a mere conceptual culture shows strong similarities with Herbert Marcuse's concept of New Sensibility. It raises the question of whether the proclaimed literature and culture of New Subjectivity represents indeed something absolutely new or rather a rediscovery of the antiauthoritarian positions that dominated the beginnings of the student movement, as Moray McGowan suggests in her assessment of the 1970s.[32]

Left-wing criticism did not use the notion New Subjectivity to discuss the literary and cultural changes in process since the early 1970s. Instead, it referred to these transformations as an emerging New Sensibility. In his *Essay on Liberation*, Marcuse summarizes his complex concept of New Sensibility and describes the student movement as its first manifestation. New Sensibility represents a transformation of both instinct and consciousness, that is, a new sensitivity to structures of domination. It has a revolutionary potential because it emancipates libidinal needs and exhibits a vital need for the abolition of injustice and misery. The student movement had indeed fought in many cases and on many fronts against injustice and social misery. For Marcuse, the liberation of the aesthetic dimension of human life does not mean a rejection or suppression of rationality. He argues that only a rationality fashioned by imagination can develop freedom. His concept aims at a reintegration of sensuous and rational experience in order to gain a new quality of knowledge.

> Beyond the limits (and beyond the power) of repressive reason now appears the prospect for a new relationship between sensibility and reason, namely, the harmony between sensibility and a radical consciousness: rational faculties capable of projecting and defining the objective (material) conditions of freedom, its real limits and chances. But instead of being shaped and permeated by the rationality of domination, the sensibility would be guided by imagination, mediating between the rational faculties and the sensuous needs.[33]

Marcuse establishes a structural correlation of New Sensibility and art by means of imagination. New Sensibility anticipates a new reality principle because it recognizes it in art while striving for the realization of the utopian content of art. Finally, Marcuse's definition of New Sensibility has a collective character. He maintains that the aesthetic universe as the foundation for liberation cannot emerge from the existing reality principle and social institutions, unless it does so as a collective practice, creating a new environment to overcome the old reality principle of late capitalism.

The concept of New Sensibility had originally gained attention in 1968 in a clash between the student movement and the Frankfurt school. It was triggered by Jürgen Habermas and his critical assessment of the students' protest.[34] Habermas attacked the oppositional students for their false interpretation of Marxism (in his opinion), their incorrect evaluation of the political and social situation in West Germany, and their self-deception as a revolutionary avant-garde. It was, however, his criticism of the student movement's mode of protest as infantile that ignited the most outrage among the generation of 1968. Habermas claimed that the students' protest exhibits the sort of confusion of reality and fantasy that is characteristic of children. He perceived the affective and sensuous dimension of the students' protest as pathological and irrational. Instead, Habermas wanted the students to stay true to the project of the Enlightenment by working to establish a merely rational discourse stripped of all emotion-laden symbolism and fantasies, of which the earlier student movement made ample use.

In his response to Habermas, Reimut Reiche, a student activist, employed the notion of New Sensibility. In accordance with Marcuse, Reiche upheld the legitimacy of the sensuous dimension in human experience as well as of imagination, and, therefore, its legitimacy in politics as well. "The ability to evaluate a political situation realistically as well as to comprehend it quickly in order to correct it with the help of imagination is part of the New Sensibility. The development of such abilities requires a greater integration of affective tendencies that have not yet been adopted by today's culture."[35] Like Marcuse, Reiche uses the concept of New Sensibility as an intrinsically collective notion. He suggests that a cure for individual psychic deformations is possible only in a collective practice. Only if the student movement succeeds in establishing rationally acceptable but also emotionally attractive images for identification can the psychic disintegration and resulting political apathy be overcome. In this context, Reiche's article discusses the significance of art as a symbolic articulation of desires and its correlation with psychic processes. Symbols are important in Reiche's conceptualization of revolutionary change because they express collective political identifications on an emotional, sensuous level. He viewed the new style of protest, for which he cites not only demonstrations but also the different lifestyle of the student movement, as a playful and successful experimentation with the new reality principle.

In contrast to traditional literary criticism's understanding of subjectivity as synonymous with individuality and in opposition to the collective and the political, the student movement's concept of New Sensibility represents the mediation of the subjective and objective dimension of human life in order to gain a new understanding of the totality of human experience and knowledge. New Sensibility encompasses and mediates individual and collective as well as rational and aesthetic needs without denying their political dimension. Thus the Marcusean concept of New Sensibility as it was adopted by the antiauthoritarian student movement and revitalized in the 1970s cannot be accused of advocating a narcissistic introspection or escapist irrationalism. Those who defended the emerging cultural paradigm of New Sensibility and its political application recognized it as a corrective to the orthodox left-wing politics of the numerous Leninist and Maoist sects that dominated the political landscape of the university in the wake of the student movement.

Those within the left who were skeptical if not outright hostile toward the cultural and political changes that the terms New Subjectivity and New Sensibility denoted indeed charged it with self-indulgent introspection and petit-bourgeois provincialism and disparagingly referred to it as the "New Narcissism." They perceived the New Sensibility of the 1970s as a retreat from politics, as expressed, for example, in Michael Schneider's criticism of the new countercultural paradigm of subjectivity:

> First the rigorous "break" with the bourgeois past, then the "break" with the left present; first the iconoclasm of use value against the sensitive emotional culture of the bourgeoisie in the name of Marxism, then the "use value iconoclasm" against Marxist theory in the name of an allegedly new emotional culture—a New Sensibility. But far from acknowledging the retreat into the private sphere as that which it is, namely, a retreat from politics, the intelligentsia still consecrates it as a political virtue.[36]

This negative evaluation of the New Sensibility of the 1970s articulates the fear that the mediation of rationality and sensuousness or of the political and the aesthetic, which the old Marcusean understanding of New Sensibility envisioned, did not take place. Reversing Reiche's argument, those hostile to the changes within the counterculture maintained that the rational and the political vanished in the onslaught of the long-repressed sensuous and aesthetic needs. They perceived New Sensibility as an escape from the burden of a socially emancipatory politics, since the former self-proclaimed liberators of the proletariat returned to their own class origins after the failure of their revolutionary project—back to the future of the bourgeoisie.

At first sight, the left's negative evaluation of New Sensibility seems to approximate that of traditional literary criticism. However, the proponents of this position did not suggest a restoration of bourgeois aesthetic culture. Instead, they drew on the tradition of a socialist aesthetics, arguing for an appropriation of the progressive forms and contents of bourgeois aesthetic culture for a Marxist aesthetics. Michael Schneider, an opponent of New Subjectivity, offers Bertolt Brecht as a positive model for a socialist aesthetic culture that would be based on an adaptation of bourgeois culture as well as on operative genres. He advocates an adaptation of Goethe, Hölderlin, and Heinrich von Kleist, while dismissing contemporary literary productions such as Peter Schneider's *Lenz*, Ulrich Plenzdorf's *The New Sufferings of Young W.* or Peter Handke's *A Moment of True Feeling*. These literary texts, which he cites in order to denounce the turn of the student movement toward a self-indulgent, introspective literature, represent in fact attempts to adopt the positive examples of bourgeois cultural traditions, as he himself suggests.[37] Plenzdorf's play uses Goethe's *Sufferings of Young Werther*, Schneider works with Büchner's *Lenz*, and Handke's hero of *A Moment of True Feeling*, Gregor Keuschnig, shows affinity with Rainer Maria Rilke's Malte Laurids Brigge as well as Franz Kafka's Gregor Samsa. Whether these adaptations are successful is, of course, another question, one that Schneider unfortunately does not address.

The split within the left could not be resolved productively in spite of voices such as Hazel E. Hazel's, which tried to make the changes understandable against the backdrop of the decline of the student movement. The negative perception of New Sensibility was dominant particularly among those remnants of the student movement that returned to orthodox Marxist political positions and totally ignored the theories of the antiauthoritarian wing of the student movement. These groups approached politics as well as aesthetic culture mainly on the level of a crude materialist critique of ideology, still using the category of class as their main analytic tool. The label "traditional New Left" therefore serves as an appropriate description to capture the essential feature that distinguishes this approach from that of the new countercultural movements developing since the early 1970s. Orthodox Marxists displayed not only a lack of self-criticism but a lack of understanding for the new concept of politics—the politics of the self. As an intellectual culture privileging conceptual cognitive processes, it was unable to communicate with the younger generation of activists who focused on the sensuous and aesthetic dimension of cognitive processes and reclaimed the legitimacy of subjective experience.

The New Personality Type (Neuer Sozialisationstyp)

This inability to come to terms with the new countercultural movements and their notion of politics led the traditional New Left to conceptualize the emerging post-1968 counterculture in psychological terms and to perceive them as merely a generational problem. Many 1968ers viewed the politics of the self not as a valid new concept but as the expression of a sociopsychological transformation or even deformation on the part of their successors in protest. As a result, they saw their successors as engaging in the criticized self-indulgent introspection and quickly labeled them as victims of a new irrationalism. To explain the differences of the post-1968 counterculture, the sociopsychological theory of the new mode of socialization, which results in a new personality type, was developed. Thomas Ziehe introduced the term "new socialization type" (*Neuer Sozialisationstyp*) in the mid-1970s, defining this new personality type by comparing it to the traditional bourgeois individual, whose identity is established in a successful resolution of the oedipal conflict.[38] He argues that owing to sociocultural transformations—particularly the increased social significance of mass consumption, the dissolution of traditional values, and the importance of extrafamiliar socialization within late capitalism—the oedipal conflict can no longer be acted out in the family. As a result, a new personality type emerges characterized by a weakness of both ego and superego, leading to an inability to cope with problematic and frustrating situations and difficulties in interpersonal relationships.

Because the proponents of Ziehe's theory based their argument on a materialist critique of political economy—a mode of analysis quite familiar to the generation of the student movement—the concept of the new personality type won rapid acceptance within the traditional left. This model postulated a basic correlation between the traditional bourgeois mode of socialization and liberal competitive capitalism, on the one hand, and a correlation between the new mode of socialization and modern consumer capitalism, on the other hand. A line was drawn between the 1960s student movement, which still leaned toward the classical bourgeois profile of socialization, and the post-1968 generation with its strong affinity to the new mode of socialization. The classical bourgeois profile of socialization was now treated positively, since it purportedly leads to political activism, and the new mode of socialization negatively, since it allegedly leads to a retreat from politics.[39]

Yet as Jörg Bopp points out, this attempt to differentiate between two generations is highly questionable. While Ziehe's theory suggests that a qualitative change took place in capitalism after the Second World War, Bopp locates such a qualitative change at the turn of the century, when today's monopoly capitalism replaced the liberal laissez-faire capitalism. He therefore views both generations as determined by the same mode of capitalism and concludes, "The relationship between the historical development of capitalism and the life stories of the generation of 1968 does not support the attempt to draw a sociopsychological distinction between this generation and the youth of today."[40]

As a stereotype, the new personality type was reduced to its regressive components and directly linked to a particularly non-dogmatic group within the new counterculture, the Spontis, who believed in spontaneous, immediate, sensuous, and authentic articulations of dissent rather than theoretical discourse and organized protest. They exerted strong influence on the universities from approximately 1975 to the early 1980s, when Sponti groups dominated the student unions at a number of universities.[41] They were stigmatized as "lascivious, libertine, and chaotic (in short, 'oral')."[42] Jens Huhn's claim that the behavior and articulations of the Urban Indians, a specific group within the Sponti left, exhibited precisely these features ascribed to the new type of socialization demonstrates the prejudices with which the generation of 1968 approached their successors.[43] He employs all of the buzzwords used to denounce the Urban Indians, and by extension the Sponti movement, drawing on the stereotype that they are unable to maintain communication or relationships because they are unable to bear any confrontation. Hence they retreat from potential disturbance into narcissistic introspection. Referring to their enmity to theory, Jens Huhn constructs a caricature of immature and infantile Spontis that even his careful choice of words—"one can understand" or "one gets the impression"—cannot veil. In his portrayal, the ecological concerns of the post-1968 counterculture become the cry of the baby that cannot yet distinguish itself from the mother nor has as yet an independent conception of reality. Huhn describes the Spontis as infantile, claiming that they project their own limited experience and imaginations onto reality, which is indeed characteristic of children. His argument resembles Habermas's critique of the student movement in the late 1960s and implies that, like children, the Spontis too will eventually grow up.

It is ironic that the same people whose political protest had once been belittled as infantile now used the same strategy to marginalize an alternative politics with which they could not come to terms. The Spontis' supposed enmity to theory showed that the traditional left was unable to deal with modes of perception and communication that did not operate on a conventional conceptual level. The traditional New Left did not take up the challenge that the new countercultural developments posed, and it failed to call its own theoretical positions into question. As Almuth Bruder-Bezzel and Jürgen Bezzel point out, the old 1968ers could not recognize that the new countercultural protest represented a return to their own antiauthoritarian beginnings: "Today's alternative scene grew out of the student movement, or at least from the early phase of the student movement. It keeps the ideas of the student movement alive in the subculture, but represents at the same time a break with the depressing lethargy."[44]

The new countercultural movements continued the assault on the student movement's original target of protest—the authoritarian structures of mainstream society. In addition, the Spontis and other parts of the nondogmatic left-wing counterculture also criticized the authoritarian structures and dogmatism that had developed within the political culture of the student movement. Hence opposition to all authoritarian structures and all modes of oppression was as much a key element for the self-understanding of the new counterculture as it had been for the generation of 1968, or, in the words of post-1968 Sponti activists:

> We belong to the generation of those who were fascinated by the distorted portrayal of the radical students, of those who identified with the stone-throwing hordes, but we found the reality to be much more harmless. The exaggerations of the media lifted us up, encouraged us. Reality was disappointing. This was the first disillusionment. Further disappointments followed in rapid succession. The former revolutionaries propagated during the ten years after their antiauthoritarian revolt a politics that was much more authoritarian than everything they had themselves attacked. They subjected themselves to a political practice, as for instance in the Communist party, that was quite a bit more authoritarian than the families from which the revolting students had broken away.[45]

The authoritarian tendencies within the traditional left manifested themselves in the hierarchical structure of their political organizations and in an ideological dogmatism, which post-1968 new social movements rejected. The Spontis subscribed to the concept of the politics of the self, arguing for the integration of one's own subjectivity and needs into politics. The "Movement Undogmatic Spring" (*Bewegung Undogmatischer Frühling*), which held the majority in the student association at the University of Göttingen, had, for example, the following plank in its platform, which is in many ways typical for the Sponti movement: "We need to create an atmosphere that allows us not only to identify what we are daily being deprived of, but beyond that to articulate our desires positively and offensively, so that they become the principles of our politics. We will not fall back into a reactive 'messing around' that only responds to the actions of the bourgeois state and subjects itself therefore to its rule."[46]

While the traditional New Left's denunciation of the Spontis closed the door to a productive dialogue with, and at the same time for valid criticism of, the newly emerging counterculture, Peter Brückner's sympathetic but critical account was more fruitful.[47]

Brückner argues that rigid insistence on the priority of subjective needs and an equally rigid insistence on the politics of the self can devalue the important rediscovery of subjectivity by the new countercultural movement. The positive aspects of the Sponti movement's understanding of politics can easily turn into a loss of a sense of responsibility for others. Brückner cautions that taken to its extremes, the concept of the politics of the self can result in a lack of solidarity with those oppressed whose needs and concerns are different from one's own, since solidarity frequently requires a denial of one's own immediate desires and interests or, at least, a compromise. Hence there is a danger that the New Subjectivist perspective of the post-1968 counterculture might lose the collective orientation contained in the student movement's understanding of New Sensibility. Still, as Thomas Waldhubel argues, the stress on subjective concerns did not necessarily mean that the Spontis slipped back into "subjective arbitrariness" but rather that they protested "against forms and structures in which they are objectified by society. They defended the individual's pursuit of happiness and self-actualization and criticized the suffering inflicted by alienated forms of socialization."[48]

Undoubtedly, the category of subjectivity had become the key reference point for the cultural and political changes of the 1970s and early 1980s. At the same time, it was used and appropriated by various groups for ideological purposes. Traditional literary criticism used the disorientation and crisis of the left in the wake of the student movement to revive traditional bourgeois concepts of aesthetic culture. The notion of New Subjectivity functioned in this setting to revitalize the concept of the autonomy of art. Within traditional literary criticism, New Subjectivity represents a synonym for the desired depoliticization of aesthetic culture and a notion of literature based on the modernist literary paradigm, namely, that literature is a fictional and purposeful interpretation of the world from the perspective of the individual. By promoting a traditional concept of aesthetic culture, traditional literary criticism also tried to further a continuation of a bourgeois system of values. Traditional left-wing criticism's account of the cultural transformations of the 1970s resembles that of traditional literary criticism, but it evaluated the new paradigm of New Subjectivity negatively. It denounced the post-1968 counterculture as a retreat from politics.

The traditional left's criticism of New Subjectivity is, however, more interesting with regard to its stance toward the newly emerging countercultural movements, particularly the Sponti movement, than its stance toward the literature of New Subjectivity. The traditional New Left did not understand that the Sponti movement's turn away from the political and aesthetic conceptualizations of the late student movement in favor of a radical subjectivism in fact represented a return to the antiauthoritarian traditions of the student movement. Traditional literary criticism and traditional left-wing criticism exhibit therefore a strong affinity in rejecting an oppositional political and cultural practice based on radical subjectivism, a basic ingredient of the post-1968 countercultural movements. The impossibility of subsuming the new counterculture of the late 1970s and 1980s under the standard models of explanation, the paradigms of either bourgeois or socialist culture, was the main reason for its rejection by both right and left.[49]

Ultimately, the generation of the student movement reacted to the challenge that the Spontis posed in a manner as conservative as that of traditional bourgeois criticism. It employed the theory of a new mode of socialization and a resulting new personality type to denounce these countercultural developments as regressive as well as narcissistic, while at the same time advocating a Lukácsian Marxist aesthetic based on an adaptation of the most advanced bourgeois culture and of socialist traditions exemplified by Berthold Brecht. The discourse on New Subjectivity in the 1970s shows that the new countercultural movements suffered a double marginalization, that is, from the right as well as from the left, while terrorism cast yet another shadow on them.

New Subjectivity and Violence: Peter Handke and the Mescalero

The previous section showed that the concept of New Subjectivity circulated not only within the literary discourse but permeated the entire counterculture. Closer inspection of the commonalities between the literature of New Subjectivity and the emerging new social movements—or, to be more precise, the Sponti movement—will allow us to determine whether the two indeed constituted one discursive field. The first methodological problem we have to face when trying to examine the discursive field of the 1970s is the question whether the notion of literature in the traditional sense is indeed a useful analytic tool. As Barbara Kosta argues, "autobiographical writing and textualizations of the self and of personal experience in West Germany flooded the literary market and dominated various literary forms."[50] The return to belles-lettres that Reich-Ranicki and others had so emphatically proclaimed represents therefore only part of the story. While a traditional concept of literature was at least programmatically resurrected, it was at the same time eroded by the new modes of writing practiced in the 1970s. Abandoning a traditional notion of literature as a highly stylized fictional aesthetic product in favor of the concept of text represents a much more productive approach and allows us to see the continuities and breaks with the student movement's concepts much more clearly.

For instance, the New Subjectivist literature was not the radical break with the 1960s that it was initially heralded to be, but instead "grew out of the focus on documentary renderings and the trend against professional writing."[51] The documentary genres of the 1960s rejected aesthetic symbolization on the one hand and, on the other hand, aimed at giving a voice to those as yet unheard and to their concerns. Erika Runge's *Bottroper Protokolle*, a collection of interviews with common men and women of the Ruhr Valley, the industrial heart of the Federal Republic up to the steel crisis in the 1970s, is perhaps the best-known example of this kind of documentary literature. The women's movement participated in the development with its consciousness-raising texts (*Verständigungstexte*), whose main goal was to present an authentic experience rather than a highly stylized literary product.[52]

From the perspective of traditional literary criticism, many of these 1970s texts would not qualify as literature and did not want to do so. Not literary stylization, but the authenticity of the experience communicated through these texts, was at the heart of the new understanding of writing also referred to as the "writing movement" (*Schreibbewegung*). But even if we draw the boundaries of literary

New Subjectivity fairly narrow, focusing on texts by such acclaimed literati as Peter Handke, Peter Schneider, Botho Strauß, or Karin Struck, the thematic scope of this literature exhibits strong similarities to that of women's consciousness-raising texts and of the writing movement. Fundamental experiences such as death and birth, alienation, the loss of meaning, introspection, and self-actualization were central to both literary New Subjectivity and the post-1968 countercultural developments. The difference between a traditional notion of literature and the counterculture's texts consists in the latter's break with literary symbolism in favor of a radical notion of authenticity that collapses author and narrator into one entity, and, in the public reception of these texts.[53] The counterculture's radical authenticity had the potential to explode the popular consensus, particularly if it touched on the issue of terrorist violence. Not solely theoretical considerations but the complexity of writing during the 1970s therefore justifies abandoning the notion of literature for a concept of writing and text in the broadest sense possible.

As we have already noted, the debate on New Subjectivity was only one issue that shaped the cultural discourse of the 1970s. Farther reaching was the confrontation with political violence, which had become more prevalent during this decade. For instance, political confrontations around ecological issues such as the construction of several nuclear power plants or the expansion of runways at the Frankfurt airport (Startbahn West) grew more violent during the 1970s and 1980s. The terrorist violence of the RAF posed, however, a special problem for the left. For one, the first RAF terrorists belong to the generation of the student movement. Second, the left had to develop a strategy of how to reject emphatically the terrorists' use of violence without denouncing the political project behind it, with which most of the counterculture sympathized. The situation was similar for the Sponti movement, whose stance toward terrorism was strongly shaped by its opposition to the government and its agencies. In spite of all the accusations to the contrary, neither the generation of the student movement nor the alternative movement condoned terrorist violence. They were, however, not willing to join the witch-hunt of "60 million" against six terrorists, as Heinrich Böll with striking clarity described the problem already in 1972.[54]

In this context, the Buback Obituary was a key event in the 1970s because it exposed the limits of the freedom of expression and the reductive understanding of New Subjectivity within the public sphere. This obituary was written for Siegfried Buback, the West German attorney general, who was killed by the RAF in May 1977. The text was signed "Ein Göttinger Mescalero," identifying it as a statement originating from the counterculture, or more precisely from the Sponti movement. Public discourse always referred to the Mescalero as a single author, although to date it has not been determined whether the obituary was written by a single or collective author. More important, however, was the response of the Sponti movement, which embraced the obituary as an articulation of their concerns and ideas. The Sponti movement immediately demonstrated solidarity with the author of the obituary when the Mescalero was threatened by criminal investigation under the new antiterrorism measures. When the public demanded a dialogue with the Mescalero, a group of counterculture activists—usually students from Göttingen—appeared on the scene so the author of the obituary, who most likely was also a Göttinger student and activist, could not be identified.[55]

The Sponti movement represented one response to the loss of meaning—including a clear political orientation—experienced by many young people in the 1970s. The loss of identity and a feeling of meaninglessness characterizes, however, the fictional heroes of literary New Subjectivity as well. For Peter Schneider's hero Lenz, in the novel of the same title, the utopia of general concepts that the student movement had tried to live no longer makes any sense, and he begins his quest for the sensuous dimension missing in his life.[56] Peter Handke's bourgeois hero, Gregor Keuschnig, in *A Moment of True Feeling* as well as Nicolas Born's main character in *The Deception*, the journalist Laschen, have similar experiences. They suddenly realize that their lives are passing by without making sense and, thrown into the vertigo of an identity crisis, they too start their quest for meaning as a search for true feeling, authentic experiences, and individual identity.

The Spontis as well as the above-cited fictional characters approach this loss of meaning from a radically subjective perspective.

The parallels between Sponti discourse and literary New Subjectivity does not stop with the theme of a lack of meaning and a radically subjective perspective. Helmut Kreuzer was the first to detect the strong interest in violence within literary New Subjectivity. "The authors of New Subjectivity (we can see this in the motto from *A Moment of True Feeling*) know that individual violence and meaninglessness are like brother and sister. Spiritual vacuums cannot be replenished at will. Since the literature of New Subjectivity still has a hard time explaining convincingly its lack of closure and halfway happy endings aside from violence and meaninglessness, violence remains a temptation for it, even though self-critically diagnosed."[57] The entire West German left from the SPD to the Spontis was equally preoccupied with the issue of violence because of the terrorism of the RAF. A comparison of one of the paradigmatic texts of literary New Subjectivity, Peter Handke's *A Moment of True Feeling*, and a paradigmatic text of the counterculture, the Buback Obituary, will shed light on this intricate discourse on meaninglessness and violence that dominated the 1970s.

True Feelings and Violence in Handke's A Moment of True Feeling

Like much of Handke's work, his novel *A Moment of True Feeling* portrays the individual in search of an authentic identity constituted through the individual's subjective experience and not determined and prescribed by the outside world. The crisis articulates itself in the protagonist's recognition of the banality of the daily routine to which he has submitted and the consequent loss of his identity. As in other Handke novels, aggression and violence play an important role in *A Moment of True Feeling*.[58] Handke places a quote by Max Horkheimer before his story almost like a guiding question or motto: "Violence and inanity—are they not ultimately one and the same thing?" The novel opens with a fantasy of violence: Gregor Keuschnig, press attaché of the Austrian Embassy in Paris, dreams one night that he has murdered an old woman for no reason. The dream haunts him throughout the day and changes his perception of daily life. Because of the dream, Keuschnig begins to experience himself as an outsider who no longer belongs to the prescribed order of the world. The loss of meaning stemming from the recognition of the uniformity of his life, which suffocates true feelings and true experiences, results in aggressive desires on the part of the hero: he wishes to hurt his wife, he is afraid of killing his daughter, and he almost beats his mistress. In short: "He wanted to beat everyone to pulp."[59]

After initial hesitation, Keuschnig indulges in his new experience without engaging in rational reflection on his violent fantasies and desires. He not only thinks and dreams in violent terms but finally acts out his aggressions when he is confronted with his double (*Doppelgänger*), the Austrian author who articulates everything that Keuschnig has experienced all day long—an intense disgust at life's uniformity and banality. When Keuschnig experiences himself in all of his outside determination and alienation, he finally shatters the superficial harmony by violating all social norms. He strips naked at the dinner table, jumps on the Austrian author's girlfriend in an attempt to rape her, smears ragout all over his face, and starts a fist-fight with the author. He regresses back into a primitive stage when conflict was resolved with physical force. Keuschnig experiences this outburst of his inner world as a cathartic moment, since he does not have to live in disguise any longer.[60] The novel thus portrays aggression and violence as potentially liberating.

At last, Keuschnig's violent inclinations, which are depicted as the result of an alienating environment, are resolved. The novel, however, explains Keuschnig's transformations not on a psychological but on a mystical level. It is a mystical solution because the dream in which he murders himself not only anticipates Keuschnig's later suicide attempt but also invokes the image of atonement, of being reborn and cleansed of one's former "sins" through death. The first cathartic moment—acting out his aggressions against his double—does not result in a reconciliation of old and new experiences. Only the second attempt to overcome his crisis, the symbolic suicide (*Selbst-Mord*), brings the cathartic development to a close. Handke's imagery suggests that Keuschnig's identity is not only reborn but is also purified of its former mendacity. Keuschnig consequently experiences the world and himself as cleansed. He has become another person, symbolized as well in his purchasing new clothes after his suicide attempt. Now he has turned into a person of true feelings. "He was free, at least for this evening and night. . . . Although he saw the same things as before, and from the same angle, they had become alien and therefore bearable."[61]

The episode in which Keuschnig suddenly sees three objects on the ground in front of him—a leaf of a chestnut tree, a piece of a pocket mirror, and a child's barrette—is crucial for understanding the novel's anti-Enlightenment, mystical model for reconstituting meaning. The three objects become *Wunderdinge*, a miracle and revelation for Keuschnig. All of a sudden his identity crisis is resolved and he finds peace only in a totally passive devotion to the thing in itself (*Ding-an-sich*), the individual phenomena and objects of the world.[62] As Michael Linstead argues, it is not the objects themselves that ignite the transformation but Keuschnig's passive, contemplative attitude that allows for the change.[63] The cause of Keuschnig's change of perception remains therefore an inexplicable inner event. Remembering a sentence about the incompatibility of the concept (*Begriff*) and the idea (*Idee*), Keuschnig clearly favors the idea. Concepts represent for Keuschnig the outside world organized in rational terms, whereas the idea stands for the unmediated, authentic, and spontaneous image, the "true feeling" that the title of the novel programmatically proclaims. Keuschnig is therefore reconciled with the inimical world and himself as soon as he no longer tries to approach it in traditional conceptual terms but permits the phenomena of daily life as such to affect him directly, thereby rediscovering the world in its enigmatic immediacy. The post-1968 countercultural groups, especially the Sponti movement, also privileged immediacy—that is, spontaneity, as they called it—and authentic sensuous experience over conceptual and theoretical discourse.

Peter Handke's novel participates in the nexus of meaninglessness and violence that Kreuzer recognized as a characteristic of literary New Subjectivity. Handke's hero never critically reflects upon or questions his fantasies of violence. These fantasies appear rather in a positive light, since they initiate and accompany the transformation of the hero. As soon as Keuschnig has reconstituted his identity simply through a passive devotion to the immediacy of the material objects of the world, his aggressions disappear. Ultimately, Handke affirms Horkheimer's rhetorical question of whether violence and meaninglessness are indeed the same without exploring the social dimension of senselessness and violence any further. It is, however, also true that Handke does not advocate or glorify violence, since he portrays his hero's aggressiveness as being destructive of human relationships. Yet the status of violence within this mystical framework of life and experience that Handke constructs remains disturbingly ambiguous.

The Clandestine Joy of the Mescalero

Whereas the ambiguity of violence in literary New Subjectivity was not thematized by the critics, the Buback Obituary was reproached with just such an ambivalent stance, and even misinterpreted as a glorification of violence. Nobody made the connection between the New Subjectivist approach the Mescalero used for his statement on terrorism and the literature of New Subjectivity, although the structural similarities are striking, as a comparison of the Buback Obituary and Peter Handke's novel *A Moment of True Feeling* demonstrate.

First of all, both texts place fantasies of violence at the beginning of their argument. Handke's novel opens with a violent fantasy—the dream in which the protagonist appears as a murderer. Basing his obituary on a true event, the assassination of the West German attorney general by members of the RAF, the Mescalero admits that in his daydreams and fantasies he has seen himself in the position of the terrorist. Second, Horkheimer's question about the intrinsic equality of senselessness and violence, which Handke has placed as a motto at the beginning of his text, is relevant for the Mescalero's reasoning as well. Third, both texts approach this question from a radically subjective perspective. The Mescalero talks about his immediate, personal feelings that the assassination of the attorney general has brought to the fore and does so from a radically subjective perspective. Handke's novel narrates the two days that changed the life of Gregor Keuschnig from his protagonist's subjective perspective.

But whereas Handke's hero attempts at first to sustain his old role and does not want to admit to himself that he has violent fantasies and is thus an outsider because of his changed perception of the world, the Mescalero accepts this status right from the beginning. The Buback Obituary opens with an adamant refusal to accept socially dominant norms or logic. Its author rejects theoretical reflection and objectification in favor of his immediate and authentic reaction. His subjective concern (*Betroffenheit*) represents therefore an example of New Subjectivity as much as Handke's literary text. "A well-balanced, stringent line of argument, dialectic, and contradiction—I couldn't care less. Some parts of this Buback story caused me to belch. I want to put those burps down on paper; perhaps they will contribute a little to a public debate. My immediate reaction, how I am affected by the execution of Buback, can be quickly described: I couldn't, didn't want to (and still don't want to) deny a clandestine joy."[64]

The general public interpreted the "clandestine joy" as a malicious joy. It consequently did not believe that the Mescalero rejected his initial delight based on ethical and moral standards, but maintained that he did so only for tactical reasons. The proponents of this reading of the article's reasoning against terrorist violence claim that it is guided only by the utilitarian logic of cost-benefit analysis; its only concern is whether this utterance could cause damage for his comrades' political project. In fact, the Mescalero's argument does not aim at such a tactical advantage, as Peter Brückner argues with reference to internal left-wing discussions and positions on the politics of the RAF. Brückner asserts that "in spite of the carefully chosen subjunctive (could disarm, might be a contribution), the author is here resisting the politics of the RAF."[65]

The Mescalero's self-understanding as an outsider with regard to the official public discourse and his approach to the problem of terrorism speak against utilitarian considerations, since he clearly states that the loss of his initial and clandestine joy over the assassination does not represent a concession to the public outcry. In the Mescalero's opinion, the West German public sphere was defunct anyway; it was a hermetic block of streamlined mass media, official statements and commentaries that did not allow for any dissenting voice in the debate over terrorism. Though fully aware of his own impotence against this media apparatus, the Mescalero still attempted to raise a critical voice, which was intended to ignite a public dispute on the problem of West German terrorism, as he frankly announced in his opening paragraph. The Buback Obituary aimed at establishing an alternative to the public sphere, which much of the counterculture felt was lacking at this moment of crisis that RAF terrorism had imposed on the Federal Republic.

Starting from his subjective enjoyment of the effects of terrorism, whose bombs created an uproar within the "capitalist high society and its myrmidons," the Mescalero ultimately questions his initial pleasure.[66] Working through his violent daydreams, the Mescalero rejects violence in general and terrorist violence in particular because he cannot legitimate it. He cites four reasons for his rejection of terrorist violence as a valid oppositional political practice. First, the Mescalero recognizes that the logic behind the single terrorist attack equals the logic of a totalitarian and violent state. Second, the Mescalero shows a high degree of moral responsibility, since he refuses to accept that innocent people might become victims of terrorism. Third, comparing totalitarian states like Argentina or Franco's Spain, where he views terrorism as a legitimate means of liberation movements, with the situation in West Germany, he poses the most important question: "But who and how many people had a (deadly) hatred for Buback? On what could I, if I belonged to the armed fighters, base my competence to make life and death decisions?"[67] The Mescalero's response to this question rejects the ideology of substitution (*Stellvertreter-Ideologie*)[68] of the RAF, realizing that its terrorist violence originates as little from the people as from the power of the attorney general. Finally, the Mescalero argues from a position of a clear political goal and ethics. A society free of any kind of terror and repression, which the Mescalero envisions, cannot be based on violence. He denies the validity of the proverbial "ends justifying the means" for his oppositional politics and vehemently rejects murder as a political weapon: "Our path to socialism (or, if you prefer, to anarchy) cannot be paved with dead bodies."[69]

Although the Mescalero, quite differently from Handke's novel of New Subjectivity, begins with his immediate and irrational impressions—happy feelings and aggressive fantasies—that the assassination of the attorney general has evoked, he develops a rational discourse that reflects critically on his violent inclinations. His reflections culminate in a critique of his immediate response to terrorist practices and ultimately in a rejection of terrorist violence. At the center of both New Subjectivist texts—Handke's and the Mescalero's—is the issue of an identity crisis that erupts violently. Whereas Keuschnig's subjectivity needs to be supplemented by mystical revelation in order to resolve his aggressions, the Mescalero's subjective approach tries to reveal his subconscious feelings of aggression in order to control them consciously and finally to eliminate them.[70] The Buback Obituary offers a rational model for dealing with an identity crisis without neglecting the subjective and affective dimension of human existence.

Furthermore, in communicating personal feelings and thoughts about terrorism, the Buback Obituary represents an attempt to reconstitute political identity within the left, which was as much disturbed by terrorism as the hegemonic culture. It shows the senselessness and unethical dimension of violence, but does not give up its critique of and fundamental opposition to the hegemonic culture itself in spite of growing pressure on the counterculture because of RAF terrorism. The Mescalero's critique of the terrorists' use of violence, namely, that it copies a logic and strategy particular to the repressive government, is in turn a critique of government-sanctioned use of terrorist means.

In addition, the obituary attacks the key elements of contemporary society: alienated labor within capitalist structures of profit maximization, institutionalized legal and psychological mechanisms of repression, and the democratic myth that all power originates from the people. It thereby articulates a vision of an alternative social order, albeit in rather vague terms—a mode of discourse typical for the Spontis: "a society without terror and violence (even if not without aggression and militancy), a society without forced labor (even if not without toil), a society without legal administration, prisons, and other correctional facilities (even if not without rules and regulations, or better, recommendations)."[71]

This statement also shows the distance between the thinking of the student movement and that of the Spontis, since they cannot be understood exclusively within the ideological framework of Marxism. As Peter Brückner points out, the Mescalero rejects the question of power (*Machtfrage*), which is always posed by the traditional left—Marxists and socialists alike. The Mescalero's statement does not call for seizing power, as many socialist and Marxist theories do and the student movement strove for, but argues instead for the dissolution of power, that is, for razing the bastions of all power—institutional, traditional, functional, spiritual. The Mescalero ultimately denounces the military arsenal and can only imagine using it to subvert power.[72]

The rational reasoning of the obituary was overlooked for a variety of reasons, but certainly not simply because of the offensive language it employs, as many critics suggested. Peter Brückner's analysis of the obituary's language is much more to the point, namely, that the linguistic structure of the obituary's argument itself has an oppositional content. It breaks with the theoretical-conceptual dimension of language characteristic of the predominant scientific discourse of today's Western world. The Mescalero insists on his subjective perception, immediate impressions and feelings, and on his subjective language, which is the language of the countercultural environment. The language of the obituary therefore represents a protest that refuses to accept a thinking and speaking that excludes the subjective and affective dimension of human existence. At the center of this understanding is, as Brückner argues, the category of authenticity. "The fact that concepts and theories, for instance, have not found entry into this text—or at best only superficially, that is, indirectly via numerous allusions—and that learned terms and rhetorical figures as we know them have been replaced by vulgarisms, is supposed to authenticate the subjective moment of this inner monologue, that is, this expression of a spontaneous sensitivity."[73]

This criticism of a mere conceptual and theoretical culture is, however, not unique to the Buback Obituary or the Spontis in general, but represents an important characteristic of the concept and literature of New Subjectivity. Furthermore, vulgarisms can be found not only in the trivial literature of the established culture, as Franz Dröge argues in his analysis of the obituary, but also in literary examples of New Subjectivity, as well as in literary culture in general, as an aesthetics of ugliness.[74]

The obvious double standard of the hegemonic culture, which denounced the Buback Obituary as an endorsement of RAF terrorism, poses the interesting question of why the subjective and anti-conceptual stance was well accepted within the confines of literary or aesthetic culture, but not within the sphere of politics, leading to the "scandal" that the obituary touched off in 1977. Dröge, who poses this question in his examination of the Mescalero scandal, gives a convincing answer based on an assumption similar to the Mescalero's opinion, namely, that a coherent and functioning public sphere no longer existed in West Germany.[75] He argues that there is, on the one hand, an established and hegemonic public sphere that is dominant, since it has the mass media at its disposal, and on the other, an alternative public sphere with its own structure, language, and goals. Dröge emphasizes that an oppositional self-understanding in terms of the categories of subjectivity and objectivity represents the main criteria for distinguishing these two public spheres. The hegemonic public sphere claims objectivity for its journalistic practices, whereas the left-wing counterculture criticizes this claim to objectivity as a mere illusion designed to cover up ideological agendas. The Buback Obituary, as an expression of the alternative public sphere, insists on its subjective approach to political issues, with regard not only to the thematic scope, but also to representational styles. Dröge observes in both public spheres the presence of violent fantasies, which are usually not theoretically or intellectually discussed, and he chooses mainstream television—to be more precise, crime stories—for comparison.

According to Dröge, television crime stories work toward the resolution of violent fantasies in a particular and generally accepted manner. First of all, they present violence as a moral deviation. Second, the deviant criminal is always caught by the authorities (the police) and handed over to the judiciary, so that justice will be done. Dröge views this mode of resolving fantasies of violence as a mechanism of repression rather than of intellectual confrontation with the problem. It precludes the crucial question of the legitimacy of violence, since the public consensus allows for the display of non-specific violent fantasies but not for a rational public discourse on their legitimacy or the legitimacy of the latent social violence they actually represent.[76] This holds true not only for television but for literature as well, as we have seen in Handke's novel, which fails to address this issue.

The Buback Obituary breaks with the social consensus in that it does not submit to this repressive mechanism, but instead works through these violent fantasies rationally and finally rejects violence as a political means. The true scandal of the Buback Obituary lies in the Mescalero's refusal to negate and denounce these fantasies as an element of his or, in a broader sense, of the Spontis' political identity; it lies as well in the Mescalero's insistence on his fundamental opposition to the government by posing the question of the legitimacy of the government's monopoly of violence. Because of this transgression of public consensus, the official public sphere misinterpreted the obituary in order to marginalize it, and so ultimately to marginalize a theme and treatment of a theme that was not supposed to become an issue of public debate. Dröge concludes: "This article was not read as a discussion about politically motivated violence but as a representation of violence."[77]

The strategy that the press employed to impute violent tendencies to the Buback Obituary was both simple and successful. It did not publish the entire obituary or even an adequate summary of it, but only the two parts where the Mescalero articulates his violent fantasies: the infamous clandestine joy about the shooting of the attorney general and the pleasure with which the Mescalero followed the hegemonic culture's confusion, fear, and uproar caused by terrorist attacks. The entirely distorted representation of the obituary by the hegemonic culture aimed at proving the standard conservative claim "that the intellectual confrontation with terror and violence is suspicious, that it is contaminated by its object of discussion."[78] The public reception of the obituary therefore represents an example of a strategy that incriminates all intellectual criticism or opposition to the officially prescribed evaluation of terrorism in spite of the constant public call for an "intellectual confrontation" with it.[79] As long as this criticism remained on a fictional-literary and nonspecific level, there was no problem at all.

The Mescalero scandal reveals that the hegemonic culture made a distinction between aesthetic and political discourse and treated them differently, even if they shared a common origin, the new cultural paradigm of subjectivity and authenticity. Traditional literary criticism had in certain ways succeeded in again separating aesthetic and political culture in the perception of the general public. Both Handke's novel and the Buback Obituary participate in the same discourse, that of New Subjectivity. But whereas the literary manifestations caused no uproar in spite of their ambivalent position toward violence, the Buback Obituary was met by a storm of protest, even though the Mescalero subjected terrorist violence to a rational critique, on the basis of which he rejected it. Considering the political insignificance of the extraparliamentary left during the 1970s and judging by the scandal the Buback Obituary evoked, radical subjectivity seems to have represented a threatening oppositional practice for the hegemonic culture.

CHAPTER 4: "Objectivity?
No, Thank You!"
New Subjectivity from
Tunix to *taz*

The Buback Obituary had tremendous sociopolitical significance. It exposed a fault line in West German society running between "two cultures." Peter Glotz, a member of the SPD and Secretary of Education and Science in Berlin during the late 1970s, argued that two totally different modes of thinking and communication, which existed parallel and separately from each other, had developed within the Federal Republic:

> The differences are so great that I have to speak of two cultures. It is as if Chinese are trying to communicate with Japanese. . . . The one side lives in a subculture within the university, reading only their own fliers and informational materials. . . . And then there exists the totally different culture of the many, who read their mainstream newspaper no matter whether the paper was produced by the Springer media conglomerate or someone else. . . . Those who have lived for three years in the subculture speak another language than those of mainstream culture, and even the common assumptions are being destroyed.[1]

Glotz certainly did not belong to those who condemned the universities as the breeding grounds of terrorism, but the theory of the two cultures that he introduced contributed more to undermine than to promote mutual understanding at a time when the rift between mainstream society and alternative projections of life and politics was growing rapidly.

The 1970s saw a proliferation of dissent that reached beyond the Spontis and the women's movement, indicating a fundamental change in the perception of politics. Many citizens were disenchanted with traditional politics because they felt that these conventional models of representative democracy failed to address their true concerns. They began to organize themselves around specific social and political issues in citizens' initiatives (*Bürgerinitiativen*) in order to influence the decision-making process more directly and effectively. Historically, the citizens' initiatives date back to the 1950s and 1960s, but there is a significant difference in self-understanding between such early initiatives as, for example, the campaigns against the rearmament and nuclear armament of West Germany in the 1950s and 1960s, or the electoral support groups for the Social Democrats in 1969, and the citizens' initiatives that cropped up after the student movement in the early 1970s. The initiatives of the 1950s and early 1960s were based on individual ethical and civil commitment. The citizens' initiatives of the 1970s, on the other hand, were conceived as a practical expression of participatory grass-roots democracy.[2]

Citizens' initiatives developed in almost all sociopolitical areas: education and the *Berufsverbote* or *Radikalenerlaß*, the status of psychiatry, physically and mentally challenged people or other marginalized social groups, the problems of the Third World and apartheid politics in South Africa, and the destruction of the urban and natural environment. Along with the women's movement, the latter initiatives on environmental issues attracted most of the public's attention in the mid-1970s. The federal government's energy policy, which was based solely on the further expansion of nuclear power, was the focus of discontent and protest. The antinuclear movement (*Anti-Atomkraft-Bewegung*)—internationally known through its symbol of the smiling sun—became most prominent. Together with the protest movement against the Startbahn West, a new runway at the Frankfurt airport, and the peace movement, the environmentalists' protest reached new heights in size, organizational structure, and ferocity. These movements not only managed to mobilize tremendous numbers of people and establish supraregional organizational structures, but also called representative democracy into question and challenged the legitimacy of the government's monopoly on decision making. If the elected representatives of the citizenry did not respond to the expressed will of the people, those organized in the citizens' initiatives were prepared to move from the level of mere demonstrative and symbolic protest to civil disobedience.

The question of the legitimacy of violence as a means of protest, posed by the Buback Obituary, was still a crucial issue in this context. The fact that the party of the Greens adopted "nonviolence" as one of their four fundamental principles attests to the significance of the issue of violence. The conflict around the Startbahn West at the Frankfurt airport, as well as the blockades of U.S. bases for nuclear weapons by the peace movement, had raised the question of whether civil disobedience, which marked a new dimension in this protest, could maintain its original nonviolent character. The question of where civil disobedience ends and violence starts was as controversial among the general public as within the counterculture. It split the counterculture into groups that were explicitly nonviolent and very small but militant and violent groups, which called themselves *Autonome* (autonomous groups).

The concrete political demands of particular activist movements represent only one aspect of the transformation of society in the wake of the student movement. The alternative concept of the politics of the self, that is, grass-roots democracy (*Basisdemokratie*), correlated with a variety of alternative lifestyles that all shared in the rejection of mainstream society. The 1970s saw the Marcusean idea of the Great Refusal revitalized in numerous countercultural projects, from ecological farming communes to women's consciousness-raising groups and physicians' coops. These projects mushroomed in all urban areas across West Germany and, since an identification with the term *alternativ* took place within the counterculture itself, were quickly subsumed under the label alternative movement (*Alternativbewegung*). As Thomas Daum points out, "alternative" became a political signifier for an anti-institutional, somehow leftist-ecological position with which the majority of the people involved in alternative projects such as eco-stores, alternative bookstores, dentists', lawyers' or any kind of craftsmen's collective identified since the mid-1970s. If people proudly referred to themselves or their projects with the label "alternative," they wanted to express their difference, their otherness from the system (*System*), as they called the hegemonic culture.[3]

In contrast to the other new social movements—such as the ecology, peace, and women's movements, which had one dominant political issue on their agenda—the alternative movement claimed to present a comprehensive alternative to the existing economic and social system, although guided by diverse concepts and worldviews. This heterogeneity in turn makes it difficult to develop a clear-cut definition of the alternative movement. We can, however, distinguish a number of subgroups within it, if only for analytic purposes. The movement of agricultural co-ops (*Landkommunenbewegung*), one of the original subgroups that can be traced directly to the student movement, had influential counterparts in the United States such as the Farm in Tennessee. The so-called New Spirituality (*Neue Spiritualität*) and the psychology movement (*Psycho-Bewegung*), or in short, the New Age movement, too, had their predecessors in the U.S. counterculture of the late 1960s, although these two major trends of practical self-assertion and self-actualization (*Selbstfindung*) gained prominence in West Germany a little later than in the United States, approximately since the mid-1970s.[4] The alternative movement also included the Sponti, ecology, and women's movements without being identical with any one of them.

All of these movements shared both ideas and individual members, to various degrees and in numerous formal and informal ways, without eliminating their differences. They in fact developed over time into a loosely structured network instead of into a hierarchical organization. Josef Huber calls the alternative movement therefore a "process of diffusion," "in which attitudes and ideas cut across all camps while taking on different modes characteristic for the respective camp."[5] We can thus, in spite of the differences, discern trends and tendencies that allow us to conceptualize the alternative movement as a specific though heterogeneous entity.

The previous chapter approached these sociocultural changes from the perspective of literary criticism in order to trace the transformation of the cultural paradigm from the student movement's utopia of a purely conceptual culture to its rejection in favor of values such as sensibility, spontaneity, authenticity, and sensuality in the post-1968 counterculture. Be it New Subjectivity, the New Spirituality, or the psychology boom, all of these movements represented an expression of the cultural changes that placed subjectivity at the center of their respective worldviews. Thus subjectivity and self-actualization were the constitutive codes and common denominator for the alternative movement.

This means, in practical terms, that the alternative movement rejected hierarchical and authoritarian structures and articulated itself in a strong anti-institutional attitude. From its very beginnings, it strove for decentralization, self-organization, and autonomy.[6] Since it had a holistic approach, alternative projects represented an attempt not only to outline theoretically but also to practice a new mode of life in opposition to the hegemonic mainstream culture. Drawing on antiauthoritarian concepts of the student movement, these projections of an alternative life world aimed at bringing together the separate spheres of private and public life, be it work or politics.

The term *movement* therefore does not adequately describe the new countercultural developments. *Movement* connotes active mobilization for political ends and mostly refers to political activism oriented around a single issue and within a limited time span, and which is clearly distinct from other protest movements because of its primary political focus.[7] The alternative movement, as we have already indicated, does not fit this definition. Hence Klaus Müschen, for instance, suggests the term "alternative milieu" for describing the network in which alternative projections of a cooperative lifestyle and an ethically responsible economy found stable forms "that were distinct, on the one hand, from the topical political activism of the movement such as protest marches, blockades, teach-ins, and so forth, and, on the other hand, from the political parliamentary focus of the Green party."[8]

For our topic—aesthetic ideas, artistic practices, and cultural politics—the notion *alternative culture* is preferable to Müschen's notion of alternative milieu. It is on the one hand a comprehensive term capturing the multiplicity described above and what we might want to call the alternative consciousness, permeating all new social movements. On the other hand, it emphasizes those aspects of the alternative culture that are the focus of this study: aesthetic concepts and artistic practices. Though much social science research has been done on this phenomenon of the new social movements, aesthetic issues in the narrow sense, that is, artistic culture and its status within society, has been neglected in comparison to the student movement of the late 1960s or to the women's movement and its feminist aesthetic. This is especially surprising considering that the alternative movement perceived itself to be in fundamental opposition to the hegemonic culture and aimed at recovering aesthetic experience in the broadest sense—an experience that it viewed as repressed in contemporary society. Moreover, the new social movements made extensive use of aesthetic symbols—the rainbow and its colors, the image of the smiling sun or the porcupine—as well as aesthetic cultural practices such as protest songs and theatrical events to express their discontent. The present chapter, which focuses on these aspects, analyzes the understanding of aesthetic culture and the cultural politics of the new social movements during the 1970s and early 1980s.

Before starting, we still need to address and discuss one methodological difficulty: How should we approach the alternative culture, since it articulated itself in a less centralized and less theoretical manner than the student movement? Each of its single movements developed its own informal network of communication independently of, if not to say withdrawn from, the communicative channels of the hegemonic culture's public sphere.[9] In comparison to the student movement, which articulated its criticism mainly in two journals, *Konkret* and *Kursbuch*, the alternative culture of the late 1970s and 1980s developed a large variety of alternative journals and magazines. Best known because of the comparably large circulation were *Emma* and *Courage* within the feminist spectrum; *Der Kompost, Humus,* and *Löwenzahn* for the ecology movement; *Middle Earth* for the spiritualists; *Der Pflasterstrand* for the Spontis in Frankfurt; and *Das Blatt* for the Bavarian alternative scene in Munich. There were still many more publications on the local and regional level as, for instance, the *Göttinger Nachrichten*, the student paper in which the Mescalero originally published the Buback Obituary. The proliferation of local alternative magazines also attests to the alternative culture's ideals of decentralization and local activism. These local magazines were of primary importance for the development of an alternative culture. They defined themselves as an alternative to the monopolized hegemonic mainstream press on the local level and are therefore subsumed under the label alternative or countercultural press (*Alternativpresse*).[10] It is impossible to work through all of this vast material, and limits must inevitably be drawn. Circulation represents a legitimate criterion for restricting the material, since a wide circulation means a wide, although not homogenous, reception.

Shortly after the escalation of terrorism, two major events took place that were of utmost significance for the constitution of the post-1968 counterculture. In 1978 the *Tunix-Treffen*, a meeting of countercultural groups mainly organized by Spontis, took place in West Berlin. It was highly publicized by a flier that not only has historical value but also gives us an insight into the self-perception of the alternative culture in its early stages, when the Spontis' influence was strongest. Second, in 1979 the first nationwide alternative daily began its circulation. This daily represents a case study of perhaps the most successful alternative project to date and demonstrates how the issue of subjectivity and the concept of the politics of the self played out in the field of journalism.

The Idyllic "Second Culture": Tunix

In January 1978 the Sponti left called on all oppositional groups to gather for three days in order to give expression to their radical opposition to the hegemonic culture. Several thousand people of various countercultural groups followed the call and met at the Technical University in West Berlin for the Tunix Gathering (*Tunix-Treffen*).[11] The rationale behind the Tunix Gathering can be summarized in three points. First of all, it was intended to remedy the identity crisis that the counterculture had suffered in the context of terrorist violence and the government's sweeping countermeasures. In the words of one of the participants, "During the fall of 1977 a political discussion took shape among us that encouraged us to initiate Tunix. We experienced the reaction of the left to the events surrounding [the RAF's kidnapping and murder of the industrialist Hanns-Martin] Schleyer and Mogadishu as a cringing before an imaginary attack on the part of the state. Many were taking cover as they would from an approaching thunderstorm and were crying, 'Don't get me wet!' Pessimism had spread even among us. We no longer believed it possible to accomplish a revolutionary project."[12] Like the Mescalero, the organizers of the Tunix Gathering did not want to join the "choir of those who distance themselves,"[13] since in their opinion, doing so would have meant a denial of their radical political identity. Many of the discussion sessions at the Tunix Gathering thus dealt with the impact of terrorism on public discourse and the political climate in West Germany.[14]

Dissatisfaction with the sociopolitical situation in the Federal Republic and with the left's traditional strategies of opposition was a second point, which accounted as well for the quantitative success of the Tunix Gathering. Finally, the meeting was supposed to provide a forum for self-assertion and mutual encouragement on the part of the alternative culture. The Tunix Gathering, as the first general and, in a certain sense, constitutive assembly of the post-1968 counterculture, therefore offers itself as a point of departure into its investigation.

The leaflet that announced the Tunix Gathering is of particular interest, since it is a longer text that goes beyond mere information of time and place. It articulated the self-perception of the alternative culture and its position to both mainstream society and the old New Left, that is, the generation of the student movement, thereby echoing the discourse of New Subjectivity. The leaflet's text was accompanied by a drawing that is in many ways a self-portrait of the alternative culture.[15] It shows an old car rolling toward the horizon, where a star resembling the socialist red star is rising. The car is packed with chaotic-looking people, and the license plate spells out the slogan of the gathering. The old clunker is decorated with the stereotypical signifiers of the alternative culture. One sticker protests against nuclear power plants, saying "Nuclear Energy—No, Thank You!" Another one plays with the meaning of the sticker that indicates the national origin of a car and was in the past legally required for all vehicles crossing inter-European borders. The *D* for West Germany has, however, been replaced with a question mark.

This single question mark covers a broad range of meanings. For one, it implies that traditional codes of identification such as nationality have become questionable within the alternative culture. Second, it articulates the alternative culture's skepticism regarding its home country, calling West German society and politics into question. Finally, inasmuch as the Tunix Gathering represented an attempt to develop a network of the various countercultural groups that emerged during the 1970s, the question mark also signaled that all of the organizational questions were still open for debate. Metaphorically speaking, the alternative movement did not know exactly by which route it could reach its dreamland of an alternative society, quite in contrast to the dogmatic left of the student movement, which always claimed to know the road to revolutionary change.

On the side of the road are the characters of "The Bremen Town Musicians," a fairy tale known to every German from the collection of the brothers Grimm.[16] They are drawn in their typical pose: four animals one on top of the other—the stronger ones carrying the weaker ones—only now it seems that they are hitchhiking. The picture has a caption taken straight from the fairy tale, supplementing the motto of the Tunix Gathering: "Come on, said the donkey, something better than death we will find anywhere." The flier offers this fairy tale as a model of identification for the alternative culture, though overlooking the ambiguities in the story's depiction of a self-help group. The four animals in the tale—a donkey, a dog, a cat, and a rooster—are threatened with death as soon as they can no longer work. But they do not submit to their fate. It takes one, the donkey, to make a beginning and to gain followers who have the same problem. The four leave their homes and workplaces to form a collective and live as street musicians (*Stadtmusikanten*). Thanks to their courage, solidarity, and intelligence, the animals win themselves a new home by chasing a gang of thieves from a little house in the woods. This tale highlights key elements of the alternative culture's understanding of itself: social marginalization, resistance (or is it escape, we may want to ask), and solidarity.

The motto of the countercultural meeting, "Tunix," reveals the fairy tale to be a more problematic emblem than it seems at first glance. What does the word *Tunix*, which translates "Don't do any-thing," actually stand for—a call for active resistance, a call for pas-sive withdrawal, or simply an expression of idleness? We can indeed understand it as a call for opposition to one of the fundamental values of capitalism, namely, to productivity, that is, the virtue of industriousness that predetermines and structures each individual's life. Rejection of the capitalist performance principle, an aspect of the student movement's opposition, demonstrates the continuation of antiauthoritarian ideals in the counterculture after 1968.

While the student movement used the Marcusean term Great Re-fusal, which connotes a deliberate activity, the Spontis chose a more polemical slogan—"Tunix!" This slogan implies also laziness and leisure (*Faulheit* and *Müßiggang*)—concepts that are as old as the capitalist work ethic itself and that experienced quite a renaissance from the late 1970s into the early 1980s.[17] In contrast to the term *lazi-ness* (*Faulheit*), which has etymologically only a negative connota-tion according to the *Deutsche Wörterbuch*, *Musze* and *müszig*, which are etymologically at the root of *Müsziggang* (leisure), originally had a positive connotation. Leisure or *müszig* implies as well "room to maneuver" and to be "free, relaxed, unencumbered."[18] Particularly the last definition expresses the self-understanding of the Spontis and the entire alternative culture, that is, its desire for freedom, spontaneity, and a nonalienated, self-determined way of life.

But do the Bremen Town Musicians indeed denounce the perfor-mance principle? Does the fairy tale take an anticapitalist stance? Closer inspection shows that the Bremen Town Musicians do not rebel against capitalism in itself. The animals do not put up any ac-tive resistance to the capitalist value system, they do not question or try to change it, but instead they quietly retreat and try to find a niche for themselves. At the same time, the fairy tale portrays the animals not as victims of the capitalist work ethic but as agents of their fate. They scare away the gang of thieves to win themselves a new home far away from society's performance principles, namely, in the German forest. The Tunix motto matches the fairy tale's ambivalent stance. The leaflet, on the one hand, seems to endorse the Bremen Town

Musicians' strategy: resistance as a mode of passive withdrawal. That reading is supported by the interpretation of Tunix by a participant of the Tunix Gathering: "Tunix celebrates falling down as a pleasurable process. To everyone who points to the hopelessness of life and demands collective mourning, Tunix replies, 'Screw You!' Tunix means, in the words of Paul Scheerbart (1898), denial of everything and staying precisely where one is—this appears to me to be the best."[19]

Both the above quote and the flier strike yet another chord. They reject an attitude of resignation and contemplate militant struggle. The rejection of capitalism's work ethic—especially of the performance principle—remains the key for understanding the Tunix motto. The Tunix generation was not calling for a reign of laziness, as the leaflet's depiction of the imaginary beach at the Tunix Gathering shows. Quite in contrast to the slogan, this beach is an industrious place where nobody goes idle; everybody is engaged in some activity, from construction work for solar technology to discussion and artistic practices. Hence the provocative "Tunix!" cannot mean "Don't do anything."

The depicted productivity differs, however, from capitalism's industriousness. It is interested not in making a profit but in fulfilling the needs and desires of the community. The alternative culture's concept of labor gains therefore a different quality, exhibiting remnants of a Marxist anthropology. Work does not mean alienated production or performance of services merely to turn a profit. Instead, work is defined as a mode of self-actualization. The flier's portrayal of the Tunix community expresses the longing for a "human and meaningful occupation," typical for the Sponti and alternative movement.[20] The alternative culture still pursued the antiauthoritarian student movement's ideal of nonalienated labor, though the alternative movement articulated it implicitly in rejecting and attacking the hegemonic culture of conformity. "We no longer want to do the same job, make the same faces over and over again. They have bossed us around enough, have censored our thoughts and ideas, checked our apartments and passports, and bashed us in the face. We will no longer let ourselves be bottled up, made small and made the same."[21]

The flier's emphasis on the collective benefits of everybody's labor refutes the criticism that the alternative movement's valorization of subjectivity and self-actualization undermines solidarity. The alternative movement was able to develop the concept of a community, even if its identity was strongly based on a common opponent—the hegemonic culture, as the above quote demonstrates. The flier's rhetoric of "we" picks up on the discourse of "us" and "them," which the theory of two cultures had generated. The pronoun "we" invokes a community that is based on solidarity in general and against oppression in particular. Hence the solidarity of the heterogeneous group of animals in the fairy tale represents the other main point of identification, since the Tunix Gathering was intended to create a group identity and demonstrate the solidarity of the alternative culture beyond its diversity. This group identity did not aim at eliminating the diversity of the alternative culture, but rather embraced the concept of difference, thereby rejecting the homogeneity of the hegemonic culture.

The flier articulates a response to the pressure it felt from the hegemonic culture, particularly institutionalized politics. The flier invokes a militant stance and concludes with the rhetoric of destruction. "We will discuss how we can destroy the 'Model Germany' and replace it with Tunix."[22] For the alternative culture, the SPD's slogan for the election campaign in 1976—"Model Germany" (*Modell Deutschland*)—was totally empty. They viewed the Model Germany not as an alternative but as a euphemistic label for the same old capitalist structures of the hegemonic culture. This ironic and aggressive reference to the SPD highlights how far the two cultures had indeed grown apart. In contrast to the activists of the student movement, many of whom found a political home within the SPD on their long march through the institutions, the SPD was meaningless for the post-1968 counterculture. The SPD represented the hegemonic culture from which the alternative culture withdrew. The alternative culture rejected not only the SPD but all left-wing groups, from staunch communists to the student movement activists, which quickly became the butt of jokes, especially among the Spontis. In naming the various left-wing groups, the leaflet uses puns and irony that express, on the one hand, the alternative culture's wit and playfulness, but reveal, on the other hand, its alienation from the traditional left and its concepts.[23]

The flier pokes fun at the concept of class—the theoretical staple for all left-wing politics in postwar West Germany. "Every ticket of our communist comrades will be a winner in the workers' lottery."[24] At first sight this sentence does not seem to make sense. It plays, however, with the communist concept of class and the institution of the state-run lottery, which is organized according to a specific system of classification of lots and is therefore called "class lottery" (*Klassenlotterie*). The flier draws an analogy between the stake of the Communist parties and that of the lottery.[25] The Communist parties' "stake" in the revolution—that is, the constantly invoked proletariat as the historical revolutionary agent/subject—and their efforts to further the revolution had become as dubious as playing the lottery. The statement implies at the same time that the West German working class supposedly pays more attention to the lottery than to communist or any other kind of left-wing propaganda, indicating that the proletariat has been integrated into the established capitalist culture through participation in increased consumption. The state lottery represents only the epitome of capitalism's deceptive powers.

The Tunix leaflet also took a shot at the movement of the socialist factory groups, or socialist cells (*Basis-* and *Betriebsgruppen-Bewegung*), which had grown out of the student movement. Many 1968ers had left the university and joined the working class at the assembly line in order to organize "cells within factory shops dedicated to the enlightening of the workers and to a correct analysis of the contradictions between labor and capital."[26] The flier ridicules these groups for acting like hard-working but misguided fools: "the socialist cells (*Basisgruppen*) dug up the yard in search of their base."[27] This short statement, analogous to the above critique of the concept of class, suggests that these socialist cells worked hard at digging up the proletarian garden, but they unfortunately never gained any fertile ground for their ideas among the working class. The satirical criticism of political groups that still employed the category of class and believed in the proletariat as the revolutionary subject demonstrates both that the alternative culture did not identify with the working class nor believed in its revolutionary potential. Consequently, the alternative culture viewed efforts at establishing a proletarian base or culture as obsolete.

Finally, the flier exhibits a similar ironic treatment of the super-stars of traditional left-wing intellectual culture. "For lunch, some of our academic comrades hunt capital stags, and Heinrich Böll prepares tea while discussing the New Sensuality with Günter Wall-raff. Uncle Biermann sings his Eurosong to the children as a lul-laby."[28] Heinrich Böll, Günter Wallraff, and Wolf Biermann were not ridiculed because of their political opinions, concepts, or ideals, since all of them were major critics of West German society and politics. By portraying them as a part of the imaginary beach of Tunix, the counterculture to a certain extent validated their criticism and invited them into their own culture. Within the Tunix culture there was no space for authorities or authority. The leaflet made fun of them in order to push them from their pedestal of left-wing idolatry and integrate them into their beach community.

As we can see by the Tunix flier, the alternative culture replaced the category of class with an ideal of community that is no longer founded on economic positioning, that is, socioeconomic class, but on the individual's opposition to the hegemonic culture. The alter-native culture envisioned this new community as absolutely egali-tarian. Nobody can have or should expect a special status, even if he or she has such in the hegemonic culture or within the tradi-tional left. The numerous alternative projects tried to organize their work in this egalitarian manner. They did not have any supervisor or boss; everybody did the same work and got paid the same base salary. These ideas correlate with the politics of the self and the grass roots. This egalitarian and antiauthoritarian stance was one of the reasons why the alternative culture preferred to retreat rather than fight against the hegemonic culture. Quite in contrast to the student movement, nobody within the alternative culture saw him- or herself in a representative or avant-garde function for the proletariat or any other group. It was imperative for the alternative culture's concept of the politics of the self that everybody raise his or her own concerns in order to attain the utmost level of authenticity.

The alternative culture's disenchantment with the West German left and its political strategies ran deeper, however. The alternative culture criticized these strategies as suffocating the imagination, that is, that which the student movement had once emphatically proclaimed: "For years we believed that actions according to the motto 'Do away with . . .' and 'Tear down . . .' would bring about change, if they were cleverly done. But it only crippled our imagination, put it to sleep, and covered it up. Instead of getting mixed up in a traditional mode of resistance, we want not only to discuss new modes of opposition but to practice them already in the way we conduct our meeting."[29]

Finally and characteristically for the 1970s' rediscovery of subjectivity and sensuality, the flier implicitly criticizes a mere conceptual culture and favors an aesthetic, that is, a sensuous and affective one. It does not invite to a "congress," although the flier uses this term once, but to a "three-day party" (*3-Tage-Fest*), an event characterized by aesthetic activities and experience. In contrast to the notion of a congress, which implies conceptual forms of presentation and discussion, the leaflet affirms its idea of organizing a festival by explicitly arguing for the aesthetic representation of one's thoughts and opinions, be it in painting, music, or another mode of expression. This holistic approach, attempting to reintegrate life, politics, and art, characterizes the alternative culture and was more significant for its members than any political resolution, as the account by the previously cited Tunix participant shows: "The fusion of theater, discussion, music, and communication was responsible for a high Tunix attendance. Where only disjointed parts were presented, the prompt result was a deeply moving failure."[30]

The key notions for comprehending the character of the Tunix Gathering are "narration" and "experience," which are used in contrast to "discussion." These two terms incorporate aesthetic and subjective elements into public debate, whereas the notion of discussion implies the idea of an exchange of controversial opinions on a conceptual level. "Let's get together at this congress of opposition before we'll all take off. Let us talk to and learn of each other and express this opposition movement, and then we'll take off together, we'll sail to the beach of Tunix, which might be far away or perhaps under the pavement of this country."[31] This preference for narration as a valid form of communicating experience connects the Tunix culture with literary New Subjectivity. The latter, too, returned to narrative forms to explore the issue of subjectivity. In contrast to both literary New Subjectivity's individualized subjectivity and the student movement's privileging of the class subject, the Tunix flier articulates the belief that the individual-subjective and collective-objective dimension of life can be reconciled, for instance, in their communitarian ideal based on subjective desires, authenticity, and solidarity.

Die taz: *A Dream Comes True*

The "German Autumn" of 1977, when RAF terrorism culminated in the murder of Hanns-Martin Schleyer and the deaths of Gudrun Ensslin, Andreas Baader, and Jan-Carl Raspe in the maximum secu-rity prison in Stuttgart-Stammheim, had a unifying effect on the diverse and diffuse counterculture, particularly in its channels of communication, that is, the alternative press. The government's in-formation blackout in the case of Schleyer, a hostage of a terrorist unit of the RAF, functioned as a catalyst to make the old dream of the left finally come true. In 1978 a radically left-wing daily newspaper got off the ground: *die tageszeitung* (the daily times), abbreviated as *die taz* and symbolized with the tiger's paw.

In his brief summary of the history of the *taz*, Wolfgang Ströbele emphasizes that the idea for an independent and radically opposi-tional paper had haunted the left since the student movement and its experience with the mainstream press during the 1960s, but it sprang as well from the dissatisfaction with the existing leftist under-ground press. "And then we were annoyed with the pamphlets of the undogmatic left, which were actually full of biased and often false information, and we were upset about the alignment of formerly left-liberal papers like *Frankfurter Rundschau* and *Spiegel*, which had in the meantime become social-democratic-liberal and loyal to the government."[32] Since the summer of 1976, when a group of people around Ströbele started to gather regularly and seriously discussed such a project, the free-floating ideas and wishful thinking gained substance, helped along as well by the successful expansion of the decentralized alternative press throughout the past years. The next historical step toward the paper's realization came in the context of the "German Autumn" and the Tunix Gathering at the beginning of 1978. The Tunix Gathering as a demonstrative assembly of the counterculture represented the ideal platform for introducing the project of an alternative daily paper that was supposed to function as a medium for the self-assertion and stabilization of the badly fragmented and demoralized West German counterculture. The alternatively inclined audience at this meeting expressed general consent as well as skepticism.[33]

The foundation of a club named Friends of an Alternative Daily (*Freunde der alternativen Tageszeitung*) in February 1978 gave the project a legal status. The seventy-page brochure *Prospekt: Tageszeitung* (Prospectus: Daily times), widely distributed two months later, in which the initiators presented and discussed their understanding of an alternative journalism, managed to mobilize more and more people for the project. Innumerable "initiatives for the *Daily Times*" (*Tageszeitungsinitiativen* or *Inis*), sprang up all over the Federal Republic. The initiatives in Frankfurt and West Berlin—the two cities with the strongest countercultural presence in West Germany—became the driving forces behind the project, and in September of the same year the first "zero issue" (*Null-Number*) was sold. After a period of organization and several experimental zero issues, the *taz* started its daily appearance on 17 April 1979 and has proven wrong all of the voices that predicted its rapid disappearance from the newspaper market. The *taz* celebrated its seventeenth anniversary in 1996, fulfilling slowly but surely its self-established goal: "The paper should have a role in shaping public opinion in the Federal Republic and West Berlin."[34] Although the *taz* is still going strong today, the paper has undergone numerous changes, and its politics looks different today than during its early years of circulation. For us, only these early years—1979 to 1983—are of interest, and I therefore refer to the *taz* in the past tense.

The question remains as to what made the *taz* so different that it could legitimately claim to represent the alternative culture. In contrast to traditional daily papers and in accordance with its political bent, the *taz* had from its inception different priorities with respect to the events and topics it covered and on which it commented, as well as with respect to the issues it raised. The second zero issue, for example, inflamed the suspicions of the right-wing defenders of law and order because it commemorated the first anniversary of the RAF terrorists' death in the Stammheim prison while calling at the same time for a general amnesty for prisoners who were serving sentences because of the new antiterrorism legislation.[35]

Not only because of this issue of the *taz*, but also because of its extensive coverage of terrorism and its critical position toward the hegemonic culture's reaction to it, the *taz* gained the odious reputation of being an intellectual collaborator (*Sympathisant*) and breeding ground for such violence. Ironically, the *taz* also came under attack from the supporters of the terrorists. In their eyes, the paper did not do enough to support the imprisoned terrorists. On 12 June 1979 the first sit-in staged by relatives and friends of the "political prisoners," as the terrorists were called by their supporters, took place at the *taz* headquarters. This action was meant to attract media attention in general and to pressure the *taz* into publicizing the hunger strike of seventy RAF prisoners, which was not covered in any other medium.

Aside from a vocal and dissident coverage of terrorism, the *taz* reported daily on ecological issues long before the traditional press became aware of environmental problems, an awareness largely due to the constitution of the Federal Party of the Greens in 1980. "From the very beginning the *taz* distinguished itself from other established dailies by the significance it attributed to ecology. The *taz* had its own department for ecological issues and reported about environmental problems on at least one page daily. That the *taz* abandoned this one ecology page in the mid-1980s had nothing to do with declining importance of ecological topics. On the contrary, the fact that other dailies had started to cover environmental scandals demonstrates that ecology had become a general social topic."[36]

A third feature that distinguished the *taz* from traditional daily papers was its coverage of women's issues. The feminist wing of its staff showed itself very critical of sexism within the left. In February 1981 a daily women's page was added because the original concept of integrating women's issues and a feminist perspective into the general journalistic work seemed to have failed.[37] Furthermore, the *taz* thematized sexuality, although as Oliver Tolmein and Detlef zum Winkel critically point out, this topic was sometimes treated quite similarly as in the other media. It functioned as a provocation in order to make the *taz* the topic of public discourse and increase its circulation, which was important for the always financially strapped paper.[38] As a result, the *taz* itself became a battlefield of the gender struggle. Finally, we should not forget that the *taz* was also the first daily paper to open its pages for lesbian and gay groups in West Germany.

Aside from social groups marginalized because of their members' gender or sexual preferences, the *taz* reported not only on the situation of the terrorists but on the grievances of ordinary prisoners as well. It printed statements and literary texts by these "jailbirds" (*Knackis*) and ran an ongoing advertisement campaign that asked its readership to donate *taz* subscriptions for prisoners.[39] Another marginalized social group the *taz* attracted attention to were psychiatric patients. Furthermore, the *taz* did not lack coverage of the Third World and supported in particular the various liberation movements there. On 3 November 1980 it started a unique and highly controversial campaign to aid the cause of the guerrilla movement in El Salvador: "Weapons for El Salvador."[40] Not only did the *taz* report extensively and favorably on the Sandinistas' victory in Nicaragua, but many of the Nicaragua initiatives that sprang up in West Germany after the revolution in support of the Nicaraguan people and the Sandinistas used the *taz* as their platform as well. In other words, the *taz* encompassed from its beginnings the whole spectrum of issues around which citizens' initiatives had formed throughout the 1970s and functioned as a public forum for all new social movements.

The militant wing of the new social movements, the *Autonome* — most active in the squatters' movement — represented, however, the crossroads for the *taz* as much as for the counterculture in general. The *taz* had sided with the squatters' movement of the early 1980s, even devoting an entire issue to it, in which the squatters could articulate their situation and demands.[41] The *taz* distanced itself from the squatters' movement when the militant *Autonome* became its driving force. The *Autonome* rejected any negotiations with city authorities or the owners of the squatted houses in order to find a legal solution.[42] In 1982 the *taz* offices in Berlin and Hamburg were invaded several times and partially destroyed by groups that identified themselves as *Autonome*. These attacks on the *taz* included takeovers, destruction of the *taz* offices, and clandestine exchanges of some of the paper's pages. The *Autonome* always articulated the same critique of the *taz*, namely, that they felt their radical position was no longer adequately represented in the paper.[43] From the perspective of the *Autonome*, the *taz* had already betrayed its journalistic principles and become mainstream.

The Concept of Grass-Roots Journalism

The founders of the *taz* had claimed that a left daily would not only be different in terms of its content but also in terms of its organizational structure and journalistic principles.[44] In other words, the *taz* was supposed to materialize as the absolutely different, true alternative to the established media. Consequently, the *taz* aimed at an antiauthoritarian, nonhierarchical, decentralized, and nonspecialized organizational structure, which would allow for "life and labor free of repression."[45] Its alternative journalism called for staying as close to the grass roots as possible, and it tried to realize this goal with the concept of grass-roots reporting or grass-roots journalism (*Betroffenen-* or *Basisberichterstattung*).

A critical approach to the dialectics of objectivity and subjectivity was at the center of the *taz*'s alternative journalistic principle. In its prospectus, under the provocative heading "Objectivity? No, Thank You!," the *taz* distanced itself from the common claim to objectivity, calling it a crude deception and a mere "fetish" of the bourgeois press: "The mass media transforms events into news items often according to rather banal mechanisms: for instance, according to their own political interest, social biases, commercial point of view, editorial routine, and so forth. The deceptive nimbus of 'duty of care' and 'objectivity' usually means not much more than the uncritical adoption of news items preprocessed by wire services, whose objectivity is at least doubtful. There is no objective news anyway, because each news report contains the subjective interest of the reporter."[46]

This skepticism regarding objectivity introduces subjectivity as a legitimate journalistic mode and reflects at the same time the shift of the cultural paradigm, which we have previously discussed in terms of the literary New Subjectivity and its psychological articulation as a new type of socialization (*Neuer Sozialisationstyp*), and which the alternative culture expressed in its concept of the politics of the self.

Based on this key notion of the alternative culture, the *taz* tried to develop a new journalistic practice—grass-roots journalism—in opposition to the hegemonic culture's media. The concept of a grass-roots journalism meant that people who are actually concerned with a political or social problem should speak for themselves by writing reports for the paper. Another institution of the alternative press, the Service for the Dissemination of Unreported News (*Informationsdienst zur Verbreitung unterbliebener Nachrichten*) in Frankfurt, had first attempted to realize this concept. The so-called ID, a press agency modeled after such countercultural projects as the Liberation News Service in the United States or the Agence de Press Libération in France, appeared weekly from October 1973 to February 1981, publishing, as the name indicates, news items that were not covered by the mainstream press.

According to Karl-Heinz Stamm, the idea behind the grass-roots report, which articulates the immediate experience of the people who are actually affected by a sociopolitical problem, can be summarized in two points.[47] First, the information of such a report has value for the reader precisely because the reported event is not mediated by an outsider, the journalist. The reader can therefore reappropriate the unmediated experience expressed in the report for his or her own political struggle. Second, the process of writing gives the people affected by a political or social problem the opportunity to work through their own experience consciously.

In contrast to established journalism, which undermines this constitution of an unmediated experience through the "objective" mediation of the journalist, the concept of grass-roots journalism was supposed to generate an emancipatory process of politicization. The founders of the *taz* described this principle less theoretically: "It is important that all news reports originate from the grass roots, because only this makes it possible to overcome the separation of reader and writer and in the long run makes emancipation (to speak up) possible."[48]

As a rejection of the false claim to objectivity, the concept of a grass-roots journalism implies a different linguistic awareness as well as linguistic plurality. The initiators of the *taz* were influenced by theories that understand language or discourse as not only reflecting but reproducing structures of domination. Hence the texts in the *taz* were supposed to be free from domination, revealing and not deceiving, accessible for everybody, and thereby possessing an informative use value.[49] Instead of translating the voices of those affected or concerned by an issue into a uniform journalistic discourse, the idea was to preserve the diversity and authenticity of those voices.[50]

Finally, the *taz* revived antiauthoritarian traditions in its attempt at reintegrating the personal and the political. This meant focusing on issues of daily private life in accordance with the postulate of the women's movement, that the personal—be it people's relationships, attitudes, fears, or desires—is intrinsically political.

The *taz* did not merely attack the hegemonic culture's concept of journalism; it also criticized the student movement's conceptualization of an alternative public sphere, which was still indebted to the ideas Habermas raised in his analysis of the structural transformation of the bourgeois public sphere.[51] Furthermore, the *taz*'s approach to the problem of objectivity implicitly rejected pseudo-materialist positions of an orthodox left and the claims to an insight into an inevitable, objective reality that can be analyzed without considering subjective implications. The *taz* criticized the actual journalistic practices of this dogmatic left.[52] In contrast to these tendentious newspapers with their dogmatic perspectives, the *taz* was designed as an "independent left daily . . . which will not become the mouthpiece for the political propaganda of any specific organization or party of the Sponti movement."[53]

As we can see from the previous description, the *taz* was a child of the alternative culture and one of its most successful projects. It was intended to develop a genuine countercultural public sphere in opposition to the established and institutionalized public sphere and aimed at the same time at overcoming its own marginalization.[54] After more than a decade of the *taz* as the self-proclaimed alternative public sphere, the question legitimately arises whether the *taz* in the 1990s still meets its original self-imposed standards. This raises yet another question, namely, for which time period can we perceive the *taz* as a representative communicative platform of the alternative culture? Tolmein and zum Winkel, for instance, claim that the *taz* failed from its very beginnings. They locate a major break as early as the first year, which showed that the cooperation with the single initiatives could no longer be sustained. In their opinion, the idea of grass-roots journalism is intrinsically connected with the concept of the initiatives, which represented the active base (*Basis*) for the *taz*. Thus they argue that grass-roots journalism ceased to exist together with the "death" of the initiatives.[55]

To count as the grass roots of the *taz*'s reader/writership only those people organized in initiatives, however, is reductive. First of all, the employees of the *taz* as well as its freelance writers were part of the alternative culture too. Without denying that reports straight from the grass roots were increasingly marginalized in favor of more professional writing, there is still sufficient evidence that the *taz* continued to report not only on but from the grass roots beyond 1980. It started, for example, a new section, the "News Report from the Factory" (*Betriebszeitung*), which appeared the first Thursday of each month since June 1982. This section introduced autonomous alternative projects either in a report or frequently as a self-description, that is, as a report from the grass roots. Furthermore, the *taz* kept publishing appeals and statements by innumerable groups across the spectrum of the alternative culture while at the same time trying to distance itself from the militant fringes.

Furthermore, one cannot substantiate Tolmein's and zum Winkel's claim that the originally alternative journalistic concept of the *taz* was altered or even betrayed predominantly for economic reasons in order to keep the project going. The confrontation between the grass roots and the journalists of the *taz* was preprogrammed because of the diversity of its reader/writership as well as because of its competing journalistic approaches. On the one hand, as already discussed, it understood itself as a platform for the entire alternative culture; on the other hand, it wanted to ovecome this limitation, thereby drawing on traditional journalistic concepts that perceive the press as a medium for criticism, for introducing new themes and issues into public discourse, and for initiating controversies and debates. As its prospectus stated, "Even as an instrument of the movement, as the carrier of reports by the grass roots, the paper should not completely surrender itself to self-presentation. . . . A specific kind of journalistic professionalism, which we cannot take as self-evident, but which we—readers and journalists alike—need to learn, is important."[56] This problem, the tension between the professional's and the layperson's work, is not particular to the *taz*, but characterizes all alternative projects. In its development toward more professionalism and political moderation—correctly observed by Tolmein and zum Winkel—the *taz* rather reflects the overall development of the alternative movement.

The development of the *taz* corresponds to three distinct phases of the alternative movement. In its first phase, the alternative movement slowly developed out of the disintegration of the student movement as a myriad of autonomous groups. During the second phase, the number of alternative projects reached an ultimate high between, roughly speaking, 1978 and 1983; the *taz*, founded in this time period, was one of those projects. Finally, from the mid-1980s those numbers declined. The alternative movement had reached its peak and started to peter out. Now only those projects that had a solid following—mainly ecological projects—survived because they catered to a large enough audience to sustain them.

The fall of 1985 represents a turning point for the *taz* as well, which became apparent in the subscription campaign it ran. The *taz* published advertisements in which it was endorsed by representatives both of the old New Left such as Hans Magnus Enzensberger, the former editor of the *Kursbuch*, and of Social Democrats such as Peter Glotz, who once claimed that one out of five students thinks like the Mescalero. The militant fringes of the alternative movement such as the *Autonome* understood this as the *taz*'s final turn away from its own radical origins. As a result, it left the level of argumentative confrontation and moved into violent action. During the night of 21 November 1985 a militant group of *Autonome* totally destroyed the offices and the layout computers of the *taz* in Hamburg.[57] This reflected the alternative culture's split into a more pragmatic wing, which developed its own institutional forms of politics such as the party of the Greens or the *taz*, and the militant wing of the *Autonome*, who were in absolute opposition to the hegemonic culture and institutionalized politics of any sort. As the *taz* participated in the overall transformations of the alternative culture, it functioned more and more as an advocate of this moderate wing that was willing to compromise and adhered to the idea of constructive criticism. Naturally, the *taz* and the militant wing of the *Autonome* became opponents.

Considering the entire development of the *taz*, it is justified to perceive it as a platform for the alternative culture at least in its very first years—from approximately 1979 to 1983—and with some qualifications up to 1985. Therefore, an analysis of the alternative culture's perception of art and culture can legitimately draw on the *taz* as an excellent source for this period, since its own development reflects in many ways that of the entire alternative culture.

"Feuilleton" versus "Kulturen"

"We are looking for an editor for our cultural section. Required are—aside from enthusiasm and a sunny disposition—experience in producing a newspaper, the ability to organize articles and thematic foci, *ideas for the daily walk along the tightrope between established and alternative culture.*"[58] This advertisement in the *taz* for an editor for its culture desk describes the paper's concept of culture in a nutshell. The advertisement expresses Peter Glotz's distinction between two cultures, but indicates at the same time the problematic status of such a distinction. Although the alternative culture defines itself in opposition to the hegemonic culture, it is difficult to make a clear-cut differentiation. The advertisement implies that there is rather an ambiguous relationship between the two cultures. This suggests using a comparative approach in order to fully comprehend and evaluate the aesthetic conceptualizations of the alternative culture. The *Frankfurter Allgemeine Zeitung*, usually abbreviated as *Faz*, offers itself for comparison with the *taz*, since the *Faz* represents the apogee of the hegemonic culture's journalism, against which the *taz* had developed its own journalistic principles.[59]

{129}

The *Faz* enjoys a large nationwide and international circulation as well as an international reputation. It not only has one of the most extensive and well regarded cultural sections but also (in contrast to the *taz*, which understands itself to be in fundamental opposition to the hegemonic culture, i.e., the *Faz*) respects and supports the established political and economic order of the Western industrialized world. In its publication *Dokumentation: Alles über die Zeitung* (Documentation: Everything about the *Times*), which spells out its official editorial policy, the *Faz* clearly states its belief in the possibility of ascertaining and communicating facts objectively, to which the *taz* had said, "No, thank you!": "First of all, the foundation for the shaping of public opinion is and remains the unbiased representation of the facts. For a paper that claims to be a leader in public opinion the up-to-date and precise coverage of news is absolutely imperative. The *Faz* stands for a balanced and mainstream approach that keeps a critical distance to all social groups. This paper intends to show the meaning and significance of our political and economic system as well as of our way of life especially to our young people, who are the leaders of the future."[60]

The idea of the necessity and meaningfulness of social order, to which this quote gives voice, articulates itself in a variety of ways. It is, for instance, already visible in the layout of the *Faz* in comparison to that of the *taz*, reflecting the different status that the two papers ascribe both to the category of objectivity as well as to their differing notions of culture. The *Faz* is thoroughly structured from the front page to the advertisement section, having the same columns in the same places day after day. They are even visually separated by vertical lines: to the left the news items and to the right the commentary, in accordance with one of the guiding journalistic principles of the *Faz*: to distinguish clearly between information and commentary. The entire paper is divided into three parts—politics, economy, culture—each of them representing a closed entity. This structure of the paper reduplicates the ideological division of social reality into autonomous spheres by the hegemonic culture and thereby veils their overwhelming interdependency. The *Faz*'s concession that there are more and more correlations between sports and the business world or politics and culture remains on the level of lip service.[61] In comparison, the *taz* showed little of such journalistic structuring in the first years of its circulation.

The layout, especially of the front pages of the two papers, serves as a good example for the differences. In contrast to the *taz*, whose front page had an eye-catching layout with a strong visual component, frequently more image than text, the *Faz* takes an anti-imagery position. Not a single photograph graces the front page of the *Faz*, and even for the cultural section the *Faz* prescribes a layout that "has always been focused on clarity, which means that decorative elements are used in a deliberately scarce fashion."[62] The *taz* did not economize with photography but employed it throughout the entire paper in a variety of ways. It installed, for example, a special section for photography called "Moments" (*Augenblicke*), which was placed at the bottom of the second page. These photographs did not function as mere decoration but were indebted to a visual aesthetics in the tradition of Siegfried Kracauer, who saw photography and film as a means to reconstitute the concrete physical reality of daily life's object world and thus allow for an equally concrete experience.[63] These photographs in the *taz* always showed human beings in situations of daily life, capturing the particularity of the accidental moment when the shutter opened. Thus the *taz* employed photography in a rather unusual manner for a daily paper; on the one hand, to reconstitute experience and, on the other hand, to make political statements. *Karikaturen*, political cartoons, represent the traditional visual artistic genre with a political intention. The *Faz* cultivates only this visual mode of political art, whereas the *taz* frequently replaced or supplemented it with photomontage and entire comic strips.[64]

While the *taz* was interested in being different and innovative, the *Faz* aimed at cultivating the traditions of hegemonic culture and its journalistic principles in order to appear as a serious and trustworthy source of information. These two different approaches articulated themselves not only in the visual makeup of the two papers but also in the language they employ. The *Faz* perceives an orderly, grammatically correct language as the basis for an objective journalism. Since the *taz* rejected this concept of objectivity as deceptive, it not only operated with nonverbal informational and artistic means but played as well with German grammar, especially with the rules of spelling. Aside from frequently neglecting to capitalize nouns, the *taz*'s linguistic style also revealed a feminist perspective. The pronoun *man* (someone) for the third person singular was by and large replaced with the feminine equivalent *frau* (woman) or with the word *mensch* (human being/person), which was considered to be gender neutral (although it is grammatically masculine). The use of feminine endings for nouns (*-in*, for example, in the advertisement quoted at the beginning of this chapter) was and still is standard practice in the *taz* and has turned into a characteristic capitalization and spelling, as in, for example, *RedakteurIn*. In contrast to other job descriptions, which usually conform to the legally required gender neutrality by adding the feminine ending as a separate and secondary suffix—*Redakteur/-in*—the *taz* style makes the feminine ending visually prominent, thereby aiming at restructuring the traditional gender codes. This innovative attempt by the *taz* to break with the traditionally gendered language has by now entered the mainstream and can be found in more and more publications.

Finally, we need to turn to an institution that was unique to the *taz*, the typesetters' annotations (*Setzer-/Säzzerbemerkungen*) that accompanied articles, statements, and letters to the editor, a practice applauded by some and rejected by others. These bracketed annotations, which were simply signed "the typesetter" and usually broke up the train of thought of an article, were not formally instituted; the typesetters spontaneously started to insert them into the text. The typesetters' annotations functioned as a kind of control mechanism and, since they represented another voice within the text, undercut the one-way communication of the printed media. They staged a debate in front of the reader's eyes, thereby encouraging him or her to engage in further questioning of the article's argument.

The typesetters' annotations also represented an attempt to recapture the many-voiced character of the alternative culture. The annotations are of significance not only for the readership but also for the *taz* as an alternative project that strives for nonhierarchical and self-determined modes of labor, as one of the typesetters explained in an interview:

No matter how funny the thing might be, however strange the thoughts of the person who wrote it, you never get that somebody else with quite different thoughts, who most likely was thinking of a holiday or has done other things or has had totally different experiences, was involved. . . . you cannot hide the fact that the people who work here are also political beings with their own thoughts, who sometimes find the ideas some authors articulate here in the paper rather idiotic but sometimes also quite good. So this means that it is not always necessarily just a negative critique.[65]

The typesetters' annotations certainly did not solve the problems and tension between the editorial staff and the other departments of the *taz* collective, but they aimed at visually breaking up the traditional division of labor that goes into a finished product. These side comments call into question the general public's hierarchy of social prestige with respect to various professions, since they draw attention to hidden but important ones—the typesetting and layout professions—thereby fostering an understanding of the collective character of production.

In the pages of the *Faz*, the typesetting and layout staff remains concealed behind the bylines of the journalists and editors. Authorship has in general a different status in the two papers. The *Faz* insists on authorship, arguing that an objective journalism requires the verification of the news item's source. Anonymously given information does not find entry into the *Faz*, since it cannot be verified. The *Faz* even refuses to publish anonymous letters to the editor.[66] In contrast, the lack of authorship particularly in the early *taz* is indeed eye-catching. Most of the articles as well as letters to the editor were signed—if at all—only with the first name.

This practice had a self-protective character if we recall the widespread fear within the West German counterculture of being charged or harassed for radical criticism of the government and its politics, especially after the experience with the Buback Obituary. Many felt that the extensive legal measures to combat terrorism made such criticism a risky endeavor. Anonymous publication within the framework of an institution, a newspaper, protects the individual and guarantees publicity at the same time, since it is the editors of the paper who are usually tried for offensive, anonymous utterances in their paper. Editors have, however, easy access to the public sphere through their own media and also to legal resources. The *taz* acquired quite an expensive history of such legal trials throughout its first decade of circulation.[67]

The comparison of *Faz* and *taz* with respect to authorship demonstrates once again the fundamental opposition of these two papers and the political camps they represent—the hegemonic culture versus the counterculture. The *Faz*'s treatment of authorship shows that it is deeply rooted in a bourgeois tradition. Authorship has been cherished since the eighteenth century as protecting the financial interests of the producer of a text, but has in turn functioned in support of censorship and social control.[68] The negation of authorship by the *taz* not only subverts the legal mechanism of social control inherent in this principle but also expresses a strong fear that authorship inevitably fosters authoritarian structures. As Hadayatullah Hübsch, himself a representative of the alternative culture, argues in his assessment of the alternative public sphere in 1980, the *taz* aimed at encouraging communication at the grass-roots level on equal grounds for everybody. Hence privileging the voice of the authority would in turn mean silencing the voice of the grass roots. "To make communication possible, to demand, foster, and expand it, represents the foremost goal of the *taz*. This is the reason why in internal discussions there is a lot of opposition to granting to VIPs any more space than is necessary, if space is granted at all. At the root is the idea of the liberation from the name, from illegitimate authority, the morality of a permanent revolution."[69]

The conceptual entwining of authorship and authority is more apparent in the cultural section of the *Faz*, its feuilleton.[70] The cultural criticism in the *Faz* is supposed to be an autonomous judgment legitimated by authority, that is, the expert status of the critic. The feuilleton of the *Faz* aims at keeping its readership informed of the current cultural developments and at articulating standards for cultural criticism. The *Faz*, therefore, represents an important element in safeguarding the cultural hegemony of the dominant social forces. In describing the function of its cultural section, the *Faz* strongly adheres to the position it already held in 1949, when the paper was refounded after having been prohibited by the Nazis in 1933. One of its main objectives was to reconstruct cultural critical positions that had been repressed by the Nazis' concept of a Germanic people's culture (*völkische Kultur*). The *Faz* refers to bourgeois German cultural traditions, including its most advanced modes of aesthetic practices, which developed between the two world wars in the Weimar Republic. We have discussed this attempt to pick up on a bourgeois tradition of aesthetic culture in analyzing Marcel Reich-Ranicki's literary criticism in the *Faz*, for which he has worked as the editor of the literary supplement since 1973.

This cultural program of the *Faz* raises two questions in particular. Can critical standards based on the bourgeois tradition of aesthetic culture still function as appropriate tools for describing and analyzing current aesthetic works and cultural developments? Second, we must also confront the problem Peter Uwe Hohendahl raised already in the early 1970s, namely, whether the critic holds such an independent position as he or she claims. In other words, can we indeed consider his or her criticism as having been developed autonomously?

Focusing on the literary critic as his primary example, Hohendahl convincingly argues that the proclaimed autonomy of the critic has vanished with the structural transformations of the bourgeois public sphere in the twentieth century. Today the critic is integrated into the apparatus of the contemporary culture industry, which restricts him or her merely to an immanent criticism. "The idea of immanent criticism, once a defense against the intrusion of private social interests, has changed its function. It makes taboo those zones of literary production and reception in which general social claims are expressed."[71] Cultural criticism as practiced in the feuilleton, especially literary criticism, had been under attack by the student movement precisely for this depoliticization of aesthetic culture. The students' critique not only undermined the status of the professional critics, revealing that they were actually subject to the mechanisms of the contemporary culture industry, but also rejected the critics' claim to the objectivity of their aesthetic judgment based on their professional competence. Hohendahl summarizes this critique of the critics with the following words: "Criticism becomes a rigid, dogmatic opinion, which no longer allows the public to form its own differing judgment. The subjective taste of the critic remains obscured and is presented as objective."[72]

The discussion of the standard practice of journalistic cultural criticism in the *taz* resembles Hohendahl's critique of the critic as a kind of absolute judge. The ideas about the feuilleton in the *taz*'s prospectus argue that such an absolute criticism forecloses on the object of criticism. The *taz* maintains that the established critical practices evaluate products of aesthetic culture only according to its own concepts and standards of "high" culture. It is, therefore, blind regarding any feature of the work of art that cannot be subjected to these standards. Concepts that reject one-dimensional readings of works of art in favor of a multitude of readings influenced the *taz*'s objections to bourgeois criticism.

For the *taz*, the guiding principle of every traditional cultural section—to be always up to date—is at the heart of this reductive criticism, since it allows only for a one-time review, mostly a short one in which the critic cannot do justice to a complex work of art. The critic can, however, sustain this image of the infallibility of his or her aesthetic judgment, since the critic does not reveal his or her standards of criticism. Instead, the critic frequently draws on the already acknowledged authoritative names, as Frank Wolff argues in an attack on an established critic of the *Frankfurter Rundschau*, another daily paper: "The point is that someone as a critic is arrogant enough to present his personal opinions, likes and dislikes, in the serious form of a rigid, obscure judgment. Tearing someone apart in a quick and mean way would be a scandal, and if so, so much the better. This, however, is the display of power, criticism as permanent verdict. It is itself deeply tendentious. The great names always guarantee value, the third rate only offer crumbs, garbage, not high culture."[73]

Since the alternative culture rejects any kind of authoritarian structures, it also articulates skepticism regarding traditional genres of criticism. The first random debates about the character of the cultural section of the *taz* discussed traditional literary critical genres. The cultural critics of the *taz* arrived, for instance, at negative conclusions regarding the important literary critical genre of the book review. In their opinion, the review represents nothing but a "thin extract concocted by a reviewer from a rather thick book."[74] Its proposal to publish more excerpts from primary texts—an entire chapter of a book, for example—not only failed for practical reasons but refuted its own line of argument against the genre of the review. It is indeed questionable whether a chapter from a lengthy book or an excerpt from a film script can represent the entire book or film better than a commentary that provides a broader context for understanding.

In comparison to the *Faz*, whose cultural section is mainly made up of reviews and critical essays, the cultural section of the *taz* drew more on primary material. There are many more excerpts from theoretical and philosophical or literary texts as well as more interviews in the *taz* than in the *Faz*. Both the excerpts and especially the interviews are an attempt to find journalistic practices for cultural criticism that resemble the grass-roots report.

In spite of its critical assessment of the traditional feuilleton and the style of the reviews therein, the *taz* itself had problems creating a truly oppositional alternative. Already in August 1979 the two competing positions regarding the concept of the cultural section clashed in a short debate. The *taz* was charged with reproducing basically the same understanding of culture as the mainstream press, that is, reducing culture to music, literature, and theater and the reviews to a mere description of the cultural events or the text. "The content of the report does not extend beyond a mere description of the events. The continuous repetition of descriptions (hot music) is as tiresome as driving on the autobahn. They do not show the surroundings, the fascinating ramifications beyond the immediate events. Streamlined and isolated, they eagerly take their places within the cultural section."[75]

This position was frequently supplemented with a critique of the inferior journalistic style in the cultural section of the *taz* compared with other daily papers and consequently with a call for more professionalism. Established left cultural critics were supposed to write for the *taz* or function at least as role models.[76] The supporters of more professionalism were accused of elitism, and their opponents made the ironic suggestion: "a column by Rudi Dutschke, an editorial by Cohn-Bendit, that looks mighty pretty."[77] Judging by the alternative paper's own attempts to give the people a space to voice their concerns, this fear of reviving a new stardom of established left-wing critics had import. Having professionals write on cultural activities and events undercuts the grass-roots journalism's emancipatory project of allowing for a process of learning for the people engaged in the subject of their writing.

The editorial staff of the *taz* rejected traditional elitist criticism without denying that the paper had not yet succeeded in developing an alternative to it. It nevertheless insisted on the validity of its twofold cultural concept as well as on the necessity to hold on to an avant-garde position: "We all associate the term *culture*—both the official culture as well as the alternative one—with something affirmative and theoretical. . . . The culture desk insists on its alleged avant-gardism. Our elitist arrogance means that we are unwilling to deliver useful help for the consumption of leisure-time activity that allows for escaping reality."[78]

For the *taz*, the supposed "elitism" was not a problem of the cultural section's editorial staff but the result of a failure on the grass-roots level; that is, the grass roots did not engage in cultural activities or was unwilling and unable to contribute to the cultural section. Hence, as Hübsch points out, the problems of the *taz* with its cultural section are caused by the concept "that the cultural section of the *taz* wants to deliver first and foremost a foundation for experience through unprofessional texts. The focus is not so much the language and the mediation of art but the powerful expression of desires that incidentally have found refuge in literary or musical form."[79]

Aside from the alleged disinterest of the alternative grass-roots constituency in cultural issues, the heterogeneity of the alternative environment posed many more problems for the *taz*'s cultural section than for the *Faz* and its traditional concept of culture. In contrast to the *Faz*, the *taz* used the plural form "cultures" (*Kulturen*) as a heading for the cultural section in its first years of circulation, because it ideally wanted to do justice to the diversity of the alternative culture. The *taz* intentionally employed this heading to remind its readership of the importance of safeguarding these cultural differences, since difference represented a positive value for the alternative culture. The acknowledgment of difference posed, however, the difficulty of choice, since such a position cannot develop distinct priorities regarding cultural events and activities. Considering the scarce space for cultural affairs in a daily paper, making choices is inevitable. Naturally, there were always groups that did not see their cultural interests adequately represented in the *taz*. The *Faz* has few problems with its cultural concept or with its acceptance by the readership. The mainstream concept of the feuilleton allows for the clear demarcation of the fields that belong to the cultural section: literature, theater productions, classical music, exhibits, and to a lesser extent cinema and TV, as well as questions of cultural politics.

The main features and distinguishing preferences regarding cultural activities of *taz* and *Faz* can be easily recognized. Music enjoyed an equally prominent position during the first two years of the *taz*'s circulation, just as in the *Faz*. The *taz*, however, did not cover events of the international high music culture, of the opera houses and the concert halls across the globe as the *Faz* does, but discussed the "lowlands" of music culture, mainly rock music and, during the festival year of 1979, folk music—popular musical genres that play a marginal role in the *Faz*. Theatrical events and literature were favored by the editorial staff as well as by the readership of the *taz*, since reports on these two fields of aesthetic culture outnumber reviews of exhibits and reports on other issues of fine arts. In contrast, the *Faz* keeps its readership well informed about art exhibits all over the world and the art market as well.

Reports on all significant national and international auctions under the eloquent heading "The Art Market" (*Kunstmarkt*) keeps the *Faz*'s readership as well informed about the value of their aesthetic assets as it does about the stock market. Today's price range for single works of visual art undoubtedly demonstrates the validity of the thesis that aesthetic culture has been totally subjected to the commodity character of contemporary society. Collecting works of art has become financially profitable, like holding stocks of multinational corporations. As a result, this mode of aesthetic culture cannot have much appeal for a countercultural movement that resents the hegemonic culture's power to commodify everything. Although the

Faz's conceptualizations construct aesthetic culture as a separate sphere without political implications, the cultural criticism of the *Faz* does not problematize the commercial tendencies of contemporary culture, but rather feeds into them.

Let us now turn from the private collection toward the public space of art, the museum and public galleries, which in Germany holds the second highest position in the allocation of government funds, together with the public libraries.[80] Here we see interesting differences between the representative of the hegemonic culture, the *Faz*, and the representative of the alternative culture, the *taz*. The *Faz* covers all major art exhibits on an international level, thereby participating in the preservation of a traditional bourgeois understanding of high art. The museum is an intrinsically bourgeois institution and functions for the larger public as the institution that sets the accepted standards of artistic quality. The art that is shown in the museum represents thus the authoritative canon of "good art." Covering mostly spectacular exhibits or artists with big names, the *Faz* clearly supports the artistic tradition that the museum and public galleries represent.

The reviews of art exhibitions in the *Faz* give an introduction into the life and work of the respective artist or the development of an artistic movement while critically evaluating its presentation in the exhibit. However, it does not thematize the problematic status of the museum as constructing a canon of art, which contributes as well to the commodification of art, especially of contemporary art. For the *Faz*, the traditional function of the museum—the preservation and presentation of art—remains unquestioned. It criticizes instead all innovations with regard to the concept of the museum that aim at opening up this institution for a broader, perhaps less-educated audience. It denounces as wrong the assumption at the heart of the debate about museum innovation. According to the *Faz*, sociologists and politicians who perceive cultural activities and their reception as class specific are simply falling prey to their own prejudice. By rejecting the class specificity of culture, the *Faz* promotes a concept of an "eternal" culture equally accessible for everybody.[81]

In contrast, the *taz* did not systematically review internationally acclaimed art exhibitions but covered them only with rather short announcements, which usually alluded in an ironic manner to the questionable status of art in late capitalism. The coverage of art events in the *taz* mirrored its general thematic focus, emphasizing the artistic work of marginalized social groups, for instance, by reporting on paintings by psychiatric patients and women's artwork.[82] Hence the *taz* aimed at breaking up the canonic understanding of art as a long list of names of predominantly male artists who have made it into the limelight of the dominant culture, that is, into the subsidized museums and public galleries. The few reviews of major exhibitions and art events of the establishment were written from a feminist angle, criticizing especially the lack of attention for women's art as well as the sexist perspective of individual artists or art critics.

In spite of these overriding differences in thematic focus, there seems to be an interesting approximation of the journalistic concepts behind the *Faz*'s feuilleton and the *taz*'s cultural reportage. In the *Faz*, the cultural section represents the designated place where the strict separation of information and commentary characteristic for its concept of objectivity is suspended in favor of subjective expression. Hence the term *feuilleton* not only functions as the name for the "culture section" but has an additional meaning indicating a different journalistic principle. "It is generally understood to be something related to literature. *Feuilleton* means something different from a treatise, a documentary, a conclusive presentation. In the feuilleton personal experiences—be they dreamt or otherwise originating from imagination—come into play."[83]

The *Faz* perceives cultural criticism as a borderline case between literary imagination and rational judgment, between subjective and objective criticism. With this understanding of the feuilleton, the *Faz* allows for journalistic subjectivity and imagination only in the sphere of cultural criticism. This restricted concession in fact supports all the more the *Faz*'s belief in the necessity of journalistic objectivity for the other sections of the paper. The acceptance of subjectivity as a legitimate category in the culture section in turn frees culture from all political implications, even if the *Faz* concedes that the modern culture section of a paper has gained "an almost political dimension" because of the manifold correlations of different spheres of life.[84] The adverb "almost" or "nearly" (*nahezu*) in this progressive-sounding statement is most revealing. It indirectly says that culture does not have a political dimension after all.

The *Faz*'s position represents a perfect example for the validity of the student movement's and the alternative culture's criticism of the dominant concept of culture as preserving the fiction of culture as a nonpolitical sphere of life, or in other words, the autonomy of art. The approximation of the *Faz* and *taz* with respect to culture reveals itself as deceptive, since it is precisely this criticism of the hegemonic culture hiding its political implications that separates the journalistic concepts of the two papers. The differences between the two cultural concepts—cultures (*Kulturen*) in the plural, expressing the diversity of the alternative culture, versus the traditional understanding of the feuilleton as High Culture in the singular—will become more clear when we look at the review practices in the respective papers.

CHAPTER 5: "Do It Yourself!"
Artistic Concepts and Practices
of the Alternative Culture

I n his comprehensive cultural history of West Germany, Jost
 Hermand devotes an entire chapter to the alternative culture,
 which he refers to as the "alternative scene" (*Alternativszene*).
He characterizes the alternative scene as a hedonistic "anti-" and "instant culture" (*Instantkultur*) that is interested not in high-quality
aesthetic production but in play, pleasure, and instant gratification.
According to Hermand, the alternative culture had a preference for
everything of low culture, including the "delights of the populist
mass media," which the upper classes despised.[1] As a result, such
traditional cultural institutions as theater, opera, symphony orches-
tras, and museums were discarded as "old fashioned." He concludes
with a devastating evaluation of the alternative culture similar to
Reich-Ranicki's verdict on the student movement's lack of artistic
achievement. "Between 1975 and 1985 an alternative artistic scene
existed, but no truly alternative art."[2]

Hermand's sweeping evaluation of the alternative culture contains
some truth but also problems of its own. For one, he appears to
speak from a position that implicitly distinguishes between "high"
and "low" culture, relegating the alternative culture wholesale to
"low" culture. The analytic value of a binary model of low and
high culture is, however, questionable for discussing the alternative
culture, which positioned itself outside these traditional conceptualizations. Secondly, such a binary model neglects the fact that
West Germany has become more and more culturally differentiated
since the student movement. It is thus more fruitful to investigate
the continuities and differences between the alternative culture's attack on the hegemonic culture and that of the student movement.
We need to trace, for instance, the fate of the Frankfurt school's

paradigms, which played such a significant role for political and aesthetic discussions during the student movement. Did the alternative culture abandon them, and if so, what did it adopt instead?

Hermand's observation that the alternative culture was indeed "anti" is correct with respect to the hegemonic culture's concepts. This did not mean, however, that the alternative culture embraced products of the culture industry, as Hermand suggests. Quite to the contrary, the alternative culture remained as critical of mass culture as the Frankfurt school and the student movement. The Tunix leaflet discussed in chapter 4 and the debate about rock music in the *taz* are excellent examples for studying the alternative culture's position on the culture industry.

Furthermore, the alternative culture did not totally turn its back on the artistic practices of the hegemonic culture. In some cases, it tried to reclaim them for its own aesthetic. The extensive coverage of theatrical events in the *taz*, including some of the hegemonic culture's subsidized theaters, demonstrates that theater enjoyed as high a popularity within the alternative culture as within the hegemonic culture and calls into question Hermand's claim that the alternative culture viewed all traditional artistic practices and genres as old-fashioned. The established theater has been a cultural battleground since the 1960s, when the student movement attacked it as "bourgeois" and developed its own politically committed street theater. Hermand's explanation of the alternative culture's critical response to the theater as a generational conflict—"old fashioned"—falls short of understanding the alternative culture's astute comprehension of the dynamics of cultural politics. The alternative culture, for example, proved to be quite aware of the powerful tool that the subsidy system represented in the hands of mainstream culture for protecting its hegemony.

We therefore need to analyze carefully the alternative culture's stance regarding the hegemonic theater culture in the Federal Republic and the theatrical practices it developed as countermodels. Moreover, close scrutiny of the alternative culture's approach to theater in this chapter not only clarifies the aesthetic categories of the alternative culture but allows us to contextualize them as well. It raises the question of the extent to which the alternative theater groups reflected the general cultural transformations from the 1960s to the 1970s, that is, constitutes a part of the New Subjectivist discourse.

The alternative culture was quite distinct from mainstream culture. It rejected the aesthetic categories of the hegemonic institutionalized culture—professionalism, high quality, originality, and stardom—in favor of a somewhat vague idea of a culture of the people. A close examination of the first years of the *taz* shows a strong interest in folk culture (*Volkskultur*) within the alternative culture. Three examples—the alternative culture's fascination with the circus, the carnival, and the clown or fool—are used in this chapter to examine its preference for folk culture.

This interest in folk culture is quite surprising in light of both German history and the contemporary culture industry. Up to the 1970s folk culture had been taboo for progressive social forces in West Germany because of the Third Reich's definition of folk (*Volk*) in chauvinistic and racist terms and its appropriation of folk culture for its own ideological ends. The culture industry showed less skepticism regarding folk culture, especially folk music (*Volksmusik*). Brass bands or individual performers of German folk songs (*Volkslieder*) have quickly become both popular and profitable in postwar West Germany. Hence the question of how to evaluate the alternative culture's bent toward folk culture gains particular significance.

As these preliminary remarks show, heterogeneity was not only the most characteristic feature of the alternative culture but also a concept it embraced and promoted. Consequently, the alternative culture could not develop a normative aesthetic and more cohesive artistic practices without contradicting its fundamental belief in diversity. The debate surrounding the cultural section in the *taz* outlined in the previous chapter attests to this problem. Still, the alternative culture had artistic preferences and its own aesthetic agenda, which can be discerned in the Tunix flier and the cultural section of the *taz*, two primary sources on which this chapter draws for its analysis.

Culture and Politics = Cultural Politics

In West Germany, aesthetic culture is more heavily subsidized with tax revenue and administered by state and municipal governments than in the United States. The allocation of the communal budget for cultural activities has therefore tremendous political implications. It has become a permanent issue of confrontation between different groups of citizens and their competing cultural concepts ever since the challenge to hegemonic culture by the student movement in the late 1960s. Throughout the 1970s the allocation of public funds largely failed to reflect the growing diversity in the sphere of culture. According to the *Handbuch der alternativen Kommunalpolitik* (Manual for an alternative municipal politics), the traditional theatrical institutions—theater and opera houses—still devoured more than one third of an average community's budget for cultural activities (38 percent), although they catered to the cultural interest of only a small percentage of the population. The museums and the public libraries, which together received only half of the subsidies of the state theaters (*Staatstheater*) (19 percent) occupied the second position, whereas adult education programs (*Volkshochschulen*), the symphony, and music schools (7, 5, 4 percent respectively) came in last.[3] This raises the question whether the distribution of public money was intended to preserve the dominant classes' understanding of culture, since it favored the traditional and institutionalized modes of aesthetic culture. In other words, did the allocation of funds marginalize certain cultural practices and ultimately function as an instrument of control?

The alternative culture was keenly aware of the organizational structure and administration of culture, that is, of the power of cultural politics (*Kulturpolitik*), recognizing that subsidies from tax revenue represented a most powerful tool for cultural hegemony. The coverage of the hegemonic culture by the *taz* problematized in one way or another this aspect of cultural politics in West Germany. For the alternative culture, the opera houses and state theater (*Staatstheater*) in particular represented the epitome of the hegemonic culture because of the content they offered, the audience they tried to address, and their privileged status in terms of public funding. Hence it was no coincidence that confrontations between mainstream and alternative culture often erupted violently around high-profile, publicly funded cultural institutions like the opera houses. The opera houses' generous public financing, however, was only the straw that broke the camel's back: the conflict between the alternative and hegemonic culture ran deeper.[4]

At the heart of this conflict was the growing tension within a society differentiated more and more into an economically defined center of power, comprising not only the economic elites and the government but also the older generations of the middle class, and the disadvantaged margins, to which more and more of the younger generation belonged. Socioeconomic and political developments promoted this stratification of society in West Germany. Since the oil crisis in 1973, which drove home the message of the impending ecological catastrophe, the West German economy exhibited signs of a lasting recession, which threatened the loss of industrial jobs. At the same time, the baby boom generation—in Germany, those born between the late 1950s (with the advent of the "economic miracle") and the mid-1960s—was beginning to enter the labor force, only to be greeted by declining employment chances and choices. In a society in which academic and vocational degrees are absolutely necessary for professional advancement, for many youths no desirable apprenticeship slot was available, which meant de facto a foreclosure of their professional future. The picture was no more rosy with respect to the academic job market. In comparison to the generation of the student activists, most of whom had settled successfully into a professional career during the 1970s despite the government's screening process for public service positions (*Radikalenerlaß/Berufsverbote*), the baby boomers were less fortunate. By the 1980s a university degree no longer necessarily translated into a well-paying job. Moreover, as a result of the SPD's reform efforts in the field of education, the universities were overenrolled, and for many popular degree programs such as medicine and pharmacy a rigid selection system based on the grade point average in high school (*Numerus Clausus*) had been implemented by the government. The constitutionally guaranteed freedom of choice regarding one's university and professional occupation was thus severely limited.[5] West German young people were faced with a large-scale economic marginalization since the mid-1970s, somewhat softened by their middle-class parents, most of whom had accumulated substantial wealth in the postwar period and were willing to subsidize their children's standard of living.

This economic marginalization was coupled with political marginalization due to the tense atmosphere terrorism had helped to create in the Federal Republic. The government's approach to combating terrorism led to a curtailing of many of the democratic reforms for which the SPD had once campaigned under its 1969 slogan, "Dare More Democracy!" Its 1976 campaign slogan, "Model Germany," which was meant to celebrate the West German economy and social safety net, was pure mockery in the ears of this young generation, which saw "No Future" written on the horizon. Those young West Germans who did not want to resolve all their problems by overadjusting to the system no longer blamed capitalism alone or society at large, but saw the government and its expanding administrative grip as the main culprit. The bleak job outlook, the new and growing consciousness of the impending ecological crisis, the rejection of the student movement's Marxist social analysis, and the role the government played in combating terrorism, all led to this shift in perspective. The alternative movement pointed its finger at the *Staat*, the government and its various executive agencies.

These economic transformations correlated with two developments within the alternative culture. The Sponti movement had reintroduced anarchist theorists who viewed the state at the heart of all oppression and consequently called for its dissolution, as we have seen, for example, in the analysis of the Buback Obituary.[6] Second, the work of the French poststructuralist historian and theorist Michel Foucault, who analyzed power structures with special emphasis on marginalized groups, gained popularity among those parts of the alternative culture that were still interested in theory, while the Critical Theory of the Frankfurt school had lost some of its luster.

Theory? Maybe: From Marx's Class to Foucault's Margins

Ute Liebmann-Schaub summarizes Foucault's appeal for the alternative culture in four points. First of all, Foucault's theory analyzes structures of domination with respect to the question of center and margins. He "describes the modern environment as a system of exclusions from society of 'useless' marginal groups," while these groups at the same time are "being put into discourse" and thus being involuntarily integrated into the predetermined power structures embodied by the government.[7] Second, Foucault's theory points to the steady reduction of the autonomy of the subject throughout the course of history. This approach and his description of how this power permeates all aspects of life appealed to the alternative culture, which cast itself in the role of the victim of the omnipresent megamachine of the state. Third, Foucault's notion of history as fractured and fraught with catastrophe, instead of the Enlightenment concept of history as a linear progress, correlated with the alternative culture's own experience, which saw the future threatened in many ways, particularly by either an ecological catastrophe or nuclear war. As Manfred Clemenz, one of the alternative voices more critical of Foucault, argues, the difference between the Critical Theory of Horkheimer/Adorno and Foucault cannot be found in the critical diagnosis of social reality, "but in Critical Theory's emphatic endorsement of the concept of the individual, freedom, and happiness, although they have not been fulfilled yet."[8]

Finally, Liebmann-Schaub mentions the "seductive" lure of Foucault's language, which represents a blatant rejection of "the long tradition of philosophical rhetoric in the West."[9] The alternative culture, which had broken with the dominant linguistic consensus, as we have seen in the case of the Buback Obituary and the language of the *taz*, viewed Foucault's mode of thinking and style of writing as an endorsement of their own break with conventional modes of argumentation in favor of a radically subjective approach and language. One of the first introductory articles to Foucault in the *taz* praises precisely this quality of Foucault's discourse in comparison to the dominant model of Western thought. "[Foucault] develops an alternative mode of thinking, a playful, flexible, and complex thinking in action. His descriptions are such that the object loses its fixed and usual contours and melts into other objects. He inventively develops new areas of knowledge/nonknowledge, because it is the only way to escape the coercive power of traditional disciplinary boundaries."[10]

Still, the theory faction within the alternative culture played only a secondary role, even though Foucault and other French poststructuralist theorists gained in popularity among the alternatively inclined students. But even for those who resented theory, the concept of center and margin offered a new model of identification after the dismissal of the Marxist concept of social class.[11]

"State/Official Culture" (Staatskultur)
and "Government Pork" (Staatsknete)

This shift from a class model of society to one of center versus margins articulated itself also in the cultural arena. Although the student movement's pet phrases "bourgeois press" and "bourgeois culture" can be found in statements of the alternative movement, the term "state" or "official culture" (*Staatskultur* or *offizielle Kultur*) became the new code words. They were the alternative culture's synonym for the centralized, institutionalized, and highly subsidized hegemonic culture that undercut any kind of autonomous culture from below and allowed for consumption only. "Culture has a particular quality in this country. There is a minister and a government agency for culture, which administer and distribute culture. Culture is a broad field, which many like to plow. Culture is produced in institutions. Like everywhere: a house for the theater, a house for the opera, a house for music, a house for culture. The government agencies promote state culture."[12] The alternative culture was "anti" with respect to this type of culture, administered from above in order to ensure the cultural hegemony of the powers that be.

In contrast, the alternative culture envisioned a decentralized neighborhood-based culture oriented at the needs of the respective residents, which became known under the name "neighborhood culture" (*Stadtteilkultur*). Since this concept was successful and found wide reception beyond the alternative culture, it attracted the attention of the hegemonic culture. Instead of supporting already existing alternative cultural projects in the neighborhoods, however, the hegemonic culture staged its own neighborhood events, quite to the dismay of the alternative culture. The latter saw their original concept threatened with decay into a public-relations gimmick for politicians as, for instance, an unnamed writer in the *taz* noted with bitterness:

Neighborhood festivals are fashionable cultural events once a year on public streets—music and cake . . . to get to know each other . . . culture for the grass roots. Grass-roots culture . . . does not exist—in spite of punk, graffiti, slogans in restrooms, and the lonely man playing the accordion in the red-light district of Hamburg. What exists is culture from above: millions for spectacular shows: Theater of Nations, literary shindigs, a party at the River Alster and at City Hall, film festival: Free and Happy City of Hamburg—simply magnificent! Thousands comfortably party along, enjoy the colorful days, forget their gray daily lives . . . a feeling of adventure and leisure time. They consume culture—nothing truly happens. Culture as a nicely packaged piece of consumer culture courtesy of the government agency and the minister for culture. Cultural politics is a specialty in this country; the establishment paints itself in pretty colors and now and then gives us a few crumbs from its table.[13]

The alternative culture recognized the integrative power of the hegemonic culture, which functioned increasingly through the reappropriation of genuine countercultural concepts and activities. If the latter were more popular than the offerings of the hegemonic culture, they were in danger of being swallowed. Attempts of the hegemonic culture to approach the alternative culture were, therefore, viewed with much skepticism, even if they came from the political left. The alternative culture sarcastically evaluated, for instance, a congress on an alternative concept of culture titled "Culture from Below" and organized by the Union for Education and Science, the traditionally left-leaning teachers' union: "It looks more like culture *for* the lower classes than culture from below."[14]

The real issue was, however, "government pork" (*Staatsknete*), that is, subsidies from the hegemonic culture. Accepting public funding was controversial from the very beginning and led to a split within the alternative culture. Some advocated making use of public funds because they perceived such offers of financial support for their projects as a positive development. They saw it, on the one hand, as an acknowledgment of the alternative culture by the hegemonic culture and, on the other hand, as a welcomed end to the frustration and self-exploitation that characterized most of the alternative projects.[15] The opponents of public subsidies countered by pointing out the heightened potential for total integration of the alternative culture into the mainstream, if the alternative culture indulged too much in governmental subsidies. For them, the acceptance of public financial support was tantamount to a loss of autonomy, which represented the foundation of the alternative culture's power of resistance.

Second, these warning voices argued that the allocation of public funds for the alternative culture could easily lead to a reproduction of the hegemonic culture's destructive structures of competition, since there would hardly ever be enough money to subsidize every alternative project. In their opinion, the hegemonic culture's financial support had only one goal: to subvert the solidarity of the alternative culture in order to reintegrate it better into the mainstream.[16] "If one takes his or her own culture away from the people, one becomes isolated. He or she becomes insecure, fearful, and no longer acts spontaneously. The individual believes he or she is alone, which suffocates feelings and hence a sense of solidarity with each other according to the old principle of divide and conquer—the centralization of culture in the *Deutsche Oper* and television and so forth, started three hundred years after Christ. Watch and consume, that's all we are allowed to do."[17]

Finally, referring to examples of alternative projects that already received public funds, the opponents argued that financial support did not mean acknowledgment of the alternative culture, but only functionalized alternative projects. Instead of investing more in badly needed social programs and services, the hegemonic culture supplied its opponents with just enough funds to perform those services perhaps more successfully than the government agencies. The alternative culture might unintentionally help to prevent the threatened diversification of the citizenry into centers of wealth and power and an impoverished, potentially explosive margin. In other words, let the alternative culture take care of those unfortunate ones who are ultimately victims of the hegemonic culture. From the perspective of the powerful elites, this was more cost effective and helped to tie the alternative culture back to the hegemonic culture.

"The famous Factory, which burned down some time ago, is being rebuilt—a shining example. Neighborhood culture is supposed to function as a reprocessing plant for dropouts, the unemployed, children, foreigners, and so forth. Integration by citizens for citizens."[18]

Both positions merit criticism for depicting the alternative culture only in the position of victim with respect to the hegemonic culture. By accepting weakness as inevitable, the alternative culture gave up prematurely and retreated into its own cozy little world of the alternative ghetto. Instead of analyzing those structural components of the counterculture that either resisted or promoted integration, the alternative culture was left with feeling vulnerable and merely keeping a "safe" distance to the hegemonic culture. This position foreclosed the possibility to intervene and change the course of cultural politics. The question thus arises whether the alternative culture gave up its position as a true counterculture in favor of a subculture similar to other subcultures, mostly limited to leisure time activities and economically dependent on those parts of the hegemonic culture that were sympathetic with the alternative culture and helped to sustain it by buying its goods and services.[19]

The Heritage of 1968: Tunix and the "Coca-Cola-Karajan Culture"

The alternative movement's statements on culture remained vague and by no means resembled the highly developed theoretical discourse of the student movement on aesthetic and cultural issues. The alternative culture attacked the highly subsidized hegemonic culture as imposed on the people "from above" and called instead for a culture "from below," that is, originating from the people. The alternative movement did not, however, define precisely what it meant by the rather problematic concept of "the people." The Tunix leaflet, which was discussed in the previous chapter, is a good point of departure for exploring this issue.

The flier describes its opponent, the hegemonic culture, in an ironic fashion as the "Coca-Cola-Karajan culture" (*Coca-Cola-Karajan-Kultur*), picking up simultaneously on two postwar cultural icons that the hegemonic culture keeps neatly apart and in a hierarchical relationship to each other. Coca-Cola stands for mass-produced consumer culture, which from the perspective of the hegemonic culture represents a "low" form of culture. The late conductor Herbert von Karajan, who had gained celebrity status beyond his artistic achievement and was often featured in West German tabloids, stands for the highly subsidized and elitist hegemonic culture (*Staatskultur*). Lumping the two cultural spheres together in the catchphrase Coca-Cola-Karajan culture shows that the alternative culture did not make a distinction between mass or "low" culture and elite or "high" culture, as the hegemonic culture did.

The phrase establishes an equation suggesting that Karajan's "high" culture is just as repressive as mass culture à la Coca-Cola, since both destroy the people's imagination and fantasies in order to integrate them all the better into the existing social reality. The Tunix flier calls the post-1968 counterculture together against this one-dimensional, hegemonic culture. "And this is what we want to see, whether we are not yet and now—or perhaps still?—alive, whether we aren't already many, who are fed up with everything, with the bleak asphalt and concrete deserts of the new housing developments, with the presence and violence of the police force armed to the teeth, and with the destruction of our dreams by Peter Stuyvesant [cigarettes] and Springer's tabloids and the television shows which are always the same, with the Coca-Cola-Karajan culture."[20]

The alternative culture's lumping together of "high" and "low" culture resembles the sps group's argument about the consciousness industry published a decade earlier. It also demonstrates that not all of the Frankfurt school's theorems had been abandoned by the alternative culture. The flier's line of argument is highly indebted to Marcuse's discussion of the status of cultural creations within today's one-dimensional society and to its later proponents such as Wolfgang Fritz Haug and his analysis of the specific function of commodity aesthetic used by the advertising industry.[21] Certain Frankfurt school concepts had become commonplaces by the end of the 1970s, although the alternative culture seemed to be at best unconscious if not suspicious of these roots. Mass culture, that is, products of the culture industry, represented a genuine culture of the people as little for the alternative culture as for its predecessor, the student movement. As opposed to the latter, however, the alternative culture no longer accepted Marxism as the only relevant theory, rejecting in particular the category of social class, as the foregoing analysis of the Tunix leaflet has explicated. It is therefore not surprising that we cannot find any references to the concept of proletarian culture in the flier or in other articulations of the alternative culture.

The fairy tale of the Bremen Town Musicians represents instead the main point of cultural reference in the leaflet. In addition, the flier uses a line from a popular German folk song—"no country more beautiful in our time"—and fuses it with an equally popular slogan of the alternative culture—"underneath the pavement lies the beach"—into "no country more beautiful than our beach,"[22] referring, of course, to the beach of Tunix. These references to folk culture are no coincidence, but echo a general trend within the alternative culture, whose artistic practices also exhibited a strong preference for folk culture. This contributed to the perception of the alternative culture as hostile to theory, which is as we have seen not such a clear-cut issue after all.

The alternative culture faced, however, a major problem—the exploitative grip of the culture industry on folk culture. This meant that the alternative culture had to excavate the common people's or folk culture by rewriting the history of artistic practices and cultural institutions, which had been either stigmatized as low culture or appropriated by the culture industry. Three examples stand out in particular: the carnival, the circus, and the concept of the fool.

The Carnival

The *taz*'s articles on the carnival in Europe are a perfect example of the alternative culture's rewriting of cultural history.[23] Today the carnivals in Cologne, Düsseldorf, and especially in Mainz appear annually as major media spectacles on people's television screens. The articles in the *taz* criticized the commercialized character of today's carnival as a final stage of a development that shows "how the structure and function of a local festival can be changed by the power of the entertainment industry."[24] In contrast to this commercialized carnival of the hegemonic culture, the *taz* stressed the origins of the carnival as a wild and uncontrolled festival of the common people.

It maintained that the carnival at first had a political nature, since during its season and behind the foolscap the established social order was suspended. As a result, the carnival represented an immanent threat to the social order and had the potential to become the vehicle for emancipatory goals spurring social and political struggle.[25]

The alternative culture's reconstruction of the history of the carnival's commercialization since the nineteenth century focused on the hegemonic classes' interest in controlling the revolutionary potential of the carnival, even if the bourgeoisie itself used the foolscap at times to subvert censorship and to express its discontent with political affairs, especially in the context of the failed bourgeois revolution in 1848. The alternative culture criticized particularly those reforms with which the hegemonic culture channeled the wild and chaotic lower-class carnival into the hierarchical structures of bourgeois society. While the hegemonic classes shaped the controlled version of the institutionalized carnival of the clubs (*Karnevalsvereine, Karnevalscliquen*), reproducing in its organizational framework the hierarchical nature of bourgeois society, the *taz* articles pointed out that there has always existed a kind of "subcultural" carnival. The articles emphasized the difference between the big organized carnival and the wild subcultural one, which took place on the streets and in the neighborhood pubs. "The improvisation, wit, quickness of repartee, and imagination of the local pub's carnival stood in striking contrast to the big organized carnival events of the clubs, which became more and more rigid and less and less funny."[26]

By retrieving the subversive roots of the carnival, the alternative culture challenged the hegemonic culture, especially the culture industry. Presenting a counterhistory, it exposed the hegemonic culture's historiography, especially of the Ruhr Valley's carnival, as a falsification. In addition, it revealed the culture industry's notion of tradition and authenticity as a mere advertising scheme. Since all of the articles concentrated on the discrepancy between the original nature of the carnival and today's commercial exploitation of it, the alternative culture's rewriting of the history of the carnival aimed at cracking the affirmative surface of the culture industry's carnival and at recovering it as an expression of genuine folk culture.

The Circus

The alternative culture's rediscovery of fairy tales, folk songs, and the carnival was accompanied by a renewed interest in the circus. One of the showcases of the alternative culture, Berlin's "Factory for Culture, Sport, and Craftsmanship" (*Fabrik für Kultur, Sport und Handwerk e.V.*), established a permanent circus as a common stage for musicians, mimes, acrobats, and all other kinds of artistic performances that had no space in the theater or other institutions of the hegemonic culture.[27] The alternative culture's interest in the circus and its specific artistic genres rested on two elements: the aesthetic of corporeality, that is, an emphasis on the body as an aesthetic and expressive means, and an understanding of the circus as a democratic space.

In their history of the circus and its specific aesthetics, which was published at the height of the alternative culture in the late 1970s, Günter Bose and Erich Brinkmann describe it as the sanctuary for the body and sensuality, which became more and more marginalized in the process of cultural differentiation that accompanied the development of bourgeois society. They argue that the body could be celebrated only within the framework of the circus, which has always been perceived as a typical manifestation of the culture of the common people, or in other words, of "low" culture, with an aesthetic that appealed more to the eye than to the brain. Nevertheless, the modern circus has always been the cultural space where the bourgeoisie could legitimately, though perhaps with a condescending smile on its lips, enjoy its repressed desires and fantasies.

Moreover, the circus represented one of the very few public spaces where all classes of society amuse themselves, in comparison to the theater, which always had a class specific audience.[28] It is therefore not surprising that the circus ring became the favored performance space within the alternative culture. Even independent theater groups, such as the Theaterhof Priessental, preferred it to the traditional theater stage (*Guckkasten-Bühne*) precisely for the reasons outlined above. In addition, the circus is mobile and can therefore come to the people in the large housing projects at the periphery of the cities that sprang up during the 1960s and 1970s.

Most importantly, the circus tent is not intimidating for an audience that has not been introduced to the "high" culture of the theater or opera house, since most people have been to a circus at least once as a child. As a writer in the *taz* described it,

> Performing in a tent is an essential element of the Theaterhof Priessental: the politics of urban planning generated in West Germany's big cities' huge newly developed neighborhoods and so-called "Satellite Cities" whose cultural offerings consist almost exclusively of communal rooftop antennas. With its tent, the Theaterhof wants to counteract the long commute to the theaters in the downtown areas and people's fear of entering these palaces of culture. The circuslike atmosphere is supposed to help the citizens out of their isolation; the mode of performance is supposed to stimulate creativity in the audience.[29]

The alternative culture was fascinated by the circus not only because of its possibilities to reach out to a nontraditional and nonprivileged audience but also because of the social status and lifestyle of its artists. One of the founders of Roncalli, another alternative circus project, explains his fascination with the circus in terms of the total otherness of circus art and life. "And then all of the sudden the circus comes and it is colorful and there everything is accepted because everything is different. They have midgets, giants; everything that is not normal is important for the circus. . . . I wanted to develop a circus as one imagines it, and this was the beginning. . . . Without making any kind of great claim, but simply a circus as one imagines it in one's dream. That is different."[30] The alternative culture's understanding of the circus is not simply an imitation of the traditional circus but the realization of an imaginative vision of circus as the embodiment of otherness and freedom from conformity.

This infatuation with otherness was in many ways problematic and points to the alternative culture's tendency to idealize marginalization. For one, the alternative culture constructs an idealized image of the circus as the sanctuary of difference, be it cultural, racial, or physical, since the "family" of the circus artists traditionally encompasses a broad variety of nationalities and ethnic groups. The alternative culture saw the circus therefore as a space of tolerance and solidarity.

Second, the circus artist's work was attractive for the alternative culture because they viewed it as nonalienated, self-determined, collective, and creative labor. This perception was fostered by statements of artists who were involved in alternative projects such as Roncalli or the Theaterhof Priessental. In an interview with the *taz*, members of Roncalli stressed that there is less competition and aggression among circus artists than within the hegemonic culture's theaters, opera houses, or dance companies, although they were critical of the metaphor of the "family" for describing the interpersonal relationships within the circus. The *taz*, relating a similar experience of the members of the Theaterhof Priessental to its readers, helped thus in constructing the circus as a model for solidarity and nonalienated, collective labor.[31]

Finally, the alternative culture's appreciation of the circus corresponded with antimodern sentiments present within parts of the counterculture. The circus represented for those groups suspicious of modern technology an alternative because of the lack of technological devices for its artistic performances, which rely solely on the physical skill of the artist.

For all these reasons, the circus artist's life appeared as authentic, and the circus itself could be understood as a last bastion against the onslaught of technological rationalization. Its all-encompassing aesthetics was perceived as stimulating sensuous experience as well as liberating imaginations and desires. From the perspective of a reception aesthetic, the immediacy of the performance, in contrast to works of art that use mechanical or technological means of reproduction, was an important aspect of the alternative culture's enthusiasm for the circus.

Ideal Types of the Great Refusal: The Clown and the Fool

A cherished figure within the alternative culture also originated within the circus—the clown, who was complemented by other members of the family of fools and traveling artists. Aside from the slapstick and clown numbers employed by many of the alternative theater groups, entire festivals of fools were organized. The Festival of Fools in Amsterdam, for instance, became the most successful and most copied one.[32] Clowns and fools enjoyed such popularity within the alternative culture that we can indeed speak of a renaissance of these two traditional characters. This renaissance was closely connected with the alternative culture's privileging of spontaneity, corporeal expression, and the issue of marginalization. The alternative culture developed its own concept of the fool, however, which became a symbol for its resistance to the hegemonic culture.

The English word *Clown* refers in German to the tradition of the circus, where the humorous figure of the clown first appeared. The humor of the clown's act draws not on complex philosophical concepts but on daily situations and therefore on experiences that everybody shares. The body of the clown, his movements and gestures, and his acrobatic and mimetic skills are at the center of the clown's artistic expression, and not verbal ability.[33] The humor of the clown is rooted as well in the abolition of common sense and the concept of rationality dominant in Western societies. The clown approaches the world and its objects like a small child who has not yet learned its logic and has not yet internalized the principle of rationality. From the perspective of the alternative culture, the clown's retention of the naïveté of the child represents a refusal to submit to the exclusive privileging of cognitive structures and rationality within the hegemonic culture.

A good case in point for the renaissance of the clown and related archetypes is the *taz* itself. The *taz*, which saw itself as a platform for those voices marginalized or even silenced in West Germany, drew strongly on the identificatory potential of the clown. Pictures of clowns, jesters, and other fools graced many pages in the early *taz*. The image of a clown decorated the front page of the very first daily issue.[34] In this first issue, the *taz* combined two significant symbols of the alternative culture—the clown and the cobblestone. The clown on the front page holds a large stone with the inscription "*taz*" in his right hand, ready to throw it. The cobblestone characterizes the street battles between the police and the militant wing of the protest movements, symbolizing not only aggression but also hope, since tearing up the stone means liberating nature and life, which have been suffocated under contemporary society's brick and concrete. It is a visualization of the alternative culture's favorite slogan—"Underneath the pavement lies the beach"—and expresses the alternative culture's self-perception: resistance to the prevalent social order and values, subversive wit and militancy if necessary. The *taz* never totally abandoned this image, although it did change over the years. Ten years down the road, the original clown of the first daily issue reappeared less menacingly colorful, smiling and throwing a birthday cake on the front page of the special issue the *taz* produced for its tenth anniversary.[35]

The alternative culture did not simply adopt the image of the clown but fused it with another tradition, the literary topos and theatrical character of the *Narr*, the witty jester, who matches the ambivalent status of the clown. In contrast to the clown, the jester, in particular the court jester, relied first and foremost on his linguistic wit, even answering philosophical questions with his witty puns. Puns, as we have seen, were deployed as critical weapons in the Tunix flier. Above all, however, the jester's wit granted him a certain freedom of speech. He was allowed to critique the social order, at least as long as he wore the foolscap. Thus the literary or theatrical topos of the jester traditionally has a subversive component. The initial laughter that greets the jester's wit often turns into a sour frown as soon as the laughing audience discovers the ugly truth the jester's speech reveals. Combining the two traditions of the clown and the jester, that is, the spontaneity and physical expressiveness of the clown with the linguistic wit and subversiveness of the jester, the alternative culture developed its own concept, that of the fool. In order to distinguish this new concept from the traditional characters like the clown and the jester, it used the English word *Fool*.

The alternative culture's concept of the fool has strong antiestablishment features. As Michael Kramer, who promoted the concept of the Fool by teaching and writing on it in the early 1980s, puts it, "Fools are dropouts, outsiders, and antiheros."[36] This definition of the fool articulates its appeal for an alternative audience. Fools, clowns, jugglers, fire eaters, and all of the other folk artists have always been a marginalized social group. In certain eras, for instance in the Middle Ages, they even had to fear for their lives, since they were not protected by law but quite literally outlawed. The fool as a social outsider naturally offered itself as an identifying figure for the alternative culture, which felt estranged from the hegemonic culture, marginalized, and frequently defamed as clandestine advocates of RAF terrorism.

The positive reception of Peter Paul Zahl's novel on the development of the counterculture since the late 1960s, *Die Glücklichen* (1979; The happy ones), demonstrates this potential for identification. Zahl's heroes are petty thieves, prostitutes, drug addicts, and street people, that is, those people who are today socially marginalized like the fools and traveling artists in former times, although they represent nothing but the flip side of bourgeois society. Zahl's novel labels this socially marginalized group with another old German term for fool, *Schelm*, (rogue), according to the subtitle of his book and the literary genre to which the author returns—the picaresque novel (*Schelmenroman*). The term *rogue* has retained only its positive connotation in contemporary language and speech, recalling such figures as Till Eulenspiegel, one of the best-known heroes of German folk culture.[37]

The review of Zahl's novel in the *taz* picks up on the term *rogue* and the context of social marginalization. The review praises Zahl's portrayal of the counterculture as socially marginalized and defines the rogue as a subversive and oppositional force from below. The review thereby articulates the alternative culture's identification with the heroes of the novel and the history of the counterculture as Zahl depicts it. "They want sun, love, and fun with their self-regulated labor. Aren't these—according to the dominant opinion—characteristics of lazy good-for-nothings, or in other words, of rogues? The traditional character of the rogue searched for material satisfaction in a society of scarcity. Zahl's rogues also search for satisfaction, for freedom and happiness in a thick, fat, and insensitive society."[38] This quotation is also characteristic of the alternative culture's main criticism of today's society: its materialism leads to alienation by imposing alienated labor and the performance principle on the individual. It implicitly makes the connection to Marcuse's concept of the Great Refusal. Marcuse defined the Great Refusal as the radical protest against the status quo by refusing to submit to its rules. He viewed the 1960s counterculture as the first movement in late capitalism that tried to practice the Great Refusal, and throughout the 1970s until his death in 1980 he looked with great hope at the emerging new social movements. The latter represent the continuation of this idea, as the concept of the fool as well as Zahl's novel and its reception within the alternative culture shows.

The alternative culture's appropriation of the image and the concept of the clown was no novelty. The clown as a subversive character has a long tradition not only in the circus but also in literature and onstage, most notably on the cabaret stage during the Weimar Republic. Joel Schechter's explanation of the clown's lure in his comprehensive study of the explicit political dimension of the clown applies as well to the alternative culture's reception of the clown. "The clown in exile or on the periphery of society remains unassimilated, naive, and does not consent to injustice or prevalent political conditions as readily as other citizens. In this sense, the clown represents a utopian freedom from oppression."[39] There were, however, also differences between the use of the clown in the cabaret or later literary or theatrical adaptations of the clown and the alternative culture's concept of the fool. For the 1920s cabaret as well as for Bertolt Brecht, Peter Handke, Dario Fo, and other playwrights, the clown functioned as an aesthetic representational device in order to critique specific political and social issues. While their concept of the fool was undoubtedly in opposition to the hegemonic culture, its political dimension remained less specific.

The alternative culture's focus was on the fool as an articulation of spontaneity, energy, and fun. One of the most prominent fools of the alternative culture, Jango Edwards, expressed his understanding of the concept of the fool precisely in these terms: "Joyous theater, maximum entertainment, energy, and audience participation."[40] The retreat under the foolscap, according to the motto often cited by the alternative culture— "be wise, be a fool"—was first and foremost meant to be a liberating experience for the individual. The concept of the fool therefore was equally significant for the idea of self-actualization as for its identificatory potential.

As with virtually all concepts and practices of the alternative culture, the fool's development was marked by controversy, expressing first and foremost the continuing anxiety that genuine alternative concepts would be absorbed by the hegemonic culture and thus commercialized. "'Just for fun'—yet another of those slogans that's catching on fast. We want to have fun, sure, but 'just for' is totally wrong. Today's capitalist fascism likes people who do things 'just for fun.' The Peter Stuyvesant generation does that, Jango does that, the disco factory turns it into leisure time."[41]

The Alternative Culture As the New Folk Culture

All of the previously discussed examples demonstrate the alternative culture's leaning toward folk culture and raises the question whether the alternative culture represented indeed a return to the tradition of folk art and folk culture (*Volkskunst und -kultur*). The turn toward folk culture was inspired by the alternative culture's desire for simplicity, antiprofessionalism and antielitism, authenticity, community, and participatory rather than representational models of politics and aesthetic culture. For the alternative culture, genuine folk culture embodied these categories and represented an attractive alternative to the hegemonic culture. Its concept of a culture of the people was therefore different from the Nazis' ideology of a Germanic folk culture (*völkische Kultur*) and a far cry from the oom-pa-pa music, folk dance groups, and other folkloristic forms to which the culture industry had reduced genuine folk culture. The alternative culture's concept of a culture of the people is rather complex. Another look at the Tunix flier can help us to gain a more precise definition of the alternative culture's concept of a culture of the people, since the leaflet expresses the self-perception of the alternative culture.

The Tunix flier described the mainstream "Coca-Cola-Karajan culture" as an all-encompassing, repressive, and ultimately destructive machine. Consumerism, competition, stifling bureaucracy, environmental pollution, philistine morals, social uniformity, and inhuman architecture and urban planning are the counterculture's key words for criticizing the hegemonic culture.[42] Worst of all, the Coca-Cola-Karajan culture condemns the majority of the people to the status of passive consumers tied to their seats in the concert hall in which a small minority—Karajan and his musicians—do all the creative work. The beach of Tunix shines bright in comparison. It is depicted as a collective, productive, and self-sufficient community, in contrast to the merely consumerist and exploitive hegemonic culture. The members of the counterculture build their own houses, provide for their own clothing and energy in an ecological manner, run their own TV shows, make their own music, grow and cook their own food. It is a "do-it-yourself culture" to which everybody contributes and in turn shares the fruits of the collective efforts.[43]

This model of a participatory culture corresponds to the new social movements' ideal of participatory, grass-roots politics. Grass-roots politics was complemented with grass-roots culture, based on a perception of folk culture as a participatory model. If everybody was supposed to become a practitioner of culture, then the hegemonic culture's cherished art forms and genres were obsolete because they require a high degree of training and professionalism. Folk culture offers instead artistic practices that had been designed by and for the layperson. The difference between the professional and the "dilettante" thus dissolved in the thinking of the alternative culture. The collective and participatory nature the alternative culture ascribed to folk culture does not even recognize this difference. In other words, the counterculture viewed folk culture as a privileged space of genuine equality. As a result, the motto of the counterculture's festival in 1978 can be understood in yet another sense. *Tunix* translates also into "do whatever you want," since the alternative culture aims at breaking down all boundaries between various cultural practices, which the hegemonic culture had erected to integrate culture into the marketplace.

Still, for Germans a return to folk culture is problematic because of the Nazis' instrumentalization of folk culture for their own ideological ends. The alternative culture's appropriation of elements of folk culture was not, however, motivated by nationalist tendencies, even if it did not distance itself actively from the Nazis' concept of Germanic folk culture. National origin or belonging was not an issue for the alternative culture. The Tunix leaflet, as we have already seen, instead questioned the "Model Germany" that filled mainstream West Germans with national pride. As the previous discussion of the

Tunix flier as well as the rediscovery of the circus shows, the alternative culture rejected nationality, race, or ethnicity as an identificatory code. It drew on a fairy tale whose characters can be understood as symbolizing difference—to be more precise, racial difference—a donkey, a dog, a cat, and a rooster. The animals demonstrate that difference does not preclude solidarity. Thus the four animals as well as the image of the circus represent from the perspective of the alternative culture successful role models of incorporating difference and of a multicultural community.

The alternative culture picked up on elements and images of folk culture that stand, on the one hand, for social and cultural marginalization but, on the other hand, for opposition to the authorities and subversive potential regarding society. It opposed a culture "from above," equating it with the petrified state cultural apparatus that allows only for the consumption of aesthetic culture, and instead argued for the spontaneous culture "from below." Hence the conflict that characterizes the new social movements—the citizen's challenge to the legitimacy of the government's monopoly of political decision making—extended as well into the realm of art and cultural politics.

We can define the self-understanding of the alternative culture as celebrating its heterogeneity, which meant the acceptance and equal treatment of the various groups and subjective concerns articulated within it. At the same time, the alternative culture perceived itself as a collective manifestation of resistance against the hegemonic culture. Because of the alternative culture's opposition to any kind of rigid organizational structure and because of its affirmation of difference, it turned toward the tradition of folk culture to bridge the gap between the supposedly contradictory concepts of a culture of difference and a collective culture. Folk culture referred to an idea of community beyond collective organizational structures based, for instance, on the category of class. It implied that community can be established among disparate groups and worldviews. The alternative culture's emphasis on the legitimacy of sensuous and affective needs and expressions, that is, its emphasis on culture's sensuous and aesthetic elements in contrast to conceptual ones, represents the missing link that accounts for a certain coherence among the organizationally autonomous and manifold countercultural groups.

The nervousness with which the alternative culture viewed the hegemonic culture's attempts to reappropriate its cultural practices demonstrates, however, that there were indeed problems with this definition of folk culture as a culture of resistance and solidarity. The main problem was that the alternative culture of the late 1970s and early 1980s simply used modes of a prebourgeois folk culture that it took to be uncorrupted by bourgeois society, thereby idealizing the culture of this premodern period. This idealization can easily lead to a regressive if not hostile attitude toward modern artistic movements. Two aspects of the alternative culture to which we will turn now seem to contradict this trend toward folk culture, namely, the popularity of theater, which for centuries has represented the showpiece of the hegemonic culture, and rock music, which many view as the epitome of the culture industry.

The Alternative Culture's Theater Aesthetic

Hardly an issue of the *Faz* goes by without a review of or commentary on a theatrical performance, since the theater has traditionally been an important institution of the hegemonic culture. The theater occupied also a favored position within the alternative culture. Yet the two papers — *Faz* and *taz* — focused on different theatrical events. The *Faz* reviews almost exclusively productions of the subsidized state theaters and the famous national as well as international theater festivals. In contrast, the *taz* concentrated on the independent theater groups of the alternative culture according to the following motto: "The state-subsidized theater is rightly avoided. This kind of theater means for us mostly philistine culture, often obsolete classics, boredom."[44]

Nonetheless, the *taz* did not totally ignore the productions of the hegemonic culture's theaters. It took, however, a critical stance toward them and reviewed their productions selectively.[45] Only four big names of the established theater culture were positively reviewed by the *taz*: the directors Peter Zadek and Claus Peymann and the playwrights Heiner Müller and Dario Fo. A critical position toward contemporary society and spectacular visual elements characterized the work of these directors and playwrights. The *taz* praised Peter

Zadek for his "down to earth" productions of the classic repertory of the theater, with which he attempted to revitalize a popular or folk theater in the Shakespearean sense, appealing more to the senses than to the intellect.[46]

Dario Fo's oeuvre was attractive to an alternative audience for similar reasons. He combined elements of the Italian folk theater tradition with his political commitment, the struggle against oppression, which was first and foremost directed against the Italian government and the Vatican. In addition, the West German counterculture saw Fo as one of their own for another reason: his politics. Because of their political commitment, Fo and his wife frequently came under close scrutiny by the Italian government authorities. In addition, they became part of the Italian counterculture after they left their successful acting careers on the bourgeois stage in favor of founding their own alternative theater in a working-class neighborhood of Milan. Fo's theater was attractive to the alternative culture because his plays are populated by fools "whose innocence (or pretense of it) enables them to question the statements of diplomats, generals, historians and other sources of authority. As the 'innocent' questioning progresses, the centers of authority look more foolish than their comic interrogators."[47] In addition, his theater productions relied heavily on the body as an expressive means. "Mime, action and gesture assume a primary importance" to the extent that language is transformed into an incomprehensible gibberish.[48]

Claus Peymann's positive reception by the alternative culture had also as much to do with his artistic ideas as with his political status during the 1970s and early 1980s. His powerful and colorful theater productions returned, like Zadek's, to a concept of the theater as spectacle, which differed from an abstract, intellectual, and logocentric theater. The political controversy that surrounded him offered, however, even more moments of identification for an alternative audience. Peymann got caught up in the political witch-hunt of the intellectual collaborators of terrorism because he had posted a letter on the bulletin board of the theater in which the mother of the terrorist Gudrun Ensslin asked for financial aid in order to pay for dental care her daughter needed. The conservative CDU majority on the city council of Stuttgart picked up on this incident and dismissed

Peymann, whose productions and repertory had slowly but surely become a thorn in the conservatives' side, since he took a critical position concerning many current political issues. Productions such as Frank Wedekind's *Spring Awakening* and Friedrich Wolf's *Cyankali*, arguing for a more liberal discourse on sexuality and particularly for a liberalization of the abortion laws in West Germany, had angered many conservative local politicians.

Furthermore, Peymann did not submit to the prevalent self-censorship in the sphere of art and culture in the 1970s, but took a position concerning the problem of terrorism and challenged audience members to develop their own perspectives. In the mid-1970s, for instance, he staged Albert Camus's play *Les Justes* and made a rather blunt connection between Russian terrorism of the 1920s and the West German terrorism of the 1970s. In the final scene of the play Peymann had a short film clip showing the subway number 5 on its course to Stammheim, the suburb where the maximum security prison for the RAF terrorists was located, projected onto the stage. Finally, during his tenure at the public theater in Bochum, Peymann publicly sided with the squatters of a factory building that he had used as a rehearsal stage. Instead of having the squatters evicted, he produced a play with overt references to the politically tense climate between the oppositional alternative movement and the city authorities in Bochum.[49] For the alternative culture, which perceived itself as the target of the hegemonic culture's persecution in the context of terrorism, Peymann represented a kind of paradigmatic fellow sufferer in the sphere of high culture.

Heiner Müller's work does not seem to fit in with this group of playwrights and directors. Müller's plays have a strong visual component, but they are not spectacles in the tradition of folk theater like Zadek's, Fo's, or Peymann's productions. The tableaus that he stages to criticize contemporary society draw on themes and motifs of "high" or "official" culture, be it a literary figure as in the play *Hamletmachine* or a historical one such as Frederick the Great in *Gundling's Life Frederick of Prussia Lessing's Sleep Dream Scream*. Using the technique of montage and collage, his tableaus demand a high degree of intellectual engagement on the part of the audience, since they refuse to give clear-cut answers to the questions Müller poses in his work.

As in the case of Zadek and Peymann, precisely this open nature of his plays, which do not allow for a merely passive attitude in the theater, made him interesting for the alternative culture. The alternative culture also appreciated Müller's work because his plays revealed the "psychopathology" of contemporary bourgeois society. The case of Müller demonstrates at the same time how uneasy the alternative culture felt about its own appreciation for an author whom the hegemonic culture—though for other reasons—also embraced. The *taz* felt obliged to distance itself from this "Müller boom" with a few introductory remarks to the reviews of his plays that it published.[50]

Since the *Faz* rarely acknowledged the alternative theater culture, the overlapping reviews of productions by the publicly funded theaters (*Staatstheater*) represents the best point of comparison for the different aesthetic concepts held by the hegemonic culture and the counterculture. The reviews in the *taz* supported critical and innovative productions of classical plays. They did not view the classical text as an end in itself but as material that should reflect upon contemporary issues. This is precisely the reason for the alternative culture's positive reception of Zadek's theater productions. His Shakespeare productions were not authentic renderings of Elizabethan drama and comedy, but connected with the life world of today's audience. "The translations by Zadek are much more precise than the ones we knew in school, but they are also no longer decent. . . . This was a brutally harsh and realistic language, today's colloquial language onstage."[51] In contrast, the critics in the *Faz* understood themselves to be guardians of the classical text against the illegitimate modernization attempts of the contemporary directors.

While the critics in the *taz* openly acknowledged their subjective approach and their individual preferences for certain playwrights and directors, the critics in the *Faz* saw themselves as holders of a quasi-public office that legitimized their professional judgments.[52] Since they all subscribed more or less to the same normative aesthetic, the *Faz* critics did not encourage alternative readings. Instead they adhered to a hermeneutics of the text that allowed for only one interpretation, namely their own, which they wanted to see onstage as the authentic reading of the play. Some critics in the *Faz* were particularly opposed to the strong visual realization of classical texts, arguing that the directors were no longer interested in the ideas and concepts that these plays discuss but only in their own theatrical techniques. In contrast to the foregrounding of theater as a visual spectacle, the hegemonic culture insists on the literary character of the theater quite in accordance with its general preference for literature as the paradigmatic bourgeois cultural practice.[53]

The hegemonic culture's critical assessment of its counterpart, the theater groups of the alternative culture, as "the theater's escape from language"[54] was consistent with the hegemonic culture's emphasis on a linguistic-conceptual theater. In addition, it refers to one of the alternative culture's most striking features. Most alternative theater groups worked without literary texts for their performances and tended to neglect the spoken word in favor of the image. A renaissance of nonverbal theatrical practices, especially of pantomime, took place within the alternative culture, which is not surprising in light of our earlier discussion of the counterculture's interest in the circus and its reappropriation of the clown and the concept of the fool.[55] The alternative culture rejected an overly literary theater as a part of the negative trajectory of Western intellectual rationality that had led to the destructive separation of cognitive and sensual recognition, that is, to a separation of "head and stomach" (*Kopf und Bauch*), as a common slogan of the time put it.

The classical bourgeois theater marginalized the body in favor of the word and the intellect, thereby undercutting sensuous experience. In contrast to language and its conceptual nature, the body stands for the lost sensuous or aesthetic dimension of experience. The alternative culture tried to replace the hegemonic culture's logocentric aesthetic with an aesthetic of the body, which often went as far as eliminating any verbal communication. One review in the *taz* describes such a nonverbal production, indicating some of the potential problems of a merely visual aesthetic of the body:

> It is always difficult to write about a theater that relies exclusively on the image. Magma, a mime troupe from Berlin, is such a theater. Not a single word is uttered during their two-hour-

long performance, and electronic music accompanies only a few scenes. Movements, lighting, and costumes alone work the magic. . . . One does not see a human face a single time during the entire performance; Magma does not want to be reduced to the old theme of man/woman. For me, it was a fascinating phenomenon to forget who is male and who is female and to observe simply two playing bodies. And this is the only concern Magma wants to communicate to its audience. No message, no demand to think along; one can let oneself go and enjoy.[56]

With pantomime, not only the image but also the body, movement, and gesture, which pantomime shares with the clown and the fool, became the primary expressive means. This focus on and appreciation of the image and corporeal expression, which was most apparent in the privileging of the art of pantomime, has problems of its own, especially regarding the relationship between performer and audience, or in other words, reception aesthetic. Precisely because pantomime requires tremendous control of the body not easily attainable by the layperson, it produces an awestruck and admiring but also passive audience and thus reproduces bourgeois modes of reception and structures such as the star system. Second, since perfection of the technique is a necessary prerequisite for successful pantomime, form often dominates the performance. Finally, those who took a more critical stance toward the alternative culture's preferred theatrical form questioned whether pantomime can indeed communicate any issue, or whether it is rather reduced to certain themes. "The well-mastered language of the body is spoken where words would in fact be proper. This does not mean that all mimes only beat the air in order to demonstrate their superb control of their bodies. Certainly, most performances are based on very sophisticated motives. But the question has to be asked whether the medium of mime is able to communicate specific contents."[57]

To put the question logocentrically, what is this nonverbal aesthetic of the body really trying to say? For one, as the review of the theater group Magma suggests, the alternative culture's emphasis on a visual and corporeal aesthetic was still a reaction against the student movement's infatuation with an abstract, conceptual aesthetic of the word. Furthermore, this review reveals that the alternative culture honored the human desire for enjoyment and pleasure without a vested interest. Hedonist tendencies were not alien to the alternative culture, but they were also not its only goal.

Among the many reviews of independent theater groups in the *taz*, the one on the Hamburg-based Grand Kanaille serves as a good example for studying the alternative culture's concept of the theater. The review lists the three fundamentals of the alternative aesthetics: privileging of the body or corporeality over the spoken word, which we have already discussed; improvisation, which represents the specific theatrical articulation of spontaneity; and personal experience. "For instance, it is very lively theater: theater that unfolds from its own ideas by way of improvisation, theater that starts from one's own experiences, and finally, theater whose focus is on bodily movements with elements of mime and acrobatics. The lack of much set design concentrates the audience's attention on the acting: there are no lighting effects; a large sheet alone with the name of the group serves as the backdrop, and only a few props, mostly chairs, are onstage."[58]

It is not surprising that spontaneity, which articulates itself as the theatrical technique of improvisation, appears as another valued characteristic of the alternative theater. Spontaneity was in general a counterconcept to the hegemonic culture's idea of organization and structure, which the alternative culture viewed as a stifling mechanism of social control. Naturally, the alternative culture tried to preserve its spontaneity, since the hegemonic culture recognized that this represents a subversive force and tried to channel it. In the context of the theater, spontaneity was supposed to guarantee the immediacy of communication between the actor and the audience. The theatrical concept of the alternative culture, therefore, was analogous to its journalistic theory, the idea of grass-roots journalism (*Betroffenenberichterstattung*). Both conceptualizations aimed at reconstructing the immediacy of communication, which allows for an authentic experience.

The alternative theater groups used their own subjective experience of life and society as material for their performances. This insistence on subjective experience as the basis for the theater event was consistent with the radically subjective approach the post-1968 counterculture took to politics as well. As opposed to the bourgeois theater of the hegemonic culture, which discusses issues in their universality and on a conceptual level, and also to the agitprop street theater of the student movement, which framed its subject matter always in terms of the concept of social class, the alternative culture emphasized nonconceptual approaches and stressed the significance of theatrical practices for the individual. Theater became an important means for its practitioners to rediscover sensuous experience and self-awareness, and ultimately for self-actualization. In the words of one of these independent theater groups, "We try to explore our own experiences, feelings, and impressions, and not according to any intellectual concept."[59]

For the alternative culture, the theater reconstructed authentic experience for the actors as much as for the audience. The successful communication of this authentic experience represented the key criterion for aesthetic reception to which all other aspects of theatrical work were subjected. As a result, the alternative culture had difficulties with such theatrical practices as the street theater, which subsumed all aesthetic means to the political end of agitation and propaganda.

While the alternative culture grew weary of the instrumentalization of the theater, it was not oblivious to the political dimension of the theater or its potential to reach out and promote a cause. Hence it argued for a modification of the traditional agitprop theater, which the student movement had reintroduced. "One of our modes of expression is an expanded agitprop theater—expanded by fun and our joie de vivre. We can do our tricks with few means; we take to the streets with a colorful mixture . . . of acrobats, fire eaters, jugglers, stilt walkers, clown skits, agitation scenes, and songs."[60] This quote neither describes a medieval folk festival nor the street carnival in the Ruhr Valley, but street theater as political protest against nuclear power plants. Instead of arguing merely on a conceptual level regarding serious issues such as death by radiation, the alternative culture wanted to resist this fate by expressing its own vitality.[61]

In the tradition of the Sponti movement, the notion of spontaneity includes the idea of having fun as well. As much as the alternative culture criticized the publicly funded theater for its inherent boredom, most of the reviews of independent theater groups in the *taz* stressed how much fun and joy the actors and spectators had with a production. The majority of the independent theater groups used comic elements—slapstick, puns, and characters such as the clown or the fool—in their performances. These elements provoked a spontaneous reaction on the part of the audience, namely, laughter. The alternative culture's theatrical practices wanted to revitalize the liberating laughter that subverts the structures of domination in ridiculing the established authorities and powers. In this context, Dario Fo's plays were especially interesting for the alternative culture's theater, since they direct this liberating laughter against the authorities.

Our discussion of the alternative culture's theater aesthetic shows the strong influence of the paradigm of New Subjectivity on the alternative culture. For the alternative culture, theater served a double purpose. The actors' subjective experiences became the thematic foundation for most theatrical performances. The actors therefore did not function simply as a representational means for a subject matter far removed from them. Instead, the theme of the production was intrinsically bound up with the actors' lives. Theater thus took on a new meaning for the actors as a form of self-actualization. From the perspective of the alternative culture, this approach to theater production guaranteed its authenticity. Finally, the return to old, often prebourgeois forms of theater underscores our observation that the alternative culture's concept of a culture of the people incorporated elements of folk culture. The alternative culture viewed both the actors' subjectivity as the basis for theatrical events and the integration of elements of folk theater to be essential for authentic communication between the actors and the audience.

It's Only Rock 'n' Roll: Popular Music and Opposition

Music, as one of the oldest artistic practices, has always enjoyed high popularity in the hegemonic culture. The same held true for the alternative culture, judging by the extensive coverage of musical events in the *taz*. In spite of the *taz*'s self-proclaimed twofold approach—reporting on the hegemonic as well as the alternative culture's events—rock music was the dominant musical genre discussed in the *taz*. The discourse on rock music in the *taz* also reflects the alternative culture's aesthetic ideas. The key codes of the alternative culture—spontaneity, experience, authenticity, and subjective concerns—permeated the discourse on rock music. Yet at the same time, this almost exclusive concentration on rock music seems to contradict the thesis that the alternative culture embraced folk culture and leads us back to our initial question: What did the alternative culture mean when it called for a culture of the people?

The alternative culture was, however, keenly aware of the power of the culture industry, as many articles and reviews in the *taz* demonstrate. While some *taz* critics argued from an Adornian position that views the culture industry as a monolithic deception machine,[62] most alternative critics did not take this stance. Instead, they insisted that authentic rock music is still possible in spite of the culture industry's obvious success in corrupting and reintegrating much of it into the mainstream. An explanation of this perception of rock rests in parts on generational differences and on the rebel image rock enjoyed since its emergence.

For the majority of postwar German youth, music, and in particular rock 'n' roll, had played an important role for their personal and political socialization. Since Bill Haley and Elvis Presley, rock 'n' roll meant rebellion against a stifling parent culture in West Germany just as much as in the United States and as illustrated already by the Halbstarken phenomenon in the 1950s. Although rock 'n' roll was quickly transformed into a profitable business, which diverted the youth's oppositional energy into channels conducive to the status quo, rock music managed to preserve its rebel image. The *taz* attests to this not only *expressis verbis* but also by constructing a history of rock analogous to the sociopolitical changes of the Federal Republic. The Rolling Stones, the Beatles, Bob Dylan, Janis Joplin, Jimi Hendrix—in short, the entire rock scene of the 1960s—represented the progressive power of music, since it reflected the youths' confrontation with the double standards and the philistinism of the parent culture. "The music reflects the revolt of the late 1960s,"[63] as one review claimed.

In turn, the 1970s appear in this historical narrative as the dark ages of commercialized rock. The alternative audience, with its skepticism concerning technology, could not identify with the heavily produced electronic sound of the 1970s, which it experienced as a far-removed, cold, and petrified professionalism. "The student movement had split into pieces, and what they said sounded cold and lifeless, just like the music of those years appears to me: synthetic, generated with a lot of technology (Kraftwerk, Genesis, Soft Machine). Reactionary forces had suffocated the youth's rebellion with big business, which corrupted rock 'n' roll. All too often new stars appeared who became rich overnight. How can you talk of the revolution, if you are a billionaire?"[64]

This nebulous analogy between the dissolution of the student movement and the style of 1970s electronic rock is especially interesting. The analogy is based on a personal or subjective approach, which marks this article as a text steeped in the discourse of New Subjectivity. The author does not establish a conclusive correlation but merely states what he or she feels comparing these two social phenomena—the failure of the student movement and the music of the 1970s. At the same time, the alternative culture's resentment of the late student movement's abstract, theoretical discourse becomes apparent and gives a first impression of the argumentative problems the alternative culture encountered when tackling rock music.

The same article, from the first year of the *taz*, prefigured a dominant line of argument regarding the culture industry. Even though the alternative culture was permanently confronted with and also recognized the integrative power of the culture industry, its narrative on rock history emphatically held on to the idea that authentic rock is still possible.[65] Against Adorno's pessimistic stance regarding the culture industry, the alternative culture struggled with a concept of rock as a double-edged or dialectic form of popular culture, reminiscent of Enzensberger's argument about the culture industry in 1962. The alternative culture argued that while the culture industry endows its products with specific ideological valences, it does not have total control over their reception. The audience might very well invest these products with its own meaning, which can indeed contradict the superimposed ideology. In other words, rock music as a part of the hegemonic culture has to rely on the complicity of the recipient. For the alternative culture, the power of rock music, like that of any other music, to cancel this complicity rests on its "emotional immediacy," which not even the culture industry can totally control.[66]

The folk revival of the early 1960s and the advent of punk rock by the mid-1970s seemed to prove this thesis right. Both musical genres represented an alternative to the electronic rock of the 1970s, which relied on high-tech equipment for its sound and large armies of human labor for its "live" performances. As a result, the 1970s rock concerts by such performers as the Who, Queen, or David Bowie were perfectly planned and computerized, contradicting the alternative culture's concept of spontaneity as a form of resistance. Furthermore, two aspects in particular made folk and punk attractive for the alternative culture. First, the simple musical forms appealed to an audience that wanted to break out of a consumer attitude in favor of a do-it-yourself culture. Second, the alternative culture defined these musical forms in terms of immediacy and authenticity, with the latter cropping up as much in reviews of rock performances as it did in the reviews of the alternative culture's theater events. Authenticity meant first and foremost that the musicians sang of their own lives and communicated their own experience, which ideally engaged the audience by addressing the latter's problems while at the same time arousing concern (*Betroffenheit*) for other issues. The alternative culture saw folk and punk as immediate expressions of the artist's subjectivity, creating in turn an immediate and therefore authentic response in the audience.

The personal was supposed to be the political in rock music as well. "You can only touch people about things that you have actually experienced, or that other people have seen or experienced. And this is, I believe, the way one has to make political music today. You can make some suggestions, how to defend oneself or whether one can still defend oneself at all. . . . Practical political work takes place in citizens' initiatives but not onstage."[67] This quote shows the same resistance toward an instrumentalization of rock for political ends that we have already discussed with respect to the alternative culture's position on the politically committed theater of the student movement.

Not surprising for the radically subjective position dominant since the mid-1970s, the alternative culture viewed the communication of experience as the essential political dimension of rock music and rejected the pathos of the pedagogical finger wagging of the 1970s *Polit Rock Bands* as an anachronistic expression of the condescension of the orthodox left. The debate following the "Rock against the Right" concert in 1979 demonstrates that the line between the preservation of rock's authenticity and its instrumentalization for political purposes was, however, thin and controversial.

Inspired by the British predecessor "Rock against Racism," a broad alliance of the diverse West German countercultural groups organized a protest concert against racism in general and in particular against the annual "Germany Meeting" of the NPD and other neo-Nazi groups on 17 June 1979 in Frankfurt. Until German unification in 1990, this day, called "Day of German Unity" (*Tag der deutschen Einheit*), was the official national holiday of West Germany. It commemorated the lost German unity on the anniversary of the citizens' uprising in the GDR against their government in 1957. Since the very first Germany Meeting of the neo-Nazis in Frankfurt in 1974, there had been political opposition and protest against the NPD's demonstration at the center of the city.[68] In 1978 the situation escalated into a day-long violent street battle between the neo-Nazis, the antifascist protesters, and the police. Hence the political groups that had organized the antifascist rally year after year were looking for a mode of protest that would express their opposition to the neo-Nazis while at the same time avoiding the violent street battles that had occurred in 1978. The ecological alliance Grüne Liste Hessen suggested organizing an equivalent to the British "Rock against Racism."[69]

The idea found a broad consensus because the alternative culture by and large still subscribed to the definition of rock music as a genuine expression of resistance. Second, it employed music because of its aesthetic and sensuous quality and because of its alleged emotional immediacy. Rational discourse was not sufficient for the alternative culture with respect to an issue such as the Holocaust precisely because it cannot be fully comprehended in conceptual terms. Instead, the alternative culture wanted to get its audience emotionally involved in the commemoration of the Holocaust and the struggle against neo-Nazism in West Germany. "'Rock against the Right' wants to express its deep disgust for the Nazis' atrocities and of neo-Nazism through the content and the emotional means of the music. Faced with the relativization of the genocide of millions of people, political analyses alone do not suffice—at issue are also the concern and the emotions of all democrats."[70]

After the national holiday had passed peacefully in 1979, critical voices questioned whether "Rock against the Right" was indeed an adequate political and aesthetic expression of opposition as it claimed, or whether it had rather abused rock as the bait to attract a larger number of people to the antifascist rally than would have come without the music. The proponents of this position accused the organizers of the rally of double standards in mobilizing the rebel image of rock merely as an advertisement strategy.[71] Others did not question the intrinsic political potential of rock music, but simply argued that nobody came only for the music. The latter position maintained that "Rock against the Right" represented a symbiotic relationship between politics and music, which managed to redirect valuable oppositional energies into politics.[72]

Neither of these two positions was able to resolve convincingly the ambivalent status of rock music in today's society. The manipulative and integrative power of the culture industry was too blatantly obvious to be ignored. On the other hand, the alternative culture was too adamant in its allegiance to rock music to give up the ideal of rock 'n' roll as an authentic mode of resistance to the hegemonic culture. As a result, the alternative culture's critical assessment of rock music mainly focused on the personal level. The criticism repeated the general outcry about musicians' double standards, namely, the discrepancy between the politically progressive claim of rock as a part of the counterculture and the personal opinions as well as attitudes of its stars. The alternative culture attacked such rock musicians as Eric Clapton, Rod Stewart, and David Bowie for their political conservatism, which they saw to be in opposition to their musical message.[73] It criticized even its very own punk rock idols for recording on big commercial labels, as in the case of Nina Hagen (CBS) and Patti Smith (EMI-Electrola).[74] As one critic put it with respect to Nina Hagen, "This attitude really pisses me off: waving the

Sponti flag and flaunting left slogans in front, but in back holding out the hand in order to take in the 'gifts' of the omnipotent record companies."75

As we have previously discovered in the heated dispute about government pork (*Staatsknete*), that is, public funding for alternative projects, a total retreat from the hegemonic culture was the only solution for part of the alternative culture. This faction therefore favored the development of a countercultural music industry with independent labels and independent festivals that would guarantee that rock music can realize its oppositional nature. "Music that rebels against oppression is the musician's response to social conditions. This music can be honest only if it remains outside the hegemonic system. In other words, only if musicians organize themselves independently in life, as a band, when disseminating their music, and organize their concerts together with other dropouts who are interested in observing how people express themselves through their music."76

However, as the development of punk rock shows, independent labels and autonomous channels of distribution did not necessarily represent a satisfactory strategy against the hegemonic culture's structures of domination. Countercultural music projects, for example, independent record labels, unwittingly provided a service for the culture industry similar to that of other alternative projects for the hegemonic culture at large. They discovered or developed new trends within the music scene or aesthetic culture in general and promoted the respective artists, who frequently then transferred to a big commercial label after their marketability had been established in the countercultural music scene. Hence the independent labels saved the music industry the high financial investments involved in launching a new star. The honorable moral position that the alternative culture exhibited, appealing to the artists that they should not commit "treason" against their own origins and should not sell out to the hegemonic culture for something trivial like money, did not solve the problem but rather promoted resignation.

Since rock music represents today a multibillion-dollar business and part of the ever-expanding culture industry, it is far removed from the concept of a decentralized and participatory culture of the people that the alternative culture envisioned. On the other hand, it is undeniably a very popular genre that once originated from the people and—one might contend—constitutes therefore a form of folk music. This line of argument is complicated by the fact that rock music was imported to West Germany, since its roots "lie deep within the historical experience of black men and women of the United States."[77] Rock music has a different origin from that of the white lower class in the United States or Europe. This did not matter to the alternative movement, which did not define their culture of the people in national terms but rather as one of the margins in opposition to the hegemonic center. Rock music not only had a rebel image but also epitomized for the alternative culture marginality because of its African American roots and its global adoption, from white lower-class youths in the 1950s to the hippies of the 1960s and punk rock of the 1970s and early 1980s. What appeared at first as a contradiction—folk culture and rock 'n' roll—makes perfect sense for the alternative movement's inclusionary concept of culture. As the Tunix flier puts it: "We put different strings on our violins, guitars, and cellos and play 'No Country More Beautiful Than Our Beach' with Tommy and the Stones."[78]

CHAPTER 6: Between Politics and Ecology: Green Ideas on Art and Culture

O ne might wonder why the Greens and the ecology movement they represent should be singled out for individual
attention from the broader context of the alternative culture. Many aspects of the Greens and their history justify a detailed
analysis of their aesthetic ideas and cultural politics. First and foremost from a historical perspective, the ecology movement had, next
to the women's movement, the most lasting impact. The ecology
movement raised the level of public consciousness in West Germany
from complete indifference and ignorance of environmental issues
to the current widely held belief that the preservation of nature has to
be a top priority. Furthermore, it successfully transformed itself from
a movement into a viable party that forced a reorientation of the
traditional parties toward more environmentally friendly policies.

The Greens had entered several state legislatures even before they
participated in the election of the federal parliament in 1980, which
initially did not meet with the same success. Most election analysts
impute the Greens' failure to enter the federal parliament at that
time to the candidacy of the late right-wing Bavarian politician Franz
Josef Strauß (csu) for chancellorship and not to a lack of support for
the Greens. In order to avert a victory for Strauß and the center-right
parties (cdu/csu), many supporters of the Greens cast their votes
for the Social Democrats and their candidate, incumbent Helmut
Schmidt, whom they saw as the lesser evil. While the alternative
movement reached its peak by 1983—reflected, for example, by the
transformations of the *taz*, which cannot legitimately be perceived as
a mouthpiece of the alternative culture after this date—the Greens
kept on flourishing. Since 1983, when they won 5.6 percent of the
vote in the federal election, the Greens have been the fourth party

in the federal parliament, allowing us to pursue our investigation of the correlation between countercultural concepts of politics and aesthetic ideas into the mid-1980s.[1]

The Greens in many ways incorporated the demands of other new social movements, as a brief look at the their founding program on the federal level (*Bundesprogramm*) shows. This platform spells out the four fundamental principles— "ecology, social responsibility, grass-roots democracy, and nonviolence"[2]— on which all Green politics rests and that exhibit at the same time the continuities and breaks between the green-alternative and the student movement. Though ecology was not an invention of the Greens but had been around for over a century, it distinguished the Greens most clearly from its countercultural predecessor, the student movement. The principle of ecology meant that the Greens not only articulated environmental concerns but also called for a transformation of the hegemonic paradigm of permanent progress and unrestrained economic growth in favor of conservation in order to avoid irreversible ecological losses and environmental catastrophes.

This concept of conservation extended well into the areas of peace and civil liberties, which the Greens perceive to be in jeopardy.[3] The platform's section on the individual and society demonstrates the impact terrorism had on left-liberal quarters, referring specifically to antiterrorism legislation passed in the late 1970s, and expressed the fear that the Federal Republic was developing into a country whose government put the entire population under constant surveillance.[4] The Green principle of nonviolence has to be understood in the context of terrorism as well, which overshadowed West German society during the 1970s. Nonviolence had, however, both a domestic and an international component. As to the latter, it articulated the Greens' commitment to the goals of the peace movement. With respect to the domestic situation, it upheld the legitimacy of civil disobedience as practiced by many ecological and peace activists.

Although the term *sozial*, which is perhaps best translated as "socially responsible," had a broad meaning for the Greens, it addressed primarily the question of fair distribution of national and internationally produced wealth and in many ways shows most clearly the influence of the student movement on the Greens' programmatic framework. The Greens perceived themselves from the very beginning as the representatives of such marginalized social groups as women, children and teenagers, old people, gays and lesbians, the Sinti and Roma community, and especially foreigners—those who migrated since the mid-1950s to West Germany to fill the labor shortage, as well as the asylum seekers, whose numbers increased during the 1980s. In terms of the global North-South divide, the Greens demanded policies that would lead to a just cooperation of the First World with the underdeveloped Third World, arguing essentially along the lines of the West German Third World Movement, which was much more vocal during the 1970s than today.

Yet the Greens' idea of social responsibility went further than welfare programs and new modes of aid to developing countries. It encompassed a vague notion of a better, nonalienated life, in which the human being will be restored to his or her full creative powers. Green politics strove for a society in which the subject is not reduced to a passive recipient either of food stamps and unemployment checks or of the commodities that the market economy provides. In contrast, the Greens advocated a model of a society in which everybody has a chance for self-actualization and political, social, and cultural participation. Naturally, this participatory model clashed with a political system based solely on representation.

At the heart of the Greens' understanding of democracy lies the paradigm of the politics of the self, now conceptualized in collective terms as a participatory versus a mere representative model of politics. The Greens did more than other new social movements in publicizing this idea of a participatory politics under the label grass-roots democracy, which represents also the fourth pillar of their politics. "Our internal organisational life and our relationship to the people who support and vote for us is the exact opposite of that of the established parties in Bonn. They are neither able nor willing to accept new approaches and ideas, nor the concerns of the democratic movement. Because of this we have decided to form a new type of party organisation, the basic structures of which are set up in a grass-roots-democratic and decentralised way; the two things cannot in fact be separated."[5] Decentralization means small and comprehensible political units at the grass roots, since "political decisions should always be taken on the lowest possible levels, thus facilitating a maximum of direct involvement of those who will be affected by the decisions."[6]

With regard to internal party organization, the Greens initially tried to secure grass-roots democracy through separation of party office and mandate, prevention of office accumulation, rotation of office holders, collective leadership, and openness to the public on all inner-party levels. Not only did this apply to the Greens' organizational structure, but they understood it as a "model for society as a whole."[7] The social groups and issues that the Green platform addresses are essentially the same as those the *taz* covered, and the Greens can therefore be viewed as another mouthpiece and the parliamentary arm of the new social movements.[8]

This leads us to another reason why an in-depth analysis of the Greens is a worthwhile undertaking. Since the ecology movement coalesced into a party, it had the strongest programmatic framework and came closest to the theoretical articulation missing in the case of the alternative culture. In addition, a holistic approach characterized the ecological thinking from which the Greens sprang, and one would expect them to pay attention to aesthetic and cultural issues as tools for bringing about a change of consciousness. Finally, we can discern a strong continuity between the generation of the student movement and the founders and supporters of the Green party. This allows for verification and sharpening of our prior observations about the development of the West German counterculture since the late 1960s.

But quite in contrast to the student movement, the Greens were weak on aesthetic and cultural issues and did not generate any extensive discussion on aesthetic culture until the mid-1980s. This lack of thorough debate of a cultural program is surprising for two reasons. First, the Greens' members and constituency came from the old and new middle class, which has traditionally been most supportive of the arts and which provides for an aesthetic education. Second, large parts of this constituency were socialized in the context of the 1960s counterculture, with its emphasis on sensuous and aesthetic experience.[9]

{186}

The Greens' reticence on aesthetic issues is also surprising in light of the fact that they received tremendous support from artists—among them such prominent figures as Joseph Beuys—and successfully used artistic means for their election campaign in 1983. The Greens arranged a professional concert tour called "Green Caterpillar" (*Grüne Raupe*), which included artists such as the songwriter Konstantin Wecker and the rock bands Kraan and Östro, traveling the entire Federal Republic on behalf of the Greens. The show was interrupted by short election statements by seven Green politicians, but their contributions did not take up more than 15 percent of the show's time.[10] In comparison to the heated dispute about "Rock against the Right," discussed in the previous chapter, the Greens did not seem to have any qualms about using music or art in general for advertising themselves and their agenda. At the same time, frustration rose among those artists who strove for an integration of their political (i.e., support of the Greens) and artistic life, because aesthetic ideas played almost no role in Green thinking. For example, Peter Altendorfer, a musician and composer from Austria who was himself involved in ecological politics, expressed this frustration by calling the Greens philistines (*Kunstbanausen*) and scolded them for their "lacking relationship to art."[11]

Instead of joining Altendorfer in his finger pointing, it is more fruitful to ask whether the ecological principle itself was at the root of the Greens' lack of a coherent discussion of art. In the beginning, the Greens dealt very little with aesthetic issues and stuck instead to the immediate problems of cultural politics with which they were confronted as elected representatives and administrators. Within the larger and more diverse framework of the ecological movement, we can nevertheless find some statements moving in the direction of an aesthetic theory. In particular, those environmental activists for whom ecology was not simply a pragmatic political program but rather an overarching philosophy were more inclined to address aesthetic issues because of their holistic approach. They saw not only environmental problems but all other social ills as a result of humanity's spiritual alienation from nature. These activists therefore aimed at a new cultural revolution, leading to an ecological paradigm that would supersede the dominant mechanistic worldview in favor of an organic, cyclical, and natural understanding of the universe.

Stephen Elkins aptly dubbed this particular brand of ecological thinking in America "deep ecology"—a term that fits the West German equivalent as well.[12] The latter's ideas exerted influence on ecological thinking in general during the early 1980s and were present in the fundamentalist wing of the Greens, although deep ecologists were not necessarily members of the party. The following analysis is thus based less on the party platforms of the Greens than on other articulations of ecological thinking.

The Greens' Dilemma: Nature versus Art

The greatest obstacle to a green aesthetic was at the same time the very premise on which all ecological thinking and the politics of the Greens rests: nature. Precisely the fact that ecological thinking places absolute priority on nature, above all the conservation of nature in view of a pending ecological catastrophe, obstructed aesthetic conceptualizations. The concepts of nature and art or culture are closely entwined, since each term can be defined only in opposition to the other. Art represents the utmost opposite to nature, since it is nothing if not human made.[13] The individual work of art is the product of human creativity and labor, or in other words, is often literally wrested from nature, a circumstance most apparent in architecture and sculpture. The course of human history is marked by the transgression of natural boundaries and limitations, a trend that articulated itself in the aesthetic realm as well. The concept of the beauty of nature has also changed in synchronism with humankind's ever more exploitive grip on nature. Though the beauty of nature and the aesthetic experience of the sublime occupied a prominent position in Kant's ethics and Schiller's ethical as well as political theory, it became secondary after Hegel's privileging of the beauty of art (*Kunstschöne*), culminating in modernity's distaste for the beauty of nature as trivial, even if single philosophers such as Adorno tried to redeem this concept for contemporary aesthetics.[14]

The aesthetic notion of nature is as much socially mediated as any other concept and is equally doomed to serve an ideological function. The concept of nature as ideology has therefore both progressive and regressive tendencies. It is progressive in its potential to evoke a utopian vision of a better world based on its criticism of the existing order, as Jörg Zimmermann points out in his historical survey of the aesthetic concept of nature: "Idealized images of nature satisfy in fictional form needs denied in reality. They are expressions of a lack, the experience of which does not lead to political practice aiming at change, but is compensated for aesthetically."[15] Zimmermann's definition of the utopian potential of the depiction of nature raises its problematic status as merely representing an aesthetic compensation. In this case art becomes affirmative in Marcuse's sense, and the concept of nature takes on a regressive tendency. As an idyllic depiction it projects a reconciliation of humankind and nature into prehistoric times or compares this state of being with the child's innocence.[16]

The privileging of nature in deep ecology runs counter not only to an aesthetic notion of nature but to the entire history of Western culture. Deep ecology attacked first and foremost the Western belief in progress through technology as well as the technological transformation and secularization of the perception of the world that the Renaissance had brought about. The Renaissance liberated the concept of nature from its religious context as a divine order and opened it up to further inquiry. This process culminated in the replacement of a metaphysical idea of nature with a scientific one, which by the end of the nineteenth century insisted on the objectivity of the laws of nature and excluded aesthetics from nature. The result was, on the one hand, an ultimate belief in science and technology's omnipotent function and applicability, and on the other hand, a critical evaluation of technology's influence under the auspices of capitalism in the twentieth century.

Horkheimer and Adorno are the paradigmatic proponents of this latter, critical position, which focuses on the correlation between the domination of nature and social structures of domination in modern capitalist society. In their *Dialectic of Enlightenment* they argue that the more humankind gained control over nature, that is, substituted mythical and mimetic approaches with rational inquiry and technological domination over nature, the more humankind became alienated from it: "Nature must no longer be influenced by approximation, but mastered by labor. . . . In thought, men distance themselves from nature in order thus imaginatively to present it to themselves—but only in order to determine how it is to be dominated."[17]

The first federal platform of the Greens was reminiscent of Horkheimer's and Adorno's analysis of contemporary society in vehemently rejecting the domination society exercised over nature and the human being. Moreover, it lamented the total commercialization of nature as well as leisure time and the resulting alienation of the individual from nature. Finally, the platform protested the bondage of human beings to the dominant economic system.[18] Although the Greens' criticism of contemporary society resembles that of Horkheimer and Adorno, even pointing out the necessity of safeguarding civil liberties and the democratic structure of the Federal Republic, the issue of the survival of the planet Earth was at the heart of their politics. Horkheimer's and Adorno's interest in the correlation between the domination of nature and of humankind, in contrast, is based on the question of freedom and autonomy for the individual and not on the conservation of nature. Quite in contrast to the Greens, Horkheimer and Adorno emphatically assert the freedom of the individual, even if this means disregarding nature.

The difference between Horkheimer and Adorno and the Greens can be explained in historical terms. The *Dialectic of Enlightenment* was written at a time when environmental problems had not yet become as blatantly visible as since the 1970s and, most importantly, would have paled in the face of fascism and the Holocaust—the historical points of reference for this study. The Greens' platform gives, however, a taste of the party's problems in shaping a coherent social and aesthetic theory out of the multitude of often opposing traditions on which the Greens drew.

The 1980 platform also illustrates the Greens' difference from the student movement. Whereas the Greens showed an apocalyptic thinking that denied any possibility for progress, since it would only lead us further along the road to ecological catastrophe, the student movement did not condemn all technological advancement but still believed in social progress driven by the technological improvement of human life. Looking at it from a Marxian perspective of class society, the students attacked only technology's undemocratic application in the service of capital as wrong. Hence the proletarian revolution represents the prerequisite for the peaceful and beneficial use of technology.

The concept of revolution played no role in the ecological movement, which favored a model of social evolution that paralleled evolution in nature. Ecological thinking therefore represented a new step in the historical development of the concept of nature, which Konrad Paul Liessmann summarizes in his analysis of the relationship between ecology and aesthetic: "The more nature actually disappears in the process of the technological transformation of the earth, the more it is stylized as a value in itself within the discourse about its end."[19] In ecological thinking, nature, that which is organically grown and untouched by the human being, stands for all that humankind has lost. Nature represents the meaningful cycle of birth and death and rebirth, in contrast to the meaninglessness of destruction. Nature is a harmonic universal network in which each particularity has its specific and necessary place and function; thus it is unity in diversity. Nature represents the unity of body and intellect or matter and spirituality. Nature is movement and change as a dialectical process, peaceful evolution instead of violent revolution. Finally, nature equals sensuality or an aesthetic experience that is repressed in contemporary society.[20]

From a green perspective, the demise of nature can be halted only by an "active partnership with nature and human beings."[21] The Greens' choice of words is not random, but an expression of the new status nature had gained by the end of the twentieth century. The term *partnership* usually denotes an egalitarian and cooperative relationship between human beings, or entities built and governed by human activity. The perception of a partnership between nature and humankind had, however, further repercussions, namely, that autonomy, "which modernity had reserved for the phenomenon of the aesthetic and for the self-conscious subject," was slowly but surely transferred onto nature itself.[22] Nature was no longer seen to be at the service of humankind, but the other way around. For deep ecologists humankind now has to be at nature's service for the sake of nature's survival. It means that humankind has to give up its autonomy and integrate itself into the predetermined cycle of nature.

In the most radical expression of this position nature gains an almost spiritual or religious quality. One of the earliest and also controversial theorists of the Green movement, Manon Maren-Grisebach, for instance, uses both the personification of nature we have already observed in the Greens' election platform and a religious rhetoric in describing the relationship between nature and humankind. She invokes the biblical image of Noah's ark and the notion of guilt, which like partnership applies primarily to interpersonal relationships.[23] "We are no longer free in our devotion to nature; we are deeply in debt. . . . The feeling of the unity of humanity and nature has been lost, overshadowed by guilt and also by the recognition that no unity can exist in the face of so much destructive potential."[24] Most importantly, she, like many other deep ecologists, attributes today's environmental problems not to structures of domination but predominantly to humanity's spiritual alienation from nature.

Her description of this spiritual alienation is reminiscent of Peter Handke's novel *The Moment of True Feeling*, discussed in chapter 3. As the title indicates, Handke addresses in this novel the problematic status of sensate experience, that is, the lack of receptivity for sensations and feelings within contemporary society. As soon as his hero, Gregor Keuschnig, becomes aware of his indifference regarding "true feelings," he is at a loss and experiences total alienation. Maren-Grisebach locates the same loss with respect to nature, as a repression of human sensuality or a loss of a feeling for nature (*Naturgefühl*): "In a written questionnaire directed to students regarding how they feel about nature, everybody wrote something about their empathy and their otherwise repressed senses. They recalled smelling the wet forest ground, blooming bushes, freezing in the icy wind; tasting roots coming straight from the ground of the earth full of sand, or strawberries on a warm mountain slope, and feeling moss and stream pebbles under their bare feet."[25] She perceives nature as the placeholder for immediate sensate experience, or ultimately for sensuality, without considering the problem that a concept such as nature is not authentic, but to the highest degree historically, that is, socially mediated.

Furthermore, both Handke's novel and Maren-Grisebach's essay suggest the same problematic remedy for resolving the contested status of the individual's sensuous experience in a world of alienation. Both call for a passive devotion (*Hingebung*) of the subject to its environment—the object world in the case of Handke and nature in the case of Maren-Grisebach. A pocket mirror, a leaf from a chestnut tree, and a child's barrette symbolize the object world that triggers the moment of revelation and thus the "true feeling," reconciling Handke's hero with the world. For Maren-Grisebach, regaining a feeling for nature represents the liberating force that reconciles humankind with nature and thus with itself.

When nature becomes the ultimate point of reference as in deep ecology, art logically has to be subjected to the primacy of nature. This means that art can relate to nature only through mimesis. It is therefore not surprising that we can find voices calling for a return to a naturalist-figurative art among deep ecologists such as that of the painter Wassili Loukopoulos-Lepanto, who rejects all abstract art: "Abstract art excludes any relationship with nature. The abstract artist does not stand within nature but opposed to nature. For him, art and nature are two separate spheres. Abstract art leaves the 'skin' of nature and its laws behind. A loss of a center is characteristic for the abstract artist. His soul is clouded and his vision is blurred. Like an orphan, he only appears to live after he has separated himself from Mother Nature. Full of envy, he gazed at her beauty, and because he was unable to imitate her radiant beauty, and he was unable to praise this beautiful glow, hatred arose in him, hatred for everything which is beautiful."[26] Loukopoulos-Lepanto summarizes his ideal of an ecological art in seven demands, which range from its definition as a naturalist-figurative art organically springing from the "inner experience" (*innere Erlebnisse*) to art's liberation from mass media and "propaganda of art" (*Kunstpropaganda*).

His two essays, even more so than Maren-Grisebach's book, are bursting with a religious, spiritual rhetoric that, for instance, compares abstract art to "idols" (*Götzenbilder*) and denounces cubism as "soulless geometry" (*entseelende Geometrie*), dada as "aesthetic nihilism" (*ästhetischer Nihilismus*), futurism as a "cult of elitism and compulsive excess" (*Kult des Elitären und des Zwanghaft-Maßlosen*), and all other avant-garde art movements of the twentieth century as a glorification of chaos and insanity.[27] All art since the emergence of the historical avant-garde is destructive, from this deep ecologist's perspective. Loukopoulos-Lepanto represented, however, a minority position even within the deep ecologist camp. As already pointed out, the majority of the ecologically inclined came from the educated middle class, whose identity was shaped by the cultural heritage of the West. Consequently, they appreciate abstract art and therefore would not go along with Loukopoulos-Lepanto's call for a return to premodernist art.

Maren-Grisebach's sketchy remarks are more characteristic examples of green aesthetic ideas. Although they show a much higher sensitivity to the question of the cultural heritage and to the shortcomings of current, ecologically motivated art, they do not amount to a coherent green aesthetic. Quite in contrast to Loukopoulos-Lepanto, Maren-Grisebach does not reject avant-garde art but cites artists from historical avant-garde movements such as Georges Braque and André Breton, taking a Lukácsian position that argues for the critical appropriation of one's cultural heritage. Aside from her positive stance toward Western culture, Maren-Grisebach tried to confront genuine aesthetic problems which Loukopoulos-Lepanto simply ignored.

For instance, she addressed the issue of the form-content dichotomy and the question of the social function of art. Based on a critical assessment of historical predecessors—idealism and materialism—she rejected the reduction of art to either form or content. "It cannot be the goal of a Green aesthetic to promote a second kind of blood-and-soil art, or even a simple realism, be it critical, socialist, or a return to a pure naturalism. A poem is not necessarily successful as soon as it criticizes and moans about humans' dealings with the environment or when it complains about exhaust fumes on a summer meadow; a picture is not necessarily superb if it simply depicts the tin cans left behind at a forest pond. Green aesthetic theory will not delight in such eco-art because it is too good for such superficial content."[28] She criticized idealism and materialism as theories that merely reflect the reductive and destructive Western thinking in binary oppositions. On the other hand, her critique of historical aesthetic positions did not result in a convincing theoretical synthesis of form and content either. She ultimately had to resort to nature, which always exists as a coherent whole and thus forbids the compartmentalization characteristic of today's world. "Good" ecological art strives precisely for this holistic representation. She too models her understanding of art on nature.

Unlike Loukopoulos-Lepanto, who used the concept of nature only in the most regressive fashion for his concept of art, thereby excluding the latter's social function, Maren-Grisebach addressed this problematic aspect of art as well. Using Braque, who compared his work to nature, and Breton, who compared his to social misery, Maren-Grisebach called for a comprehensive art that not only synthesizes the beauty of nature and that of art but also reintegrated ethics into aesthetics. "Regarding nature, the beauty of nature and of art would move closer together and reunite an aesthetic torn apart by analytic modes of thought into formal-abstract and concrete-content principles. With regard to social misery, ethical considerations would be integrated, which would agree with our consciousness of the responsibility for the entire ecosystem of the earth. Therefore, ethical and aesthetic aspects are entwined in our philosophy of art."[29]

From behind her aesthetic ideas lurk pretty much all the major names of German aesthetic theory except for Hegel, since it was the latter who put the beauty of art on the highest pedestal of bourgeois culture. Maren-Grisebach failed to fulfill her own Lukácsian postulate. She did not critically appropriate these historical positions but simply lined them up by using their rhetoric, as the following quote demonstrates: "In play we approach such a disinterested activity, not in a rigidly regulated game, but in one of purposelessness, imagination, dreams, and surprising novelties. . . . To play is a curative for the mentally sick, comfort for learning children, source for artistic creation."[30] She borrows from Kant a comprehensive notion of aesthetic, which still includes ethics and the definition of art as the only mode of disinterested perception. Her notion of play recalls in a vague sense Schiller and Nietzsche, but she also draws on Freud's concept that art represents the sublimated fantasies, desires, and dreams of humankind.

The above quote is characteristic of the eclectic and random approach to aesthetic issues within green culture. By only alluding to these aesthetic concepts dominant throughout centuries of Western thought, Maren-Grisebach can evade the problem that some of these concepts cannot easily be brought together into the organic whole so dear to ecological thinking. For instance, she does not explain how to reconcile Kant's ethical view of aesthetics with Nietzsche's notion of art as an amoral liberating force or with Freud's insistence on repression as a necessary constituent of all culture.

The Notion of Play

It is a futile effort to make sense of Maren-Grisebach's vague and indiscriminate pillaging of the wealth of intellectual history. Instead, we might want to focus on the element of play, which is featured prominently in her statements on a green aesthetic culture. She endorses the concept of play as the foundation for a green aesthetic, since play resembles nature. Like nature, play does not pursue any utilitarian purpose in its creative endeavors. In addition, though creation takes place purposefully in nature as an ecological system, it does not serve any particular interest. Hence nature and play are equally opposed to the intentionality and vested interest that characterize capitalist society. "Also because we like the element of uselessness in playing, because we therein oppose in an almost revolutionary manner the economic thinking of profit maximization. Breaking out of the rules of the market economy and the use value, and playing against the superior force of money, against technology's utilitarian rationality."[31]

This emphatic praise for the subversive potential of play, based on the Kantian definition of beauty, is not, however, convincing in a society that has successfully managed to subject almost all artistic production to the laws of the market economy. What is more, play does not seem to have quite the anti-instrumental character that deep ecologists such as Maren-Grisebach claim. If it has healing powers, as Maren-Grisebach implies, then perhaps it turned into a therapeutic means that compensates for the mental and physical disorders generated by the social system and forms a profitable sector of the economy to boot. Play can be just as affirmative as art.

The notion of play fits well into the general trend toward a concept of art as a nonprofessional and participatory cultural activity popular with the entire alternative culture. As Maren-Grisebach defines play, namely, without rigid rules, it does not require any knowledge, especially not professional knowledge. In other words, the Greens too leaned toward the do-it-yourself culture, discussed in the previous chapter. Maren-Grisebach's aesthetic theory combines the concept of a participatory culture with the idea of a material asceticism also typical for the entire alternative culture: "to reduce one's possessions and wealth as much as possible, to give things away, to like only very few things around, homemade things, whose production we can reconstruct and which are closer to the heart than to one's wallet."[32]

This notion of a participatory culture for everybody leaves no space for professional art and explains why the Greens had no relationship to art. Green thinking in this most radical fashion claims that the replacement of "shopping," that is, buying whatever one needs, with homemade and handmade products liberates one from alienation. This line of argument ascribes to homemade products an aura of immediacy and therefore of authenticity that allows for the individual to experience itself as a subject and thus promotes self-actualization. We can discern a fetishization of "self-production" and "handmade" within the entire ecological movement, expressing not only an antitechnology stance but also a deep-seated yearning for a premodern life imagined as that harmonious cohabitation of humankind and nature. Ultimately, the green-ecological milieu thus replaced art with crafts.

The Greens on Art, Culture, and Politics

The founding platform of the Greens, the *Bundesprogramm* of 1980, was perhaps not the best place for an elaborate theoretical discussion of aesthetic. The Greens' apparent lack of interest in aesthetic culture, however, seems to have rendered them oblivious to the importance of this battleground in their wider struggle against all modes of social hegemony. The platform's section on culture was squeezed onto one page, a third of which was taken up by a photograph of two street musicians in front of a happily smiling audience in some urban center.[33] The cultural section of the platform was not brimming with innovation, but represented rather an eclectic collection of ideas taken from the alternative culture at large. For instance, the platform picks up on the alternative culture's criticism that the government-subsidized hegemonic culture caters only to the interests of a small part of the population and that its institutions are exclusively located in the cities, neglecting those living on the periphery. Consequently, the Greens call in their platform for a decentralization of cultural offerings by way of traveling exhibits and events by traditional cultural institutions such as the museum or theater, and for support for the creation of neighborhood and community-oriented cultural centers. In addition, they want to strengthen those cultural initiatives that specifically address the needs of children, senior citizens, women, foreigners, those suffering from substance abuse, recently released convicts, and other at-risk social groups. In contrast to the discussion within the alternative culture, the Greens did not seem to be concerned that the alternative cultural projects might become cheap substitutes for welfare programs.

Although the cultural section opens with a reference to the diversity of cultural production in society, behind its pluralist approach lurks an attitude typical of the educated middle class (*Bildungsbürgertum*), which is not surprising considering the social makeup of the Greens. As a result, the Greens stress the significance of education for the appreciation of aesthetic culture. At the same time, the platform operates with the binary model of a society divided into two cultures—mainstream and alternative—which Peter Glotz had originally introduced and with which the Spontis had readily identified. The platform contrasts the publicly subsidized hegemonic and professional culture with a "democratic cultural movement at the grass-roots."[34]

The key criterion distinguishing the grass-roots culture from the hegemonic culture is, of course, its participatory nature. The Greens' platform thus articulates the primary goal of the alternative culture, which focused on removing the barrier between the production and the consumption of culture in favor of a model in which everybody becomes a cultural practitioner and artist. Without any hesitation, the Greens demand more public funding for this grass-roots culture, siding with those voices of the alternative culture that favored accepting government pork (*Staatsknete*) for alternative projects.

Finally, the platform uses the Adornian term *culture industry*. This term remains vague, however, in comparison to the Tunix flier's "Coca-Cola-Karajan culture." The Greens do not make clear whether they see both "low" and "high" culture as the culture industry, or only "low" culture. The platform's more specific criticism of the culture industry follows the student movement's line of argument: the culture industry fosters a consumptive and passive attitude on the part of the audience, promotes stardom and the commercialization of culture, and adjusts and compensates for cultural underdevelopment instead of trying to change it. Even if a party platform is not the place for elaborate theorizing, it cannot be excused from clarifying the concepts it employs. On the other hand, the vagueness of the platform's cultural section was characteristic of the Greens, who had to forge at least a minimal consensus from the broad and diverse range of positions and ideological preferences within it.

While the Greens' platform matched their silence on cultural issues on the federal level, cultural committees had formed on the city level during the early 1980s. As a result, the Green cultural committees in Hamburg and West Berlin, which held quite opposing views, dominated the first Green congress on culture in January 1984, where the Federal Cultural Committee (*Bundesarbeitsgemeinschaft Kultur*) constituted itself.[35] The Greens' involvement with cultural issues intensified by the mid-1980s and was briefly pushed into the limelight by a controversial position paper that Christoph Ströbele and Udo Knapp delivered in March 1986 in the context of the federal parliament's ongoing discussion on culture. This paper triggered much debate and a publication by the Greens that collected the various Green positions on art and culture.

This publication—entitled "Brushing through the Struwelpeter's Hair: Toward a Green Cultural Politics"[36]—represents the state of the Greens' aesthetic discussion and its cultural politics in the mid-1980s. Jost Hermand's evaluation of this brochure sums up its problems. He argues that the Greens' analysis of the situation of contemporary culture is quite accurate, but that they are rather weak on articulating alternatives. He also points out another important aspect: "One can clearly see that this brochure was produced because of the pressure of the other parties' cultural-political offensive rather than because of their [the Greens'] own initiative."[37] Since the shift toward the issue of culture was not self-induced but the result of pressure from outside, we need to contextualize the Greens' discussion by examining why the Greens started this short but intense discussion on culture in the mid-1980s.

For one, the Greens' success in entering city councils and municipal administrations forced them to confront this issue, since West German cultural activities are in large parts publicly funded. This posed a challenge for which the Greens were little prepared, as the *taz* critically commented: "Their self-understanding was based on the fact that they had to decide about the allocation of money, which does not necessarily go hand in hand with competence. Rubbing their hands with glee, joyfully awaiting a rich flood of money, the independent artistic groups line up; on the other hand, the Greens have to watch helplessly as the budget for culture is cut."[38] However, Bernd Wagner, himself a member of the Greens and deeply involved in the Greens' search for a coherent aesthetic and cultural politics, contradicts the *taz*'s assessment of the budgetary situation. He argues that the overall spending for cultural affairs increased on all levels—municipal to federal—during the 1980s.[39]

These two observations are not as mutually exclusive as they appear at first glance to be. Even if the total amount spent on culture increased, this did not necessarily mean that the alternative culture benefited from it. In many cities, and particularly on the federal level, large sums of money were allocated to such prestige projects as the two new historical museums in Bonn and Berlin, which the CDU chancellor Helmut Kohl commissioned when he took office in 1982.[40] While the new emphasis on culture started in the 1970s on the municipal level and was driven by economic considerations—the growing competition of the cities to attract business headquarters—Wagner interprets the increased funding of culture on the federal level as a part of the neoconservative offensive in the struggle over cultural hegemony. He explains the renewed interest in culture in general as an attempt to distract from the economic, ecological, and political crisis of West Germany and in particular an attempt by the CDU/CSU to instrumentalize culture for creating a new national identity.

Wagner cites as one example the attacks on the West German cultural institutions abroad, the *Goethe Institut*, by the late CSU politician Franz Josef Strauß. According to Strauß, the Goethe Institutes operated with too broad a concept of culture, which included all aspects of daily life from environmental pollution to minority issues. In addition, Strauß criticized the institutes for focusing too much on the problems of West Germany instead of sticking to the eternal values of high culture, as the institution's namesake might suggest, and instead of emphasizing the achievements of the Federal Republic. Strauß's far-right position was complemented by Helmut Kohl's own agenda for a new positive perception of German history freed from the shadows of the Nazi past and thus as a tool to generate cultural and political meaning.[41] Kohl's agenda was indeed supported by historians, first and foremost Michael Stürmer, who functioned as advisor and speech writer for the chancellor, and Ernst Nolte, who taught during the 1980s at the Free University of Berlin and ignited the Historians' Debate with his article in the *Frankfurter Allgemeine Zeitung* that tried to dispel the singularity of the Holocaust.[42]

While this hard-core conservative position was exclusive, attempting to return to a 1950s notion of culture as truth, beauty, and goodness, the CDU's modernization wing proposed an inclusive approach to culture similar to that of the SPD. Since the 1970s the SPD had been under pressure by the new social movements and finally by the Greens, which emerged to the SPD's left and posed the danger of taking away constituencies. The SPD tried to reintegrate the growing alternative culture according to the concept of culture for everybody (*Kultur für Alle!*), which Hilmar Hoffmann, the longtime head of cultural affairs in Frankfurt and a SPD member, had developed and tried to implement in his city.

This SPD concept simply meant recognizing the diversity of cultural needs and interests in contemporary society and distributing public funding in a more equal manner. Instead of subsidizing only such established cultural institutions as the theater, opera house, and museum, the SPD supported community-based sociocultural centers (*Sozio-Zentren*) such as the adult education centers (*Volkhochschulen*) and youth centers or even alternative projects like the Factory for Culture, Sports, and Crafts in Berlin.[43] The SPD picked up on the demands of those within the alternative culture who wanted to have more public subsidies forthcoming for their projects. Wagner criticized the SPD's concept of culture for everybody on the same grounds as the conservative CDU position. Both, in his opinion, turn to culture as a means to substitute for the loss of meaning and social cohesion in a society whose traditional codes of identification—labor and economic success—are in crisis.[44]

By the mid eighties the cultural and political lines of confrontation had sharpened even within the federal legislature, which had to decide on numerous cultural issues. Among them was one of the most significant changes for postwar West Germany, the opening up of the hitherto state-organized radio and television markets to private competitors. The Greens were forced to show their colors and did so with the infamous Ströbele/Knapp position paper "Art and Culture—This Is Like Mustard and Whipped Cream,"[45] which was written mainly in response to the SPD.

Ströbele and Knapp criticized the SPD's cultural politics first and foremost as an attempt to depoliticize art and trap it in the ghetto of leisure time activity or on an elitist playground separate from the sphere of politics. Instead, they defined art in terms similar to those of the student movement, namely, as an articulation of the repressed desires and dreams of the people and artistic creativity as a means of resistance and opposition. Second, the antitechnology stance of many Greens found expression in the position paper's rejection of the SPD's call for equal access to the newly privatized media instead of condemning the media altogether. Ströbele and Knapp viewed the media merely as government-sponsored thought control and suggested that citizens disconnect themselves from the media. Third, they attacked the affirmative character of the government-sponsored cultural activities, particularly the proliferation of museums and historical exhibitions, since they smoothed over historical and social contradictions. Finally, they demanded the separation of art and government. No longer should government officials but the artists themselves have the power to determine how public funds for cultural and artistic activities and projects be spent.

These are only the core demands of the position paper, which was immediately challenged by other Greens. The distinction that Ströbele and Knapp made between art, which they defined positively as a mode of resistance, and culture as the government's instrumentalization of art for its own ideological ends came under special attack for setting up an artificial binary opposition between art and culture—or rather cultural politics—instead of recognizing how they are mutually entwined.

Aside from all its shortcomings, it was no surprise that the Knapp/Ströbele paper was controversial from the very beginning. The dispute about it only attests to the Greens' diversity, which rendered theorizing and programmatic statements much more complicated than for other parties, especially since the Greens aspired to act based on a consensus rather than on simple majority rule. This minimal consensus resulted in the idealized image of a green-alternative culture as the "totally different" defined by such categories as "decentralized, grass-roots oriented, democratic, contemporary, provocative, lively, and self-determined."[46] Certainly every member of the Green party could subscribe to these categories, since they did not define aesthetic culture in itself but described its formal framework.[47] Beyond this minimal consensus, the different factions within the Greens all made their distinct contributions to the debate on culture with one exception. The fundamentalists, which represented deep ecology within the party of the Greens, did not contribute much for the reasons discussed earlier in this chapter. Their privileging of nature made it ultimately impossible for them to develop a coherent aesthetic or cultural theory. Green aesthetic and cultural statements on art and culture show traces of various political traditions and persuasions, from hard-core socialist to more pragmatic and reconciliatory ones.

Eco-Socialist and Eco-Liberal Ideas

The most ideologically distinct contribution was the eco-socialist position on art and culture presented by the Green-Alternative Alliance Hamburg (Grün-Alternative-List Hamburg or GAL Hamburg). The concept of culture put forth by the GAL Hamburg followed a standard Marxist line of argument. It conceptualized West German society as a class society in which aesthetic culture fulfills a specific social function, namely, as an instrument of repression. "We assume that the masses are culturally deprived; that means we want to tear the privileges and exclusive monopoly over art and cultural institutions from the hands of the ruling classes of this society."[48] This did not, however, mean that the GAL Hamburg viewed aesthetic culture as inevitably affirmative. It argued that those in power control the access to cultural institutions in order to prevent a dissemination of aesthetic culture's potentially critical and emancipatory quality. In addition, aesthetic culture is neutralized through open censorship by integrating works of art and artists into the mainstream through commodification and by strict separation of art and politics.

This position followed the Adornian equation of mass culture with mass deception. Consequently, it attributed the differentiation of aesthetic culture into "low" and "high" to the class structure of society and rejected any kind of integration of "low" and "high" culture or alternative and hegemonic culture, particularly if it took on the form of cultural education in order to make high culture accessible to those who had been excluded from it. Instead, the proponents of this concept of cultural class struggle argued for a culture "of and with many and against the few (namely, the ruling classes of this society)."[49] They called on the Greens to promote the artistic creativity of the people in order to develop genuine collective cultural and artistic practices. The GAL Hamburg did not address aesthetic problems like form and content, but claimed that all the questions about qualitative criteria for aesthetic culture would fall into place without the authoritarian judgment of the professional critic characteristic for bourgeois culture.

{204}

At the center of this position, which opposed in particular Hilmar Hoffmann's (SPD) concept of culture for everyone, was the demand to seize power over cultural institutions in order to break the social structures of domination permeating all cultural production and reception:

> The target of cultural politics are the institutions of cultural production and dissemination in the broadest sense in their role as instruments of domination or emancipation in the class struggle. If it is the task of green-alternative cultural politics to safeguard the freedom of art, it always means the emancipatory side of culture, and not the freedom to make stupid, to distract or neutralize by ghettoizing art as the playground of the elites. Thus, we cannot stop with the idea of "culture for everybody" in the sense of a wider distribution of leisure time activities.[50]

Though this position refrained from prescribing the proper form aesthetic culture should take, its argument gained a normative dimension nevertheless. For one, the GAL Hamburg suggested a reorientation of Green aesthetic and cultural theory and practices toward the tradition of working-class culture during the Weimar Republic, particularly toward the Communist party's cultural concepts at that time. Secondly, it called on the artists to take a partisan position, that is, that artists join relevant social movements.[51] In other words, it argued for artistic production that actively promotes the class struggle, quite similar to the student movement's notion of art as a means of agitation and propaganda. The category of class was decisive for this wing of the Green party; nature as a significant concept was absent from its aesthetic conceptualizations.

The eco-socialist position on culture was not well received by the majority of the party, which quickly rejected it as a mechanical vulgar materialism.[52] Bernd Wagner, for example, took issue with the suggestion that a Green cultural politics should model itself after the Communist party during the Weimar Republic, pointing out that the Communist party's aesthetic was rather conservative and initially rejected such artists as John Heartfield and Georg Grosz cherished today by the entire left. Furthermore, he chided the GAL

Hamburg for a simplistic approach that reduces culture to art and cultural politics to budget politics. This criticism refers already to the position of the Alternative Alliance West Berlin (Grün-Alternative Liste West Berlin or AL West Berlin), which shaped up as a challenge for the GAL Hamburg's understanding of art as an instrument of the class struggle, although eco-socialist positions were not alien to the AL West Berlin.

The AL West Berlin's approach to art and culture was influenced both by the presence of a strong alternative culture in West Berlin and by a bourgeois understanding of culture, while it still engaged in some Marxist rhetoric. The AL West Berlin represents thus in a nutshell the fundamental problem of the Greens—their heterogeneity. Sabine Weißler articulated the alternative culture's ideas and demands more aggressively than her fellow activist Hajo Cornel, who was the other leading figure on the cultural committee of the AL West Berlin.[53] Weißler still applied Marxist theorems, viewing capitalism as the source of all alienation and stifling of human creativity. In addition, she used the Adornian notion of the culture industry but emphasized that the culture industry was itself only a product of capitalism and should therefore not be held solely responsible for the cultural passivity of the people.

The influence of the alternative culture on the AL West Berlin was evident in two ideas that Weißler adopted for a Green notion of culture: cultural self-determination and a broad concept of culture with an antiprofessional tendency. The notion of cultural self-determination, which was originally put forth by the Greens in Hessen, endorsed the idea of a participatory culture. Weißler pushed this concept, however, beyond the deep green or fundamentalist fetishization of do-it-yourself culture, arguing that the reception of cultural and artistic events or products represents a form of participation as well. "Autonomous cultural activity also occurs—and this is often forgotten—when someone reads a book, watches a movie, or writes a letter. It is everything that allows a person to reflect on his/her personal situation and to relate it in some way to the state of his/her environment."[54] Weißler defines culture in the broadest terms as encompassing the entire life world. Therefore, everybody is a cultural practitioner as soon as one recognizes oneself as an acting subject, recognizes one's own needs and desires, and reflects upon them with respect to one's entire environment.

Weißler is not interested in the objectification of culture, that is, art in the narrow sense produced by professional artists, but in culture as a process of reflection because "permanent reflection on the existing everyday world enables humanity to develop projections of a society that transcends the existing reality and becomes utopian. Every person in whatever social position is in principle able to do this, and not only artists and scientists, as the bourgeois understanding of culture would have us believe."[55] Weißler did not stop at a simplistic reflection theory but maintained that aesthetic culture projects at the same time a utopian vision of a better life as an alternative to the contemporary life of alienation. Weißler's position moved toward a bourgeois understanding of art and culture as a refuge for the desires and dreams of a better life, but at the same time she breaks with the bourgeois tradition that gives the artist a privileged position for cultural production.

Hajo Cornel's contribution to the discussion represented the influence of bourgeois concepts on Green cultural politics. For one, he took the green-alternative culture to task for its ghetto mentality, which looked only at its own countercultural navel and did not address pressing issues within the hegemonic culture. Second, he opposed the instrumentalization of aesthetic culture and argued instead for the autonomy of art. His idea of the autonomy of culture was distinct from conservative attempts to depoliticize culture in order to return it to the higher sphere of truth and beauty. Cornel was concerned with the destruction of a genuine bourgeois public sphere that raised the possibility of censorship by government and business. He argued that only the autonomy of culture allows art to be oppositional. Cornel's definition of culture as founded on a functioning public sphere thus encompassed such classical bourgeois values in the tradition of the Enlightenment as the ideas of emancipation, plurality, tolerance, difference, and democracy.

The return to the concept of the autonomy of art and culture within the Greens' debate did not abstract from culture's embeddedness within a particular sociohistorical context including structures of domination. The insistence on the autonomy of the sphere of culture grew out of the disenchantment with the late student movement's reduction of art to a means of propaganda and agitation for the class struggle. Traces of the latter's approach could be still found in the eco-socialist position of the GAL Hamburg. The dispute between the two most distinct positions, the GAL Hamburg's eco-socialist one and the AL West Berlin's eco-liberal one, which one might want to describe as a pragmatist or integrationist position, was nothing new but simply a replay of an old controversy. "Art instrumentalized as a weapon in the class struggle and art as an autonomous force of resistance are only the two sides of the same coin, which in all its various nuances permeates almost two centuries of our history in the discussions of *l'art pour l'art* versus committed art, but remained fruitless, because the question it posed was and still is reductive and beside the point."[56]

Though Bernd Wagner was in general right in his critical assessment of the Greens' debate on aesthetic culture, the reconciliatory position cannot be compared to an art-for-art's-sake paradigm, since this position showed itself to be aware that culture does not develop in a social and historical vacuum. It represented rather an attempt to mediate between opposing cultural needs and demands. The eco-liberals' pragmatic position worked well, for instance, in securing funding from municipal and state administrations for alternative cultural projects, but did not and could not succeed in articulating a genuine green aesthetic theory beyond the call for the absolutely different, whatever that might mean.

CONCLUSION: As the Story Ends

As we have seen, the new social movements of the 1970s and 1980s that constituted the green-alternative counterculture were both influenced by and at the same time opposed to the student movement. Hermann Glaser has convincingly summed up the discrepancy between the generation of 1968 and the following generations of the counterculture: "The student movement talked a lot about the liberation of sensuality, but did not develop a sensuous relationship to objects or even nature."[1] The later student movement's ossified Marxism had nothing to say about these two aspects of human existence—nature and aesthetic-sensual experience. The Sponti movement, most visible and influential at the universities from the mid-1970s, represented the first direct response and challenge to the student movement. It challenged the authoritarianism of both the hegemonic culture and the orthodox Marxist groups that dominated the late student movement. Often without being aware of it, the green-alternative culture instead revitalized aspects of the early student movement, namely, its antiauthoritarian concepts and practices.

The use of aesthetic practices for individual emancipation and as a means for expressing dissent had become popular again. These symbolic forms of protest included the extensive use of folk tunes, particularly within the ecology movement, the use of face paints among those countercultural groups that called themselves Urban Indians (*Stadtindianer*) or Mescaleros, the use of witch costumes by the women's movement in events like "Taking Back the Night," or the various die-ins staged by the peace movement. These aesthetic and at the same time political practices are strongly indebted to the antiauthoritarian tradition of 1960s protest, from Fritz Teufel's satirical response to the establishment's court authorities to teach-ins, sit-ins, and go-ins, which the student movement introduced into the political culture of postwar West Germany.

{209}

The student movement had also left its mark on subsequent countercultural developments on the theoretical level. Horkheimer and Adorno's theory of the culture industry remained a crucial element for the green-alternative culture's criticism of the hegemonic culture, but with a different bent. The students used this theory to explain the failure of the West German working class to become a revolutionary subject, blaming first and foremost the universal system of deception that capitalism creates by means of the culture industry. The students saw themselves, however, as outside this system of deception and, since their conceptualization of society worked with a hierarchical model of base and superstructure, the students understood themselves to be in an avant-garde position for the working class and the revolution.

In contrast, the alternative culture did not operate with a class model of society but in terms of the paradigm of center versus margins. It applied this paradigm to its own situation in contemporary West Germany, seeing itself as socially marginalized and as such endangered by the integrative power of the culture industry. This is most visible in the models of identification that the green-alternative culture chose: the fool and marginalized ethnic groups like Indians, as the name Urban Indians indicates. The heated debates about whether alternative projects should accept state subsidies or not also articulates this problem in terms of cultural politics. Yet the student movement and the green-alternative culture agreed in their criticism of another aspect of the culture industry. They attacked the passivity and consumer attitude that the culture industry cultivates in its audience.

While the early antiauthoritarian student movement believed in the emancipatory function of aesthetic culture for the oppressed individual, a class-based conceptualization of art became the dominant paradigm as the student movement turned toward a reductive application of Marxist theory. Two consequences of this turn thereby distinguish the student movement from the green-alternative culture. First, the students replaced the privileging of the individual within bourgeois society with the privileging of a collective class subject. Second, the students' interest in aesthetic culture focused mainly on the political application of art, that is, art's function as a means of agitation and propaganda for the class struggle. It is therefore not surprising that the student movement modeled its own aesthetic practices on the agitprop techniques of the left during the Weimar Republic, for instance, in their street theater performances.

As we have seen, the alternative culture had a quite different position. Analogous to the new social movements' idea of a participatory politics in opposition to the hegemonic culture's representative politics, the green-alternative culture developed the idea of a participatory culture in contrast to a mere representative one. Its model of a participatory culture adhered to the principle "Participation is everything!" Although many of the green-alternative culture's aesthetic practices were collective ones or designed to constitute community, its focus was on individual participation.

Aesthetic practices, therefore, had a different meaning for the green-alternative culture than for the later student movement. Since bourgeois aesthetics had always privileged the individual subject, the students promoted an aesthetics that gave voice to the collective, documented "objective reality," and took an overt political stance, as in the many forms of documentary literature and the street theater. At the center of the green-alternative culture's interest in aesthetic practices was the desire for self-expression and self-actualization, for the rediscovery and expression of individual subjectivity in accordance with the concept of the politics of the self.

The generation of the student movement watched the alternative culture's turn away from conceptualizing the subject solely in terms of class and toward matters of individual subjectivity and the notion of the politics of the self with much suspicion and often a clear lack of understanding. For many in the generation of 1968, the new cultural paradigms of the self and subjectivity amounted to treason, to a sellout to the hegemonic culture, especially in light of the ideological reappropriation of the alternative culture's interest in subjectivity.

By the mid-1980s the argument that the alternative culture had sold out the countercultural project seemed to be substantiated by the changes a visitor might observe in the small university towns of West Germany, which had been bastions of countercultural life. Tübingen, for example, had been one of the first strongholds of an alternative lifestyle and for the Greens in the late 1970s and early 1980s.[2] During that time, the alternative culture's "uniform" — purple overalls and Indian clothing — and the improvised chaos and secondhand interior design of numerous bookstores, Third World shops, and health food cafés dominated the city's landscape. Returning to Tübingen in the mid-1980s, the same visitor could suffer quite a culture shock; the display of overalls and Indian dresses had been replaced by the national and international chain-store couture from Benetton to Marco Polo; the seedy comfort of the alternative culture's health food cafés had given way to the slick facades of high-tech and neon-lit bistros, preferably with a touch of Italy: gentrification the German way.

Matthias Horx's observation regarding the changing eating culture of the West Germans can be cited in support of this "yuppification" of the alternative culture by the mid-1980s. Horx maintains that the student movement was far removed from any gourmet pleasures; the revolutionary student simply wolfed down any kind of food indiscriminately as long as it kept him or her going for the next protest march. Eating was just a means to sustain life for the revolution. The alternative movement's concern with the body and indulgence in health food from whole grains to tofu replaced the student movement's obliviousness to dietary issues. According to Horx, when the alternative movement slowly dissolved in the mid-1980s, it discovered the sensuous pleasures of gourmet cooking.[3]

The question remains whether we can legitimately conclude from these changes in diet and clothing that the post-1968 counterculture had sold out to the hegemonic culture. Perhaps this one-way description of the cultural transformations within the alternative culture is rather reductive and based on a misunderstanding of the function and development of countercultures. The complex history of continuations and breaks between different generations of the counterculture and of the struggle between resistance and reintegration of the counterculture into the mainstream can be illustrated with two slogans popular during the student movement and the alternative culture. Slogans and graffiti played, after all, an important role for the counterculture as an alternative means of communication and self-expression. They could be found everywhere; on public buildings, the pavement, and on clothing, particularly within the punk/squatters' movement.[4]

The slogan "All Power to the Imagination!," which adorned many walls and other public spaces during the late 1960s, captures the students' adaptation of Marcuse's reinterpretation of Freudian theory. It expressed not only the students' belief in imagination's potential for self-actualization but also their belief in the necessity of transforming the desires and demands articulated in imagination into revolutionary energy. The slogan itself, a demand on or maybe even a threat to the hegemonic culture, calls for the realization of the desires repressed in contemporary society. It thereby addressed the question of power and power relationships and furthermore, if stated as an imperative—Fantasy, take power!—a willingness to be in power. It articulates the intention to transform the material and political conditions of life in order to make dreams come true.

The post-1968 counterculture's slogan picked up on the student movement's call for imagination and demonstrates the continuation of ideas from the student movement to the alternative culture. The emancipation of the repressed imaginative and creative faculties of the human being were still an issue for the alternative culture. However, the slogan now reads differently: "Meer Fantasie—und Muscheln," perhaps best translated as "The Ocean/More Imagination—and Mussels/Shells."[5] The linguistic play with phonetic similarity and written difference—"Meer/Mehr"—was typical of the alternative culture's sense of irony and use of puns. Whereas the students' slogan referred only to an intangible and immaterial power—imagination—which it wanted to see take power, the alternative culture's slogan embeds imagination in the material world; the ocean and mussels or shells. But why the ocean and mussels/shells in particular? we might ask.

The ocean, or rather the beach, has for a long time functioned as an idyllic place, a *locus amoenus* in Western culture. Both the alternative and mainstream culture make use of this old, positive imagery to articulate their repressed desires and hopes. The alternative culture employed it in the Tunix flier, as we have seen, and also in the name of one of its main publications *Pflasterstrand* (Pavement beach), thus reappropriating as well as popularizing the slogan "Underneath the pavement lies the beach," which dates back to the student movement. However, the beach and the ocean signify for most Germans the best time of the year, namely, their vacation. The beach in mainstream culture symbolizes not only the economic achievements of West Germany but also pleasure, spontaneity, authenticity, or in other words, the breaking free from the boredom of day-to-day lives.

Does this mean that the desires of the hegemonic and the counter-culture have converged into one idyllic image of vacation and leisure time by the mid-1980s? This understanding of the slogan is only one of its possible readings. If one resolves the pun *Mee/hr* (the ocean/more) differently, the alternative culture seemed to call for more imagination, expressing discontent with the results of the first call for fantasy in the 1960s. Still, even this reading does not dispel the most significant alteration of the original: More imagination *and* mussels. Mussels are considered gourmet food in Germany and the epitome of elitist culture. This complicates an interpretation of the slogan even further and raises many questions. For instance, does the alternative culture want to have it all: the status of a countercul-ture as well as the blessings of yuppie consumer culture — mussels for supper? Has the establishment once again successfully reinte-grated the counterculture by means of the culture industry's repres-sive desublimation? Or can the slogan perhaps be understood in a different manner?

Let us begin unraveling this ambiguous statement and the de-velopment of the counterculture that it describes with a reference to the worst-case scenario — the reintegration hypothesis. Applying Marcuse's concept of repressive desublimation, one can read the slo-gan as an expression of the alternative culture's reintegration by the hegemonic culture. Such an argument would claim that the slogan no longer calls for imagination to take power but simply asks for a few more crumbs from the table of the hegemonic culture. Late capitalist society's repressive tolerance allows only for an immediate gratification of desires on the surface without changing the material conditions of life and thus precludes true gratification.

In this context, the double meaning of the German word *Muschel*, namely, "mussel" and "shell," gains significance. The shell does not necessarily have a content; it can very well be empty. This is exactly the nature of repressive desublimation; it offers only the illusion of gratification in order to reconcile the individual with his or her unsatisfying conditions of life. The strategy of repressive desublimation helps to contain the counterculture's subversive potential, expressed in its desire for the rule of imagination in opposition to instrumental rationality. In short, the alternative culture has become more interested in the superficial bliss that the hegemonic culture happily grants—the German's annual travelmania to the Mediterranean shores, as well as the preoccupation with gourmet cooking since the 1980s—in order to prevent imagination from being turned into revolutionary energies and structural change, as the student movement desired. Thus one could indeed read the slogan simply as "The Ocean, Imagination—and Mussels," that is, as signifying the seduction of the alternative culture by the hegemonic culture's material offerings.

This interpretation of the slogan, or rather the development of the post-1968 counterculture, is characteristic of a social theory that considers change in today's world to be impossible. Horx, who has written extensively on the alternative culture, does not buy into the argument that the alternative movement has been successfully contained by the hegemonic culture. He maintains that the alternative movement had a tremendous impact on postwar West German society even though it also seemed to have come to an end in the mid-1980s. He argues that the diversity of the alternative culture allowed for a dissemination of alternative values and ideas into society on a broad scale. The multitude of cultures—ecological, feminist, gay/lesbian, and many more—enriched each other while dissolving the sharp dogmatic outline characteristic of the innumerable orthodox left-wing groups in the wake of the student movement. They were less threatening than the students' rigid class analysis and privileging of the collective. "As a result, the new desires made inroads into the old world. Alternative movement: this is for quite some time now no longer a label for a small, brave, radical social stratum. There is hardly anyone in this society who hasn't been confronted with these alternative impulses, whether directly or indirectly, even if it was only in doubting the old certainties or in desires that were buried behind career goals and utility, old habits and discouragement."[6]

Horx's argument rests on a theory of cultural hegemony that argues that this hegemony is always contested. As a result, the hegemonic culture's strategy of co-opting through repressive desublimation does not inevitably succeed—an idea that the scholars of the Birmingham Center for Contemporary Cultural Studies have put forth with respect to the 1960s counterculture. They argue that " 'repressive desublimation' is a dangerous, two-sided phenomenon. When the codes of traditional culture are broken, and new social impulses are set free, they are impossible fully to contain."[7]

This perception of society opens up a different way of conceptualizing what happened to the West German counterculture from the 1960s to the mid-1980s. Horx suggests that the alternative culture dissolved into three groups: at one extreme, a totally reintegrated minority that returns to the maw of the hegemonic culture, and at the other end, a marginalization of those parts of post-1968 counterculture that did not manage to leave their alternative ghetto situation behind. Between these two groups, an alternative middle class emerged, which he describes as follows: "Their income is by now close to that of the bourgeois middle class; their consciousness is no longer strictly alternative, but rather green. They do not feud with the old ideals, they do not reject them, but neither do they return to the old values. This countercultural middle class no longer desires alternative purity. It leaves the rigid value system of the totally different behind, but still insists on alternative values. Treason is carried to extremes: one wants to have both money and meaning, stable relationships and a reliable circle of friends, collective spheres and radical slogans—also and particularly in parliament."[8]

Based on Horx's description of the alternative culture, the slogan "The Ocean/More Imagination—and Mussels/Shells," gains yet another meaning. By the mid-1980s the alternative culture wants to have it all and, for the alternative middle class, can also afford it: enjoying the ocean and beach, more imagination, and mussels for supper. The alternative middle class did not necessarily commit treason. It was certainly willing to compromise, but without completely renouncing its former radical ideas, as Horx points out. Instead of continuously striking an oppositional pose based on rigidly defined principles, which easily leads into ghettoization, the alternative middle class aimed at developing strategies for affecting the hegemonic culture. The counterculture indeed fell back on more traditional means, but this was a strategic retreat similar to the student movement's long march through the institutions in order to obtain influence and affect change. A reappropriation of sensuous pleasures associated with a more affluent bourgeois lifestyle can be one result and should not be mistaken for a sellout to the hegemonic culture. It is part of the process of negotiation characteristic of the ongoing cultural struggle, which in turn accounts for the counterculture's continued influence on German society.

If the counterculture was or is successful in implementing some of its values and ideas into mainstream culture, it also has lost some of its oppositional profile. Defining itself once and for all as a counterculture is simply impossible. The clear distinction between hegemonic culture and counterculture will always be in flux. Thus the counterculture will also be always challenged to define itself anew when facing the fact that it has successfully influenced the dominant culture, that is, its ideas and values have been reintegrated into the mainstream. For instance, only after the ecology movement had "gone mainstream" by founding a party to enter parliament did it achieve its goal of making ongoing environmental destruction a top issue of the political discourse. Today all parties have—more or less convincingly—responded in their platforms to this new political challenge. The transformation of the *taz* represents another example of this process of cultural negotiation. The *taz* developed a more moderate profile by distancing itself from the utterly radical fringes of the alternative culture at the same time that we can locate the dissolution of this culture into dropouts and an alternative middle class.[9]

The history of the West German counterculture should therefore not be mistaken as a cyclical one, that is, the eternal return of the same. It is perhaps better described with the image of an upward spiral. The post-1968 counterculture revisited the ideas of its predecessors in dissent, taking up those that proved to be still valid, such as antiauthoritarian concepts, but at the same time introducing new ideas to respond to the redefined terrain of discontent and social conflict. These demands remained contentious until they were addressed by mainstream culture, often by means of an appropriation of countercultural ideas. Environmentalism was just one idea that the counterculture successfully launched into public consciousness. Others were and are less visible.

"Meer Fantasie—und Muscheln" indeed articulates the broader horizon of the post-1968 counterculture, namely, that opposition to the hegemonic culture can take various and different forms. No one said that the road to the beach of Tunix would be a short one—and given the chaotic and turbulent history of West Germany's counter-cultural movements, how could anyone expect it to be straight?

NOTES

INTRODUCTION

1. See, for instance, Sarkar, *New Social Movements*; Wasmuht, *Alternativen zur alten Politik?*; Roth and Rucht, *Neue soziale Bewegungen*; Brand, *Aufbruch in eine andere Gesellschaft*; Raschke, *Soziale Bewegungen*; Schäfer, *Neue soziale Bewegungen*, 1983.

2. Williams, *Sociology of Culture*, 11.

3. Clarke et al., "Subcultures, Cultures and Class," 10–11.

4. See Gramsci, *Selection from the Prison Notebooks of Antonio Gramsci*.

5. Clarke et al., "Subcultures, Cultures and Class," 40.

6. Clarke et al., "Subcultures, Cultures and Class," 40.

7. Clarke et al., "Subcultures, Cultures and Class," 40–42.

8. Clarke et al., "Subcultures, Cultures and Class," 60–63; see also their schema on p. 70.

9. Hirsch, *Der Sicherheitsstaat*, 151–53.

10. For a discussion of the so-called *Schreibbewegung*, see *Literaturmagazin* 11: "Schreiben oder Literatur" (1979).

1. HEGEMONY AND SUBCULTURES IN THE 1950S

1. See Harald Thon's comment in Hoche, ed., *Die Lage war noch nie so ernst*, 231. On the band Geier Sturzflug, see Döpfner and Garms, *Neue deutsche Welle*, 34, 213. The original lyrics read: "Ja dann wird wieder in die hände gespuckt/wir steigern das bruttosozialprodukt" (Geier Sturzflug, "Bruttosozialprodukt," *Heiße Zeiten*). All translations except where noted are my own.

2. For historical accounts of the 1950s of more or less critical value, see Eisenberg and Linke, *Fuffziger Jahre*; Franck, *Die fünfziger Jahre*; Grube and Richter, *Die Gründerjahre der BRD*, and Siepmann, *Bikini: Die fünfziger Jahre*. "Heimweh nach den falschen Fünfzigern," *Spiegel* 14 (3 Apr. 1978): 90–111; see also Brock, "Löcher im Himmel" *Spiegel* 14 (3 Apr. 1978): 114.

3. See, for instance, *Schlager* hits such as *Eine weiße Hochzeitskutsche* (1952; A white marriage carriage), *Florentinische Nächte* (1952; Nights in Florence), and *Ganz Paris träumt von der Liebe* (1955; All of Paris dreams of love).

4. Von Trotta, *Die Bleierne Zeit*.

5. According to Hardach, monthly wages increased from DM243 in 1950 to DM512 in 1960. See his "Die Wirtschaft der fünfziger Jahre: Restauration und Wirtschaftswunder," 58. For more statistical material on the 1950s

economic development see also Morsey, *Die Bundesrepublik Deutschland.*

6. Siepmann, *Bikini*, 28, and Grube and Richter, *Gründerjahre der* BRD, 106–9.

7. In 1957 the first secretary of economics, Ludwig Erhard, published a book, *Wohlstand für alle* (published in English as *Prosperity through Competition*), outlining and legitimizing his economic agenda.

8. On "nivellierte Mittelstandsgesellschaft" see Glaser, *Kulturgeschichte der Bundesrepublik Deutschland* 2:75–81, 94, and Hermand, *Kultur im Wiederaufbau*, 255–56.

9. Bürger, "Das Erbe der fünfziger Jahre," 165–66, and Danzmann, "Bericht über die fünfziger Jahre in der Schule," 205–6.

10. Noelle and Neumann, *The Germans: Public Opinion Polls 1947–1966.*

11. For a critical evaluation of the empirical data, see Manfred Wannöffel, "Auf politischem Gebiet kriegen Sie keine guten Antworten von mir," 26–27.

12. Schelsky, *Skeptische Generation*, 75–78.

13. Wasmund, "Leitbilder und Aktionsformen Jugendlicher nach dem Zweiten Weltkrieg bis zu den 60er Jahren," 218–19.

14. Hermand, *Kultur im Wiederaufbau*, 263.

15. Clarke et al., "Subcultures, Cultures and Class," 39.

16. Hermand, *Kultur im Wiederaufbau*, 387.

17. Hermand, *Kultur im Wiederaufbau*, 409.

18. See Hartung, *Experimentelle Literatur und Konkrete Poesie*; Gumpel, *"Concrete" Poetry from East and West Germany*; and Kessler, *Untersuchungen zur Konkreten Dichtung.*

19. The most significant papers read at this conference are collected in *Germanistik: Eine deutsche Wissenschaft.*

20. Glaser, "Das Exil fand nicht statt," 260–84.

21. Glaser, "Das Exil fand nicht statt," 268.

22. Doehlemann, *Germanisten in Schule und Hochschule*, 153.

23. Glaser, "Das Exil fand nicht statt," 265.

24. Achim S. (b. 1934), in Krüger, "Viel Lärm ums Nichts? Jugendliche Existentialisten in den 50er Jahren," 264–65.

25. Hebdige, *Subculture*, 17.

26. Hebdige, *Subculture*, 18.

27. Curt Bondy's claim that the Halbstarken did not come from one socioeconomic strata seems strange, judging by the statistical data he himself provides. He states that 68 percent were apprentices in industry or crafts, 25 percent were apprentices in white collar professions, and only 7.4

percent were students, a category that he does not specify any further (*Jugendliche stören die Ordnung*, 55).

28. Krüger, "Exis habe ich keine gesehen: Auf der Suche nach einer jugendlichen Gegenkultur in den 50er Jahren." See also his article "Viel Lärm ums Nichts?"

29. Krüger, "Exis habe ich keine gesehen," 143.

30. Hebdige, *Subculture*, 130–31.

31. See Bondy, *Jugendliche stören die Ordnung*, 26.

32. Krüger, "Exis habe ich keine gesehen," 143.

33. Von Wensierski, "Die Anderen nannten uns Halbstarke," 103.

34. Fröhner, *Wie stark sind die Halbstarken?*, 10.

35. Bondy, *Jugendliche stören die Ordnung*, 84.

36. Bondy, *Jugendliche stören die Ordnung*, 18.

37. Clarke et al., "Subcultures, Cultures and Class," 62.

38. Von Wensierski, "Die Anderen nannten uns Halbstarke," 107–13.

39. Bondy, *Jugendliche störten die Ordnung*, 79.

40. Von Wensierski, "Die Anderen nannten uns Halbstarke," 109–10.

41. Lindner, "Jugendkultur: Stilisierte Widerstände," 14. Although Lindner uses here the term *boogie-woogie*, which denotes 1930s and 1940s popular dance music, Lindner discusses primarily the reception of rock 'n' roll during the 1950s in West Germany. Rock 'n' roll historically developed out of boogie-woogie, and the response to this wild new dance in the 1930s was not much different from that to rock 'n' roll in the 1950s.

42. See Kuhnert and Ackermann, "Jenseits von Lust und Liebe? Jugendsexualität in den 50er Jahren," 43–81.

2. "ALL POWER TO THE IMAGINATION!"

1. Clarke et al., "Subcultures, Cultures and Class," 62.

2. Clarke et al., "Subcultures, Cultures and Class," 61.

3. On Picht, see Glaser, *Kulturgeschichte der* BRD 2:308–9.

4. For an extensive discussion of this issue see Bopp, "Faszination durch Gewalt," 119–23.

5. The following publications demonstrate this and represent the most comprehensive studies and accounts of the student movement: Bauß, *Die Studentenbewegung* (1977); Zimmer, "Wo sind sie geblieben?" *Die Zeit* 24–26 (3–17 June 1977); Mosler, *Was wir wollten, was wir wurden* (1977); Bieling, *Tränen der Revolution* (1988); Cohn-Bendit and Mohr, *1968* (1988); *Früchte der Revolte* (1988); Mündemann, *Die 68er* (1988); Seibold, *Die 68er* (1988); Dahrendorf, "Die Revolution, die nie stattfand," *Die Zeit* 20 (13 May 1988): 3; *Spiegel-Spezial: Die wilden 68er* (1988); and

the following three contributions in *Aus Politik und Zeitgeschichte* B20/88 (13 May 1988): Leggewie, "1968: Ein Laboratorium der nachindustriellen Gesellschaft?" 3–15; Lübbe, "Der Mythos der 'kritischen Generation,'" 17–25; and Sontheimer, "Rebellion ist gerechtfertigt," 36–46.

6. McCormick, *Politics of the Self*, 47; see also Hohendahl, "Politisierung der Kunsttheorie: Zur ästhetischen Diskussion nach 1965," in *Deutsche Literatur in der Bundesrepublik seit 1965*, ed. Lützeler and Schwarz, 282–99.

7. Bock, *Geschichte des "linken Radikalismus,"* 208–21; Cohn-Bendit and Mohr, *1968*, 106; and Bauß, *Studentenbewegung*, 300.

8. McCormick, *Politics of the Self*, 32. I am following by and large McCormick's periodization, though I differ in viewing the Spontis already as a new countermovement rather than an integral part of the student movement; see also Hübner, "Klau mich, oder Die Veränderung von Verkehrsformen," 230, and Schmid, "Die Wirklichkeit eines Traumes," 11.

9. Markovits and Gorski, *German Left*, 47.

10. Markovits and Gorski, *German Left*, 54–56.

11. Bauß, *Studentenbewegung*, 187.

12. Kuckuck, *Student und Klassenkampf*, 60–61.

13. "Ein Gespräch über Zukunft," 149.

14. See Marcuse's line of argument in his *One-Dimensional Man*.

15. McCormick, *Politics of the Self*, 47.

16. Cohn-Bendit and Mohr, *1968*, 7–8.

17. For a very detailed account of Marcuse's influence on the student movement see Lehnardt and Volmer, *Politik zwischen Kopf und Bauch*, 63–83, and Juchler, *Rebellische Subjektivität und Internationalismus*. For a very critical evaluation of the student movement's adaptation of psychoanalysis see Reich, who was himself an active participant, "Sexuelle Revolution: Ein Rückblick aus dem Reich der Mitte," 45–72.

18. See Sigmund Freud, "Civilized Sexual Morality and Modern Nervous Illness" (1908); "Totem and Taboo" (1912–13); and "Civilization and Its Discontents" (1929).

19. Marcuse's *Eros and Civilization* appeared in German translation as early as 1957, and in a second edition in 1965.

20. Jameson, *Marxism and Form*, 107.

21. Marcuse, *Eros and Civilization*, 142.

22. Marcuse, *Eros and Civilization*, 143.

23. Marcuse, *Eros and Civilization*, 181.

24. Marcuse, *Eros and Civilization*, 179–80.

25. Schmid, "Wirklichkeit eines Traumes," 13; see also Peter Schneider's novel *Lenz*.

26. Schneider, "Phantasie im Spätkapitalismus," 1–37.

27. Schneider, "Phantasie im Spätkapitalismus," 17.

28. Marcuse, *Eros and Civilization*, 185.

29. Marcuse, *One-Dimensional Man*, 63, and *Eros and Civilization*, 148–49. See as well his *Essay on Liberation*, in which he calls for the Great Refusal as a mode of political activism. He also saw in the student movement the beginning of such a Great Refusal.

30. Marcuse, *On Liberation*, 43.

31. Marcuse, *Eros and Civilization*, 144–47, and *One-Dimensional Man*, 66–69.

32. Schneider, "Phantasie im Spätkapitalismus," 21.

33. Schneider, "Phantasie im Spätkapitalismus," 31–32.

34. Scharang, "Thesen zur Kulturrevolution," 28–29; Schneider, "Phantasie im Spätkapitalismus," 30.

35. Bauß, *Studentenbewegung*, 301.

36. Schneider, "Phantasie im Spätkapitalismus," 3–4. See also Rudi Dutschke on the cultural revolution, "Die Widersprüche des Spätkapitalismus," 63.

37. Schneider, "Phantasie im Spätkapitalismus," 1.

38. Scharang, "Thesen zur Kulturrevolution," 26.

39. Marcuse, *One-Dimensional Man*, 12.

40. Marcuse, *One-Dimensional Man*, 31.

41. Marcuse, "Repressive Tolerance," 81–117.

42. Dutschke, Rabehl, and Semler, "Ein Gespräch über die Zukunft," 151–58.

43. Schneider, "Phantasie im Spätkapitalismus," 20–32.

44. Schneider, "Phantasie im Spätkapitalismus," 29.

45. Schneider, "Phantasie im Spätkapitalismus," 31.

46. Büscher, *Wirklichkeitstheater*, 7; Huyssen, *After the Great Divide*, particularly the chapter "The Cultural Politics of Pop," 141–59.

47. Scharang, "Thesen zur Kulturrevolution," 52–53.

48. See the chapter "The Culture Industry: Enlightenment As Mass Deception" in *Dialectic of Enlightenment*, 120–67.

49. Adorno, "Culture Industry Reconsidered," 86.

50. Adorno, "Culture Industry Reconsidered," 90.

51. See also Adorno, *Aesthetic Theory*, 210–12, 355–57, and 443–45.

52. Berman, "Adorno, Marxism and Art," *Telos* 34 (1977–78): 163.

53. SDS-Gruppe "Kultur und Revolution" (Berlin), "Kunst als Ware der Bewußtseinsindustrie," *Die Zeit* 48 (3 Dec. 1968): 12.

54. Hohendahl, "Politisierung der Kunsttheorie," 283.

55. Huyssen, *After the Great Divide*, 150.

56. The debate continued into 1969. See also Peter Handke, "Totgeborene Sätze," *Die Zeit* 49 (6 Dec. 1968): 17–18; Dieter E. Zimmer, "Die große Liquidierung," *Die Zeit* 49 (6 Dec. 1968): 18; Peter Hamm, "Versäumte Solidarität. Eine Erwiderung auf Peter Handkes Aufsatz 'Totgeborene Sätze,'" *Die Zeit* 50 (13 Dec. 1968): 18; Bazon Brock, "Warum kürzere Röcke?" *Die Zeit* 52 (27 Dec. 1968): 9–10; Dieter Wellershoff, "Puritaner, Konsumenten und die Kritik," *Die Zeit* 1 (3 Jan. 1969): 9–11; Uwe Nettelbeck, "Recht hat, wer zuletzt lacht," *Die Zeit* 2 (10 Jan. 1969): 11–12; Erich Fried, "Ja, aber . . . und . . . Der Warencharakter der Kunst ist kein Grund zur Verzweiflung," *Die Zeit* 3 (17 Jan. 1969): 13; Helmut Reichel and Gert Schäfer, "Was heißt hier 'Ware?' Die Antwort des Karl Marx," *Die Zeit* 4 (24 Jan. 1969): 12; Michael Buselmeier (for the association Arbeitskreis Kulturrevolution in Heidelberg), "Gesellschaftliche Arbeit statt Kunst: Schluß der Diskussion," *Die Zeit* 5 (31 Jan. 1969): 11–12.
57. SDS-Gruppe, "Kunst als Ware," 12.
58. SDS-Gruppe, "Kunst als Ware," 12.
59. SDS-Gruppe, "Kunst als Ware," 12.
60. SDS-Gruppe, "Kunst als Ware," 12.
61. Huyssen, *After the Great Divide*, 150.
62. Hillach, "Walter Benjamin: Korrektiv Kritischer Theorie," 64–65.
63. See Scharang, "Zur Emanzipation der Kunst," 67.
64. Huyssen, *After the Great Divide*, 9.
65. Lethen, "Zur Materialistischen Kunsttheorie Benjamins," 228.
66. Scharang, "Zur Emanzipation der Kunst," 72.
67. Scharang, "Zur Emanzipation der Kunst," 78.
68. Scharang, "Zur Emanzipation der Kunst," 80.
69. Scharang, "Zur Emanzipation der Kunst," 81.
70. Benjamin, "The Work of Art in the Age of Mechanical Reproduction," 242.
71. Enzensberger, "Industrialization of the Mind," 4.
72. Enzensberger, "Industrialization of the Mind," 13f.
73. Michel, "Ein Kranz für die Literatur," 177.
74. Michel, "Ein Kranz für die Literatur," 176.
75. Enzensberger, "Commonplaces," 39.
76. Enzensberger, "Commonplaces," 43.
77. Michel, "Ein Kranz für die Literatur," 170.
78. Michel, "Ein Kranz für die Literatur," 171–73.
79. Michel, "Ein Kranz für die Literatur," 186.
80. Enzensberger, "Commonplaces," 37.
81. Enzensberger, "Commonplaces," 43–44.

82. Enzensberger, "Commonplaces," 44.

83. Berghahn, "Operative Ästhetik," 279.

84. Weiss, *Discourse on the Progress of the Prolonged War of Liberation in Viet Nam*, 65–230; Enzensberger, *The Havana Inquiry* and *Der kurze Sommer der Anarchie* (The short summer of anarchy).

85. For material on street theater see first and foremost the collection of plays and statements by street theater groups in Hüfer, *Straßentheater*; Büscher, *Wirklichkeitstheater*, and Kändler, "Das Straßentheater stellt sich vor," 1366–71.

86. See the dispute that Peter Handke's position on street theater ignited: Peter Handke, "Straßentheater und Theatertheater," *Theater Heute* 4 (1968): 4–7, and "Für das Straßentheater gegen das Straßentheater," *Theater Heute* 7 (1968): 6–7, as well as "Theater und Revolte: Eine Debatte" in the 1968 yearbook of *Theater Heute*, 25–37.

87. The label independent or free theater groups referred not only to the fact that these groups received no public subsidies, but also that they understood themselves to be an alternative to the hierarchically structured, highly subsidized public theaters; see Büscher, *Wirklichkeitstheater*, 10–11.

88. Büscher, *Wirklichkeitstheater*, 9.

89. Das Sozialistische Straßentheater Berlin (West), "Kritik und Selbstkritik," 292.

90. See, for example, the "Franz-Gans-Kampagne" of the Munich group POFO, described in Hüfer, *Straßentheater*, 279–82.

91. See Buselmeier, "Bedingungen des Straßentheaters," 332.

92. For a detailed description of the predecessors see Stourac and McCreery, *Theatre As a Weapon*, and for the connection to the street theater of the 1960s and early 1970s Büscher, *Wirklichkeitstheater*, 91–95, 146–49.

93. Von zur Mühlen, "Straßentheater," 216; Ulla Hahn, *Literatur in der Aktion*, 89, and Hüfer, *Straßentheater*, 248.

94. Hüfer, *Straßentheater*, 257.

95. Meinel, "Möglichkeiten eines sozialistischen Straßentheaters," 306–12, and Buselmeier, "Bedingungen des Straßentheaters," 320–33. Das Sozialistische Straßentheater Berlin (West), "Kritik und Selbstkritik," 292.

3. POST-1968 BLUES

1. On this issue and the women's movement from the perspective of its early activists see Schwarzer, *So fing es an! Die neue Frauenbewegung*; von Soden, *Der große Unterschied: Die neue Frauenbewegung und die siebziger Jahre*; and Altbach et al., eds., *German Feminism*.

2. McCormick, *Politics of the Self*, 72.

3. Kraushaar, "Thesen zum Verhältnis von Alternativ- und Fluchtbewegung," 12.

4. Kramer, *New Subjectivity*, 41.

5. See Koebner, *Tendenzen der deutschen Gegenwartsliteratur*, 215–19.

6. Beicken, "Neue Subjektivität," 164–81. Barbara Kosta also cautions against using the term New Subjectivity too broadly in *Recasting Autobiography*, 39–40.

7. See Hohendahl, *The Institution of Criticism*, 75–76.

8. See Winter, "Von der Dokumentarliteratur zur 'neuen Subjektivität,'" 95–113.

9. Kramer, *New Subjectivity*, 8.

10. For historical accounts of RAF terrorism see Peters, *RAF: Terrorismus in Deutschland*, and Aust, *Der Baader-Meinhof Komplex*.

11. See Heckelmann and Heumann, "Herbert Marcuse und die Szene 1978." Both authors are members of the conservative Ring Christlich Demokratischer Studenten (RCDS). Their article represents an excellent example of this line of argument. See also Holthusen, who tried to prove that Jean-Paul Sartre and Max Frisch were the intellectual fathers of terrorism in "Sartre in Stammheim: Literatur und Terrorismus."

12. For a short chronology of the legal measures see Schröder, *Terrorismus*, 86–87.

13. Buch, "Vorbericht," 12.

14. Rutschky, *Erfahrungshunger*, 133, 157.

15. Sandford, *New German Cinema*, 148; see also Schreitmüller, *Filme aus Filmen*, 237.

16. As another example of articulating the changes within the political culture see Botzat, *Deutscher Herbst*, 9–16.

17. Quote from the film *Deutschland im Herbst* (Germany in Autumn).

18. The Buback Obituary was originally published in the *Göttinger Nachrichten* 25 Apr. 1977: 10–12. Since the mass media represented the text only in distorting quotations, it was reissued by numerous other groups, for instance, by a group of university professors under the title *"Buback: Ein Nachruf": Eine Dokumentation*, 3–6, and distributed at cost price. I am quoting from this edition of the text. The obituary can also be found in the following publications: Brückner, *Mescalero-Affäre*, 24–25; Glotz, *Die Innenausstattung der Macht*, 169–73; Hoche, ed., *Die Lage war noch nie so ernst*, 197–201; and Dietz et al., eds., *Klamm, Heimlich & Freunde*, 122–24.

19. Kosta, *Recasting Autobiography*, 36.

20. Reich-Ranicki, "Rückkehr zur schönen Literatur," 21.

21. See as well Hans Dieter Zimmermann's contribution to the question of literary New Subjectivity, "Die mangelhafte Subjektivität," 468–78. Jörg Drew's polemic criticism of the poetry of New Subjectivity had triggered the so-called Poetry Debate in 1977. The debate was originally carried out in the periodical *Akzente*, but the single articles were again published in Hans, *Lyrik-Katalog Bundesrepublik*.

22. Stephan, "Das Gedicht in der Marktlücke," 509–10.

23. Reich-Ranicki, "Rückkehr zur schönen Literatur," 21.

24. Reich-Ranicki, "Schriftsteller am stillen Herd," 1.

25. Reich-Ranicki, *Entgegnungen*, 21.

26. Stephan, "Das Gedicht in der Marktlücke," 511–12.

27. Reich-Ranicki, "Schriftsteller am stillen Herd," 1.

28. Zimmermann, "Die mangelhafte Subjektivität," 475.

29. Winter, "Von der Dokumentarliteratur zur neuen Subjektivität," 95.

30. Hazel, "Alte und neue Sensibilität," 131.

31. Hazel, "Alte und neue Sensibilität," 132.

32. McGowan, "Neue Subjektivität," 53–69.

33. Marcuse, *On Liberation*, 30–31.

34. Habermas, "Die Scheinrevolution und ihre Kinder," 5–15.

35. Reiche, "Verteidigung der 'Neuen Sensibilität,'" 100.

36. Michael Schneider, "Von der alten Radikalität," 182.

37. Michael Schneider, "Von der alten Radikalität," 174–75.

38. Ziehe, *Pubertät und Narzißmus*, first published through the Psychology Department of the University of Hannover in 1975. See also Häsing, *Narziß*.

39. Schülein, "Von der Studentenrevolte zur Tendenzwende," 102–4.

40. Bopp, "Vatis Argumente," 13–19.

41. On the Spontis see Schütte, *Revolte und Verweigerung*.

42. Whereas Matthis Dienstag uses the term *oral* in an ironic manner in his satire on the Sponti movement ("Provinz aus dem Kopf," 155), this term and the complementary *anal* for the bourgeois mode of socialization were taken seriously; see, for example, Schülein, "Von der Studentenrevolte zur Tendenzwende," 114.

43. Huhn, "Die Stadtindianer auf dem Kriegspfad," 129–47.

44. Bruder-Bezzel and Bruder, "Unter den Talaren der Muff von 10 Jahren," 23.

45. Autorenkollektiv: Quinn der Eskimo, Frankie Lee, Judas Priest, "Zum Tango gehören immer zwei," 126. Leineweber and Schibel ("Die Alternativbewegung," 95–128) give a portrayal of their work within an agricultural commune that they had started in the early 1970s. They explain

their "dropping out" from their "left career" as a failure to realize the "new human being," i.e., the New Sensibility that the New Left had once propagated.

46. "Wählt Liste 8," in Schütte, *Revolte und Verweigerung*, appendix 5.

47. Brückner, "Thesen zur Diskussion der 'Alternativen,'" 68–85.

48. Waldhubel, "Sponti-Bewegung," 10.

49. See also Roberts, "Tendenzwenden," 290–313.

50. Kosta, *Recasting Autobiography*, 35.

51. Kosta, *Recasting Autobiography*, 35; while Kosta makes this point only with respect to autobiographical literature and film, I view this as a general trend.

52. On the *Verständigungstexte* see Keitel, "Recent Literary Trends."

53. For an early and insightful discussion of the new category of authenticity and its relationship to the canonic literary tradition see Ursula Krechel, "Leben in Anführungszeichen: Das Authentische in der gegenwärtigen Literatur," 80–107.

54. Heinrich Böll, "Will Ulrike Gnade oder Freies Geleit?" *Spiegel*, 10 January 1972, 54–57.

55. For an interview with the Mescalero see "Unheimlich klammheimlich."

56. See Rutschky, who perceives the student movement as an attempt to live a "utopia of general principles" (*Utopie der Allgemeinbegriffe*), subsuming the individual to general concepts such as the category of class (*Erfahrungshunger*, 32–33). Michael Schneider expresses the same idea in his notion of a "intellectual-conceptual culture" (*Verstandeskultur*) in "Von der alten Radikalität," 176.

57. Kreuzer, "Neue Subjektivität," 99.

58. See as well Handke's earlier texts *The Goalie's Anxiety at the Penalty Kick* and *Short Letter, Long Farewell*.

59. Handke, *Moment of True Feeling*, 7, 96, 23, 15.

60. Handke, *Moment of True Feeling*, 78–79; see as well 82, "I'm free, he thought, I don't have to talk any more. What a relief!"

61. Handke, *Moment of True Feeling*, 128–30.

62. Handke, *Moment of True Feeling*, 63–65.

63. Lindstead, *Outer World and Inner World*, 160–61.

64. Buback Obituary, 3.

65. Brückner, *Mescalero-Affäre*, 28.

66. Buback Obituary, 4.

67. Buback Obituary, 4–5; see also Brückner, *Mescalero-Affäre*, 28.

68. Brückner, *Mescalero-Affäre*, 29.

69. Buback Obituary, 6.

70. Gottschalch, "Gutachterliche Äußerung," 212.

71. Buback Obituary, 5–6.

72. See in contrast Dutschke, Rabehl, and Semler, "Ein Gespräch über die Zukunft," 155: "Still, the experiment of the hippies is a total experiment. The hippies' attempts to reactivate quasi-biological, physical tendencies are an important move that perhaps points us into the future. The only thing they forget is the question of power. This is the limit of this movement."

73. Brückner, *Mescalero-Affäre*, 36–37.

74. Dröge, "Mescalero-Sprache," 194.

75. Dröge, "Mescalero-Sprache," 184–185.

76. Dröge, "Mescalero-Sprache," 184–185 and 198–199.

77. Dröge, "Mescalero-Sprache," 200.

78. Dröge, "Mescalero-Sprache," 200.

79. See the documentary of parliamentary debates on this issue: *Die Anti-Terror-Debatten im Parlament.*

4. "OBJECTIVITY? NO, THANK YOU!"

1. "Jeder fünfte denkt etwa so wie Mescalero," *Spiegel* 41 (1977): 58.

2. Brand, *Aufbruch in eine andere Gesellschaft*, 86.

3. Daum, *Die 2. Kultur*, 115. See also Hiltl, "Die Alterantivbewegung: Ansprüche, Praxis, Perspektiven," 29.

4. Brand, *Aufbruch in eine andere Gesellschaft*, 163–64.

5. Huber, *Wer soll das alles ändern*, 27.

6. Offe, "New Social Movements," 829.

7. Raschke, "Zum Begriff der sozialen Bewegung," 19–29.

8. Müschen, "Praktisch unübersichtlich, unübersichtlich praktisch," 260–71.

9. See the preface to Hermand and Müller, *Öko-Kunst?* 4.

10. See Emig, *Alternativpresse.*

11. The gathering took place 27–29 January 1978. Most major daily newspapers as well as the alternative press reported on the Tunix Gathering. For information on the event see Hoffmann-Axthelm, *Zwei Kulturen?*

12. Autorenkollektiv, "Zum Tango gehören immer zwei," 127.

13. Autorenkollektiv, "Zum Tango gehören immer zwei," 128.

14. The Tunix flier lists five events that deal with terrorism and the hegemonic culture's response to it. Among the events were a discussion with the author of the Buback Obituary and discussions about the situation of RAF inmates in the maximum security prison in Stammheim and about the laws prohibiting the promotion of politically motivated violence in

writing, speaking, or images. See Stein, ed., *Bohemien—Tramp—Sponti*, 301–3.

15. The "Treffen in Tunix" leaflet can be found in the following publications: Hoffmann-Axthelm et al., eds., *Zwei Kulturen?* 92–93; Stein, ed., *Bohemien—Tramp—Sponti*, 296–303; and Schütte, *Revolte und Verweigerung*, appendix, pp. xxiv–xxvi (only the text without the drawing). My references are to the reprint of the leaflet in Hoffmann-Axthelm et al., eds., *Zwei Kulturen?*

16. The story of the Bremen Town Musicians can be found as "The Travelling Musicians" in *Grimms' Fairy Tales*, 11–15.

17. Not only did Paul Lafargue's pamphlet *Das Recht auf Faulheit* [The right to laziness] enjoy popularity, but the well-established Insel-Verlag found it worthwhile to market this concept in its *Inselbuch der Faulheit* [The book of laziness]. This represented a response to the CDU/CSU's emphasis on industriousness and economic growth.

18. Jakob Grimm and Wilhelm Grimm, eds., *Deutsches Wörterbuch* 6:2771–81.

19. Micky, "Berlin, 1. Februar," 305.

20. Waldhubel, "Sponti-Bewegung," 10; see also "Wählt Liste 8."

21. "Treffen in Tunix," 93.

22. "Treffen in Tunix," 93.

23. See also Autorenkollektive, "Zum Tango gehören immer zwei," 129–130.

24. "Stets ein Gewinn wird jeder Einsatz der Genossen Kommunisten in der Arbeiter-Klassenlotterie" ("Treffen in Tunix," 93).

25. The word *Einsatz* has a double meaning in German: (1) the bet or stake in any kind of gambling, and (2) the efforts one makes to achieve something, or one's engagement in or commitment to a specific project.

26. McCormick, *Politics of the Self*, 60

27. "Treffen in Tunix," 93.

28. "Treffen in Tunix," 93.

29. "Treffen in Tunix," 93.

30. Micky, "Berlin, 1. Februar," 306.

31. "Treffen in Tunix," 93.

32. "Die Anfänge der *taz*," 11.

33. "Chronik," 17 Apr. 1984 (on the occasion of the fifth anniversary of the *taz*).

34. *Prospekt: Tageszeitung*, 5.

35. [Zahl], "Alle Türen offen: Amnestie für alle!"

36. Introductory remark to the chapter on ecology in Bröckers, *Die Taz: Das Buch*, 10.

37. Bröckers, *Die Taz*, 63.
38. Tolmein and zum Winkel, *Tazsachen*, 147–48.
39. In 1989 this campaign was briefly interrupted in favor of the people in the GDR until the *taz* could be legally obtained there as well.
40. "Waffen für El Salvador," 1; See as well Tolmein and zum Winkel, *Tazsachen*, 37–42.
41. "Sachschaden: Häuserkampf und andere Kämpfe," *taz-Journal* 3 (1981). The *taz* occasionally published a whole journal on a specific theme.
42. Tolmein and zum Winkel, *Tazsachen*, 49–51.
43. Bröckers, *Die Taz*, 645.
44. *Prospekt: Tageszeitung*, 5.
45. *Prospekt: Tageszeitung*, 5.
46. *Prospekt: Tageszeitung*, 4.
47. Stamm, *Alternative Öffentlichkeit*, 110–12.
48. *Prospekt: Tageszeitung*, 19.
49. Simeon, "Fetisch Objektivität," 281–83.
50. *Prospekt: Tageszeitung*, 19.
51. Habermas, *The Structural Transformation of the Public Sphere*.
52. Stamm, *Alternative Öffentlichkeit*, especially 54–69, "Zerfallsprozesse der linken Öffentlichkeit: Kaderparteien, Basisgruppen und 'bewaffneter Kampf' " [Dissolution of a left public sphere: Cadre parties, grass-roots groups, and the "armed struggle"].
53. *Prospekt: Tageszeitung*, 4.
54. *Prospekt: Tageszeitung*, 4–5.
55. Tolmein and zum Winkel, *Tazsachen*, 32–34.
56. *Prospekt: Tageszeitung*, 4
57. "Anschlag auf die Hamburger-*taz* 'wg. Lochte,' " 1, 3; Interview with Lochte, *taz*, 16 Oct. 1985, 5. The *taz* interview with the head of the *Verfassungsschutz*, Lochte, in Hamburg provided only a superficial cause for the crusade of the *Autonome* against the *taz*. See also Tolmein and zum Winkel, *Tazsachen*, 69–72.
58. Job advertisement for a "KulturredakteurIn," *taz*, 7 May 1984, 9 (my emphasis).
59. My analysis is not based on either a one-to-one or a quantitative comparison of these two papers. Since the aesthetic conceptualizations of the alternative culture are the main focus of scrutiny, the *Faz* as the mainstream counterpart to the *taz* functions more as an illustrative background.
60. *Dokumentation: Alles über die Zeitung*, 3.
61. *Dokumentation: Alles über die Zeitung*, 106.

62. *Dokumentation: Alles über die Zeitung,* 79.

63. Kracauer, *Theory of Film.*

64. For a beautiful example of photomontage see the front page of the *taz,* 3 Dec. 1979, which comments on the party convention of the SPD, or *taz,* 4 Mar. 1983, which comments on the bribery scandal of the Flick conglomerate. For comics see *taz,* 9 May 1980, 9: "Deutschland: Ein Dschungelmärchen" (Germany: A jungle tale).

65. Bröckers, *Die Taz,* 730.

66. *Dokumentation: Alles über die Zeitung,* 42–43.

67. For a documentary of the legal confrontation between the *taz* and the state see Bröckers, *Die Taz,* 690–702.

68. See Kiesel and Münch, *Gesellschaft und Literatur im 18. Jahrhundert,* 104–22, 141–43.

69. Hübsch, *Alternative Öffentlichkeit,* 101. Note as well the cultural difference between the United States and West Germany. In the United States, the anonymous articles of the wire services are considered to be the most objective source of information.

70. All conventional German daily newspapers use the heading "Feuilleton" for their cultural sections.

71. Hohendahl, *The Institution of Criticism,* 78.

72. Hohendahl, *The Institution of Criticism,* 46.

73. [Wolff], "Kulturkritik: Erster Klasse," 9.

74. *Prospekt: Tageszeitung,* 67.

75. [Chris Kelly and Petra Kelly], "Diskussion über Kultur in der Tageszeitung: Eine Autobahn," 9.

76. "Nee, ich faß kein Buch mehr an: Literatur ??? da wird mir übel!" 9.

77. "Zur Autobahnkritik von Chris und Petra," 9. The late Rudi Dutschke was one of the best-known theorists and activists of the student movement. Daniel Cohn-Bendit also played a major role in the student movement and in the post-1968 counterculture as the editor of the Sponti paper *Pflasterstrand.* Still active in politics today as the proponent of the concept of the multicultural society, he is the coordinator of multicultural affairs for the city of Frankfurt am Main.

78. "Liebe Frauen, lieber Leser, liebe Initiativler," 8; see as well "Die Kulturen in der Tageszeitung," 13.

79. Hübsch, *Alternative Öffentlichkeit,* 101.

80. See Cornel, "Kultur" in *Handbuch der alternativen Kommunalpolitik,* 293.

81. See Beaucamp, "Fetisch Öffentlichkeit," 21.

82. See "Johann Hauser Ausstellung in Köln," 9; "Pictures of an Exhibition," 8; "Wir sind wahnsinnig," 8; "Die Bedeutung des Körpers: Frida Kahlo

und Tina Modotti," 12–13; "Jacoba van Heemskerch," 11; "Frauenkunst: Amsterdam–Berlin '83," 11; "Zum Thema 'Haut' zeigen 61 Künsterlinnen ihre Werke," 10; "Frauenräume," 9.

83. *Dokumentation: Alles über die Zeitung*, 80.

84. *Dokumentation: Alles über die Zeitung*, 106.

5. "DO IT YOURSELF!"

1. Hermand, *Kultur der Bundesrepublik Deutschland*, 516.

2. Hermand, *Kultur der Bundesrepublik Deutschland*, 518.

3. Cornel, "Kultur," in *Handbuch der alternativen Kommunalpolitik*, 293. Jost Hermand confirms this allocation of public funds in *Kultur der Bundesrepublik Deutschland*, 58–67.

4. The most famous case occurred not in West Germany but in Switzerland. The exorbitant subsidies that the opera house in Zurich was supposed to receive from public funds, at the same time that the autonomus youth center was closed down, triggered street battles between alternative youth and the police that has become known today as the Youth Revolt of 1981. This event had a ripple effect on West Germany, where opera houses also became a target of criticism and protest rallies of the alternative culture.

5. Watts, *Contemporary German Youth and Their Elders*, 11–12.

6. Huber, *Wer soll das alles ändern*, 26.

7. Liebmann-Schaub, "Foucault," 145.

8. [Clemenz], "Meine Theorie ist eine Werkzeugkiste," 12.

9. Liebmann-Schaub, "Foucault," 143–44.

10. Heidi, die Piepmaus, "Die Brille von Foucault," 12.

11. Another case in point to study the alternative culture's dispute about the necessity of theory are the responses to the coverage of Herbert Marcuse's death in the *taz*. In addition to excerpts from Marcuse's position on the new social movements in "Die Angst des Prometheus" (*taz*, 31 July 1979, 3), the *taz* published only obituaries written by the generation of 1968. Their highly theoretical discourse was harshly criticized by a number of *taz* readers in letters to the editors (see *taz*, 7 Aug. 1979, 3). This antitheory position elicited protheory responses. The protheorists called, however, for a comprehensible theoretical language, demonstrating that even they were weary of the student movement's rhetoric (see *taz*, 31 Aug. 1979, 3).

12. "Kultur Politik in Hamburg," 9; see also [Günter], "Die eigene Kultur: Auf dem Weg zur kulturellen Demokratie," 9.

13. "Kultur Politik in Hamburg," 9. The last sentence reads: Kulturpolitik ist hierzulande eine Spezialität, das System malt sich ab und zu bunt an und zeigt uns die lange Nase—der Macht."

14. "Kultur von unten!" 20.
15. On the problem of self-exploitation see Huber, *Wer soll das alles ändern*, 51.
16. "Knete vom Staat, ja oder nein?" 7, and "Zwischen Geldnot und Integrationsgefahr," 6.
17. "Olympiade der Kultur," 10.
18. "Kultur Politik in Hamburg," 9. The Factory was an alternative performance space in Hamburg that was, as the name indicates, located in an old factory building. The alternative culture typically used old factories and warehouses as autonomous cultural centers for pragmatic and ideological reasons. Pragmatically speaking, these old industrial buildings were inexpensive and offered plenty of space for a variety of groups and purposes. From an ideological perspective, the alternative culture saw these old buildings as more appealing for an audience that either consciously rejected or was afraid of entering the cultural temples of the hegemonic culture. Using old factory buildings was also in the spirit of "recycling" cherished in the alternative culture. Often the building's old and familiar name was retained. Cultural centers of this kind can be found in all major cities and in many mid-sized towns in the Federal Republic.
19. For a discussion of the alternative projects' dependence on progressive parts of middle-class West Germany see Huber, *Wer soll das alles ändern*, 110–11.
20. "Treffen in Tunix," 93.
21. Haug, *Kritik der Warenästhetik.*
22. "Kein schöner Land in dieser Zeit," "Unter dem Pflaster liegt der Strand," and "Kein schöner Land als dieser Strand."
23. See the following articles: [Tutzer], "Karneval in Venedig," 12; [Hallerbach], "Karnevalsutopie: Zurück zu den Wurzeln," 8; [Bauer and Link], "Lalü: So schön wie nie," 6; [Bauer and Link], "Mainz bleibt Mainz," 10–11; and [Hallerbach], "Dr Morgestraich isch eifach schaurig schö . . ." 8.
24. [Bauer and Link], "Mainz bleibt Mainz," 10–11.
25. [Hallerbach], "Karnevalsutopie," 8.
26. [Bauer and Link], "Mainz bleibt Mainz," 10–11.
27. See the advertisement for the Fabrik für Sport, Kultur und Handwerk, 14.
28. Bose and Brinkmann, *Circus.*
29. "Der Theaterhof Priessental auf Tournee," 8.
30. "Die Reise zum Regenbogen," 8.
31. "Die Reise zum Regenbogen," 8. See also "Der Theaterhof Priessental auf

Tournee," 8, and Claußen's positive evaluation of the circus in "Politisch-kulturelle Bildung im Circus?" 215–27.

32. On the Festival of Fools see Kramer, *Pantomime und Clownerie*, 109–14; see also *taz*, 31 May 1979, 9, reporting on a Festival of Fools in Recklinghausen and a letter to the editor about the Festival of Fools in Berlin (*taz*, 16–17 July 1979, 3).

33. Von Barloewen, *Clown*, 94.

34. *taz*, 17 Apr. 1979, 1.

35. "Hoch taz: 10 Jahre Pressefrechheit," *taz* Juchz- & Jubel- Sonderheft 10 (Apr. 1989). See also the use of clown images in the controversy about theory that erupted in the *taz* in the context of covering Herbert Marcuse's death (*taz*, 31 Aug. 1979, 3).

36. Kramer, *Pantomime und Clownerie*, 107.

37. Jakob Grimm and Wilhelm Grimm, *Deutsches Wörterbuch* 8:2506–10; see also Kluge, *Etymologisches Wörterbuch der deutschen Sprache*, 628–29.

38. "Quer zu allen: Wir Kinder des 30jährigen Friedens," 9, a positive review of P. P. Zahl's *Die Glücklichen*.

39. Schechter, *Durov's Pig: Clowns, Politics and Theater*, 22.

40. Edwards, *Ich lebe Dich*, 80.

41. Rabotti Clownstheater Duo, "Be wise, be a fool, but please no FOOL!" 7.

42. "Treffen in Tunix," 93.

43. "Treffen in Tunix," 93; see also Klaus Röder, "Thesen zur Alternativkultur," 156.

44. "Spaß beiseite," 9.

45. [Ege], "Es muß mal wieder gesagt werden," 7.

46. "Spaß beiseite," 9. It is interesting to note that the student movement had evaluated Zadek's productions very negatively; see chapter 2.

47. Schechter, *Durov's Pig*, 142.

48. Mitchell, *Dario Fo*, 12.

49. "Märchen, Muff, Mief," 6.

50. "Leben Gundlings Friedrich von Preußen Lessings Schlaf Traum Schrei," 9; "Müller-Boom oder wie mache ich am besten von mir reden," 9.

51. "Spaß beiseite," 9.

52. Hohendahl, *The Institution of Criticism*, 46–47.

53. See, for example, Georg Hensel's reviews of Schiller productions, "Don Carlitos, der Infantile von Spanien," *Faz*, 1 Oct. 1979, 23, and "Der Infant von Spanien und sein Vogel," *Faz*, 6 Oct. 1979, 25, and Sibylle Wirsing's review of a production of *Antigone*, "Die Tragödie als Luxusartikel," *Faz*, 28 Mar. 1979, 21. See also Wirsing's criticism of the annual theater meetings (*Theatertreffen in Berlin*) as a "circus" (*Szenen-Zirkus*) rather than

a collection of high-quality productions of the theater (*Sprechtheater*) in *Faz*, 28 May 1979.

54. Hensel, "Fluchtwege des Theaters aus der Sprache," 22–23.

55. See as well "Pantomime—Phantomime—Pammime," 9.

56. [Zucker], "Mimentheater Magma," 9.

57. "Pantomime—Phantomime—Pammime," 9.

58. "Grand Kanaille: Theater-Tagebuch aus Hamburg," 10.

59. "Spiderwomen," 9.

60. "Straßentheater: Atomlobbyisten von 'angeblichem' Strahlentod entführt," 9.

61. This concept of a politically engaged theatrical practice resembles the idea embodied in the fool and also articulated by the countercultural band Mobiles Einsatzorchäster. Instead of chanting political slogans and carrying posters, the band suggested a rally full of various music groups and different performance styles. They argued that the aesthetic, sensuous nature of such protest represented its political dimension, since it refused to take the predetermined paths of expressing political protest and mobilized energy.

62. "Rock und linke Kulturpraxis," 9; [Müller], "Wenn die Nacht am tiefsten," 13; "Gimmicks: Rock 'n' Roll Schmetterlinge," 10.

63. "Das Geld macht die Musik: 25 Jahre Rock 'n' Roll," 9.

64. "Das Geld macht die Musik," 9.

65. "Das Geld macht die Musik," 9; "Wahrscheinlich liest's (hört's) wieder kein Schwein," 9; "Als linke Rockgruppe überleben," 9.

66. "Das Geld macht die Musik," 9.

67. "Als linke Rockgruppe überleben," 9.

68. The NPD usually did not get permission from the city authorities for their rally, so they went to court in order to compel permission legally.

69. Leukert, *Thema: Rock gegen Rechts*, 19–38.

70. "Rock gegen Rechts. Kein Nazi-Treffen in Frankfurt und anderswo!" flier reprinted in Leukert, ed., *Thema: Rock gegen Rechts*, 153–54.

71. Wolf, "Alter Wein in alten Schläuchen", 10–11; Beck, "Wenn Vergangenheit Mode wird," 5.

72. Kraushaar, "Rockmusik als politischer Deckmantel?" 69–86.

73. "Wahrscheinlich liest's (hört's) wieder kein Schwein," 9.

74. "Rock und linke Kulturpraxis: Eine Auseinandersetzung mit der Rezeption von Nina Hagen und anderen," 9.

75. "Über Nina Hagen kann man so und so denken," 3 (letter to the editor).

76. "Umsonst und Draußen: Porta Westfalica 1979," 9.

77. Chambers, "A Strategy for Living: Black Music and White Subcultures," 157.

78. "Treffen in Tunix," 93.

6. BETWEEN POLITICS AND ECOLOGY

1. This chapter draws on the following research on the party of the Greens: Raschke, *Die Grünen*; Frankland and Schoonmaker, *Between Protest and Power*; Kolinsky, ed., *The Greens in West Germany*; Hülsberg, *The German Greens*; Langguth, *The Green Factor in German Politics*; and Weinberger, *Aufbruch zu neuen Ufern*.

2. The original German reads, "Ökologisch, sozial, basisdemokratisch, gewaltlos" (Die Grünen, preamble, *Programme of the German Green Party*, trans. Porritt, 6–9). All references in this chapter are to this translation.

3. See Offe, "Griff nach der Notbremse," 85–92.

4. Die Grünen, *Programme of the German Green Party*, 36–37.

5. Die Grünen, *Programme of the German Green Party*, 8.

6. Poguntke, "Organization of a Participatory Party," 610.

7. Poguntke, "Organization of a Participatory Party," 610. Poguntke analyzes as well to what extent the Greens realize their self-proclaimed goals and to what extent the German Basic Law hampers a full realization of grass-roots democracy.

8. Poguntke, "Organization of a Participatory Party," 624.

9. Wagner, "Kulturpolitik und Politik des Kulturellen," 37; see also Frankland and Schoonmaker, *Between Protest and Power*, 87, which summarizes empirical research on the Greens, and Brockmann, "Streit um die grüne Kulturpolitik," 25.

10. Holler, "Grüne Kulturpolitik und kulturelle Bewegung 'von unten,'" 56–58.

11. Altendorfer, "Die Kunstbanausen," 123–25.

12. Elkins, "The Politics of Mystical Ecology," 52.

13. See the entry "Natur" in *Geschichtliche Grundbegriffe*, 215–45, and Zimmermann, "Zur Geschichte des ästhetischen Naturbegriffs," 118–54.

14. See Adorno, *Aesthetic Theory*.

15. Zimmermann, "Geschichte des ästhetischen Naturbegriffs," 140–41; see as well Huyssen, "Das Versprechen der Natur," 2.

16. Zimmermann, "Geschichte des ästhetischen Naturbegriffs," 141.

17. Horkheimer and Adorno, *Dialectic of Enlightenment*, 19, 39.

18. Die Grünen, *Programme of the German Green Party*; see especially the section on "Economy and Work," 9–10.

19. Liessmann, "Natura Mortua," 64.

20. These key categories of early Green thinking are best explicated in Manon Maren-Grisebach, *Philosophie der Grünen*, 14, 31–33, 49, and 24; see also Wolf-Dieter and Connie Hasenclever, *Grüne Zeiten*, 53.

21. Die Grünen, *Programme of the German Green Party*, 7.

22. Liessmann, "Natura Mortua," 65.

23. Maren-Grisebach, *Philosophie der Grünen*, 34. In addition, this comparison to the ark rocking back and forth on the waters of the great flood evokes the image of the potential ecological catastrophe.

24. Maren-Grisebach, *Philosophie der Grünen*, 26.

25. Maren-Grisebach, *Philosophie der Grünen*, 24

26. Loukopoulos-Lepanto, "Kunst für den Menschen," 15. He published this essay together with the essay "Für eine Überwindung der abstrakten unverpflichtenden Kunst" and called them together "A Manifesto."

27. Loukopoulos-Lepanto, "Kunst für den Menschen," 19, 31.

28. Maren-Grisebach, *Philosophie der Grünen*, 129.

29. Maren-Grisebach, *Philosophie der Grünen*, 126.

30. Maren-Grisebach, *Philosophie der Grünen*, 129.

31. Maren-Grisebach, *Philosophie der Grünen*, 130.

32. Maren-Grisebach, *Philosophie der Grünen*, 23. On this issue of "Selbstgemachtes," see also Kos on the Austrian Greens: "Landgemacht und Handgemacht," 126–34.

33. Die Grünen, *Programme of the German Green Party*, 48–49; The English translation does not, however, contain the photograph I am referring to. For the photograph see p. 42 of the German version.

34. Die Grünen, *Programme of the German Green Party*, 49.

35. See Wolff, "Kultursterben," 54–56, Wagner, "Zwischen Klassenkampf und Lebensphilosophie," 38–44, and Brockmann, "Streit um Kulturpolitik," 24–36.

36. Die Grünen, *Dem Struwelpeter durch die Haare gefahren: Auf dem Weg zu einer grünen Kulturpolitik. Der Struwelpeter* is a nineteenth-century anthology of stories and pictures by Heinrich Hoffmann that illustrates what happens to ill-mannered children who do not follow their parents' rules. The Struwelpeter, who refused to have his hair and nails cut, is depicted with long nails and unruly blond hair standing up in all directions.

37. Hermand, "Dem Struwelpeter durch die Haare gefahren," 189.

38. " . . . ich hab' einfach keinen Nerv mehr! Gespräch mit Paul E. Pauly, dem scheidenden Kulturreferenten der Grünen," 9.

39. Wagner, "Von der Parteien Gunst getragen," 9–10.

40. On these two museums projects see Stölzl and Tafel, "Das Deutsche Historische Museum in Berlin," 17–26, and Schäfer, "Das Haus der Geschichte der Bundesrepublik Deutschland," 27–34.

41. Wagner, "Von der Parteien Gunst," 15.

42. For the Historians' Debate of 1985–86 see *Historikerstreit*. In addition, see Evans, *In Hitler's Shadow* and "The New Nationalism and the Old History"; Eley, "Nazism, Politics, and the Images of the Past"; and Maier, *The Unmasterable Past*.

43. See also Büscher, *Wirklichkeitstheater*, 195–209, and Glaser, *Kulturgeschichte der Bundesrepublik Deutschland* 3:147–51.

44. Wagner, "Von der Parteien Gunst," 18–19.

45. Ströbele and Knapp, "Kunst und Kultur—das ist wie Senf und Schlagsahne," 30–33.

46. Wolff, "Kultursterben," 55: "dezentral, basisnah, demokratisch, gegenwartsbezogen, anstößig, lebensvoll und selbstbestimmt."

47. Wagner, "Zwischen Klassenkampf und Lebensphilosophie," 40.

48. Schröder, "Kunst als Klassenkampf oder Kultur für Alle?" 23.

49. Schröder, "Kunst als Klassenkampf," 24.

50. Schröder, "Kunst als Klassenkampf," 25.

51. Schröder, "Drei Fallen grün-alternativer Kulturpolitik," 6, "Kunst als Klassenkampf," 25.

52. Wagner, "Zwischen Klassenkampf und Lebensphilosophie," 39.

53. Weißler, "Grüne Selbstverständlichkeiten," 56–57; Cornel, "Rahmenbedingungen für eine 'Kultur im Widerspruch'" and "Fortschreibung 1985," 57–59.

54. Weißler, "Grüne Selbstverständlichkeiten," 56.

55. Weißler, "Grüne Selbstverständlichkeiten," 57.

56. Wagner, "Zwischen Klassenkampf und Lebensphilosophie," 39.

CONCLUSION

1. Glaser, *Kulturgeschichte der Bundesrepublik* 3:113.

2. The Greens won seats in the state legislature of Baden-Württemberg, where Tübingen is located, in its first election campaign in 1980, that is, three years before the Greens entered the federal legislature. While the Greens averaged 5.3 percent of the popular vote statewide, in university towns such as Tübingen they collected up to 15 percent.

3. Horx, *Das Ende der Alternativen*, 75–81, and "Du bist, was du ißt." See also [Enard], "Die Neuen Feinschmecker oder Die Linke als Gourmands." This *taz* article, originally published in *Le Monde-Dimanche*, makes the

same observations as Horx but with respect to the French post-1968 counterculture.

4. Benny Härlin lists a number of slogans popular within the alternative culture in his report on the squatters' movement, "Von Haus zu Haus," 15. See also Keitel, "Recent Literary Trends," 445–47.

5. The slogan can be found in Härlin, "Von Haus zu Haus," 15.

6. Horx, *Das Ende der Alternativen*, 9.

7. Clarke, "Subcultures, Cultures and Class," 61.

8. Horx, *Das Ende der Alternativen*, 116.

9. See also Brand, "Kontinuität und Diskontinuität in den neuen sozialen Bewegungen," 30–32.

BIBLIOGRAPHY

ARTICLES FROM *DIE TAGESZEITUNG* (*taz*)

"Als linke Rockgruppe überleben." 17 Sept. 1979: 9.

"Anschlag auf die Hamburger-*taz* 'wg' Lochte.'" 23 Oct. 1985: 1, 3.

Bauer, Gerd, and Rita Link. "Lalü: So schön wie nie." 21 Feb. 1980: 10–11.

———. "Mainz bleibt Mainz." 15 Feb. 1980: 10–11.

Beck, Johannes. "Rock gegen Rechts: Wenn Vergangenheit Mode wird." 18 June 1979: 5. Reprint. *Thema: Rock gegen Rechts: Musik als politisches Instrument*, edited by Bernd Leukert, 39–51. Frankfurt am Main: Fischer, 1980.

"Die Bedeutung des Körpers: Frida Kahlo und Tina Modotti." 14 May 1982: 12–13.

"Chronik." 17 Apr. 1984: 4–7, 9–20.

Clemenz, Manfred. "Meine Theorie ist eine Werkzeugkiste . . . Erfahrungen und Schwierigkeiten mit der Theorie von Michel Foucault." 7 Sept. 1979: 12–13.

"Deutschland: Ein Dschungelmärchen." Cartoon. 9 May 1980: 9.

"Diskussion." Letters to the editor about *Umsonst & Draußen*. 30 Aug. 1979: 3.

Dorsten, Dagmar. "Wir sind der Rost, der die Rüstung frißt: Premiere am Theaterhof Priessental: Nach 'Wir Nibelungen' und 'Johanna' ein neuer Volltreffer: 'Frauenschuh.'" 25 May 1982: 8.

Ege, Gert. "Es muß mal wieder gesagt werden." 12 Feb. 1980: 7.

Enard, J. P. "Die Neuen Feinschmecker, oder Die Linke als Gourmands." 10 Mar. 1980: 8.

"Fabrik für Sport, Kultur und Handwerk/Anzeige." 25 Oct. 1979: 11–14.

Fool illustrations. 17 Apr. 1979: 1. "Festival of Fools in Recklinghausen." 31 May 1979: 9. Letter to the editor about Festival of Fools in Berlin. 16/17 July 1979: 3.

"Frauenkunst: Amsterdam–Berlin '83." 31 May 1983: 11.

"Frauenräume." 4 Oct. 1983: 9.

"Gema! Bericht der Fabrik für Kultur, Sport und Handwerk über ihren Konflikt mit der GEMA." 27 Jan. 1981: 8.

"Gimmicks: Rock 'n Roll Schmetterlinge." 15 Apr. 1980: 10.

Günter, Roland. "Die eigene Kultur: Auf dem Weg zur kulturellen Demokratie." 12 Nov. 1979: 9.

Hallerbach, Jörg. "Dr Morgestraich isch eifach schaurig schö . . ." 22 Feb. 1980: 8.

———. "Karnivalsutopie: zurück zu den Wurzeln." 14 Feb. 1983: 8.

Heidi, die Piepmaus. "Die Brille von Foucault." 22 June 1979: 12.

"Hoch *taz*. 10 Jahre Pressefrechheit." Juchz & Jubelsonderheft 10 (1989).

" . . . ich hab' einfach keinen Nerv mehr! Gespräch mit Paul E. Pauly, dem scheidenden Kulturreferenten der Grünen." 11 Nov. 1984: 9.

"Jacoba van Heemskerch." 2 May 1983: 11.

"Johann Hauser Austellung in Köln." 5 Feb. 1980: 9.

Kelly, Chris, and Petra Kelly. "Diskussion über die Kultur in der Tagszeitung: Eine Autobahn." 6 Aug. 1979: 9.

———. "Diskussion über Kultur: Zur Autobahnkritik von Chris und Petra." 16 Aug. 1979: 9.

"Knete vom Staat, ja oder nein? Erstes Nachdenken über staatliche Integrationsversuche der Alternativen." 30 Sept. 1980: 7.

"Die Kulturen in der Tageszeitung." 19 Dec. 1980: 13.

"Kultur Politik in Hamburg." 9 Oct. 1979: 9.

"Kultur-RedakteurIn." Job advertisement. 7 May 1984: 9.

"Kultur von unten!" 4 Mar. 1980: 10.

"Liebe Frauen, lieber Leser, liebe Initiativler." 12 Sep. 1980: 8.

"Märchen, Muff, Mief." 11 June 1982: 6.

Marcuse, Herbert. Letters to the editor. 31 July 1979: 1–3; 7 Aug. 1979: 3; 31 Aug. 1979: 3.

Meier, Reiner. "Open-Ohr-Festival in Mainz." 7 June 1979: 1, 9.

Müller, F. "Wenn die Nacht am tiefsten . . . Wie Medienmultis Rockmusik verwerten." 17 Aug. 1979: 13.

"Müller-Boom, oder Wie mache ich am besten von mir reden." 30 May 1979: 9.

Müllrich, Uwe. "Umsonst und Draußen." 17 Aug. 1979: 12.

"Nee, ich faß kein Buch mehr an: Literatur ??? da wird mir übel." 6 Aug. 1979: 9.

"Olympiade der Kultur." 21 July 1980: 10.

"Pantomime—Phantomime—Pammime." 27 June 1979: 9.

Photomontages. 3 Dec. 1979: 1. 4 Mar. 1983: 1.

"Pictures of an Exhibition." 17 Mar. 1980: 8.

"Porta Westfalica 1979: Umsonst und Draußen." 13 June 1979: 9.

"Quer zu allen. Wir Kinder des 30jährigen Friedens." 29 Jan. 1980: 9.

Rabotti Clownstheater Duo. "Be wise, be a fool, but please no FOOL!" 12 Feb. 1980: 7.

"Die Reise zum Regenbogen." 24 Oct. 1980: 8–9.

Review of Heiner Müller, *Leben Gundlings Friedrich von Preußen Lessings Schlaf Traum Schrei*. 16 May 1979: 9.

"Rock und linke Kulturpraxis: Eine Auseinandersetzung mit der Rezeption von Nina Hagen und anderen." [Michael O.R. Kröher] 23 Apr. 1979: 9.

Sontheimer, Micha. "Die Grenzen eines alternativen Festivals." 22 Aug. 1979: 9.

"Spaß beiseite." 27 July 1979: 9.

"Spiderwomen." 18 Oct. 1979: 10.

"Straßentheater: Atomlobbyisten von 'angeblichem' Strahlentod entführt." 17 Dec. 1979: 9.

Ströbele, Wolfgang. "Die Anfänge der taz." 17 Apr. 1984: 4.

taz-Ini/Hamburg. "'Das Geld macht die Musik': 25 Jahre Rock 'n' Roll: Rockausstellung in der Hamburger Markthalle." 20 Jan. 1979: 9.

———. "Grand Kanaille: Theater-Tagebuch aus Hamburg." 10 June 1980: 10.

"Der Theaterhof Priessental auf Tournee." 27 Apr. 1981: 8.

Tutzer, Inge. "Karneval in Venedig." 4 Feb. 1983: 12.

"Über Nina Hagen kann man so und so denken . . . über die taz-Berichte auch." Letter to the editor. 22 Aug. 1979: 3.

"Viel Folk fürs Volk? Alternative Kulturindustrie und emanzipatorische Musik." 8 May 1979: 9.

"Waffen für El Salvador." 3 Nov. 1980: 1.

"Wahrscheinlich liest's (hört's) wieder kein Schwein." 23 July 1979: 9.

"Wir sind wahnsinnig." 7 Oct. 1981: 8.

Wolff, Frank. "Alter Wein in alten Schläuchen." 13 June 1980: 10–11. Reprint. *Thema: Rock gegen Rechts: Musik als politisches Instrument*, edited by Bernd Leukert, 97–102. Frankfurt am Main: Fischer, 1980.

———. "Kulturkritik. Erster Klasse." 30 Nov. 1979: 9.

Zahl, Peter Paul. "Alle Türen offen: Amnestie für alle!" 0, no. 2 (Oct. 1978).

Zucker, Renée. "Mimentheater Magma." 21 Oct. 1983: 9.

"Zum Thema 'Haut' zeigen 61 Künstlerinnen ihre Werke in Bonn." 4 Oct. 1983: 10.

"Zwischen Geldnot und Integrationsgefahr." 13 Oct. 1980: 6.

OTHER ARTICLES AND BOOKS

Adorno, Theodor W. *Aesthetic Theory*. Translated by C. Lenhardt. London: Routledge & Kegan Paul, 1984.

———. "Culture Industry Reconsidered." Translated by Anson G. Rabinbach. *New German Critique* 6 (fall 1975): 12–19. Reprint in *The Culture Industry: Selected Essays on Mass Culture*, edited by J. M. Bernstein, 85–92. London: Routledge, 1991.

———. "On the Fetish Character in Music and the Regression of Listening." In *The Culture Industry: Selected Essays on Mass Culture*, edited by Andrew Arato and Elke Gebhardt, 26–52. London: Routledge, 1991.

Altbach, Edith Hoshino, et al., eds. *German Feminism: Readings in Politics and Literature*. Albany: State University of New York Press, 1984.

Altendorfer, Peter. "Die Kunstbanausen: Über das (Nicht)Verhältnis der Grünen zur Kunst und Kultur: Versuch einer Herausforderung." *Kunstforum International* 93 (1988): 123–25.

Die Anti-Terror-Debatte im Parlament. Reinbek: Rowohlt, 1978.

Aust, Stefan. *Der Baader-Meinhof Komplex*. Hamburg: Hoffmann & Campe, 1985.

Autorenkolletiv: Quinn der Eskimo, Frankie Lee, Judas Priest. "Zum Tango gehören immer zwei, wenn ich gehe, kommst du mit! (Malcolm X)." In *Zwei Kulturen? Tunix, Mescalero und die Folgen*, edited by Dieter Hoffmann-Axthelm et al., 125–38. Berlin: Ästhetik und Kommunikation, 1978.

Barloewen, Constantin von. *Clown: Zur Phänomenologie des Stolperns*. Königstein: Athenäum, 1981.

Bauß, Gerhard. *Die Studentenbewegung der 60er Jahre in der Bundesrepublik und West-Berlin*. Cologne: Pahl-Rugenstein, 1977.

Beaucamp, Eduard. "Fetisch Öffentlichkeit: Zur Neueröffnung des Sprengel-Museums in Hannover." *Frankfurter Allgemeine Zeitung* 11 June 1979: 21.

Beicken, Peter. " 'Neue Subjektiviät': Zur Prosa der siebziger Jahre." In *Deutsche Literatur in der Bundesrepublik seit 1965*, edited by Paul Michael Lützeler and Egon Schwarz, 164–81. Königstein: Athenäum, 1980.

Benjamin, Walter. "The Author As Producer." In *Understanding Brecht*, translated by Anna Bostock, 85–103. London: NLB, 1973.

———. "The Work of Art in the Age of Mechanical Reproduction." In *Illuminations*, translated by Harry Zohn, 217–52. New York: Schocken, 1969.

Berghahn, Klaus L. "Operative Ästhetik: Zur Theorie der dokumentarischen Literatur." In *Deutsche Literatur in der Bundesrepublik seit 1965*, edited by Paul Michael Lützeler and Egon Schwarz, 270–81. Königstein: Athenäum, 1980.

Berman, Russell. "Adorno, Marxism and Art." *Telos* 34 (1977/78): 157–66.

Bieling, Reiner. *Die Tränen der Revolution: Die 68er 20 Jahre danach*. Berlin: Seidler, 1988.

Bock, Hans Manfred. *Geschichte des 'linken Radikalismus' in Deutschland: Ein Versuch*. Frankfurt am Main: Suhrkamp, 1976.

Böll, Heinrich. "Will Ulrike Gnade oder Freies Geleit?" *Der Spiegel* 10 Jan. 1972: 54–57. Reprint in *Heinrich Böll: Freies Geleit für Ulrike Meinhof: Ein Artikel und seine Folgen*, edited by Frank Grützbach. Cologne: Kiepenheuer & Witsch, 1972. 27–33.

Bondy, Curt, et al. *Jugendliche stören die Ordnung: Berichte und Stellungsnahmen zu den Halbstarkenkrawallen.* Munich: Juventa, 1957.

Bopp, Jörg. "Faszination durch Gewalt." In *1968–1988: Eine Pädagogengeneration zieht Bilanz,* edited by Johannes Bastian, 119–28. Hamburg: Bermann & Helbig, 1988.

———. "Vatis Argumente." *Kursbuch* 58 (1979): 2–20.

Born, Nicolas. *The Deception.* Translated by Leila Vennewitz. Boston: Little, Brown, 1983.

———. *Die erdabgewandte Seite der Geschichte.* Reinbek: Rowohlt, 1976.

Bose, Günter, and Erich Brinkmann. *Circus: Geschichte und Ästhetik einer niederen Kunst.* Berlin: Wagenbach, 1978.

Botzat, Tatjana, et al. *Ein deutscher Herbst: Zustände, Dokumente, Berichte, Kommentare.* Frankfurt am Main: Neue Kritik, 1978.

Brand, Karl-Werner. "Kontinuität und Diskontinuität in den neuen sozialen Bewegungen." In *Neue soziale Bewegungen in der Bundesrepublik Deutschland,* edited by R. Roth and D. Rucht, 30–44. Frankfurt am Main: Campus, 1987.

Brand, Karl-Werner, et al. *Aufbruch in eine andere Gesellschaft: Neue soziale Bewegungen in der Bundesrepublik.* Frankfurt am Main: Campus, 1986.

Brock, Bazon. "Löcher im Himmel. Die 50er Jahre werden mythenfähig." *Der Spiegel* 14 (3 Apr. 1978): 114.

———. "Warum kürzere Röcke?" *Die Zeit* 52 (27 Dec. 1968): 9–10.

Bröckers, Mathias, et al., eds. *Die Taz: Das Buch: Aktuelle Ewigkeitswerte aus zehn Jahren "tageszeitung."* Frankfurt am Main: Zweitausendeins, 1989.

Brockmann, Stephen. "Der Streit um die grüne Kulturpolitik." In *Öko-Kunst? Zur Ästhetik der Grünen,* edited by Jost Hermand and Hubert Müller, 24–36. Hamburg: Argument, 1989.

Brückner, Peter. *Die Mescalero-Affäre: Ein Lehrstück für Aufklärung und politische Kultur.* Hannover: n.p., [1977/78].

———. "Thesen zur Diskussion der 'Alternativen.'" In *Autonomie oder Ghetto? Kontroversen über die Alternativbewegung,* edited by Wolfgang Kraushaar, 68–85. Frankfurt am Main: Neue Kritik, 1978.

Bruder-Bezzel, Almuth, and Klaus-Jürgen Bruder. "Unter den Talaren der Muff von 10 Jahren: Die Theorie vom Neuen Sozialisationstyp." *Psychologie und Gesellschaft* 3 (1979): 19–32.

Buch, Hans Christoph. "Vorbericht." *Literaturmagazin* 4. Special issue reprinted as *Die Literatur nach dem Tod der Literatur: Bilanz der Politisierung,* edited by Hans Christoph Buch, 11–23. Reinbek: Rowohlt, 1975.

Büchner, Georg. *Lenz.* Translated by Henry J. Schmidt. In *Georg Büchner: Complete Works and Letters,* 139–62. New York: Continuum, 1986.

Bürger, Peter. "Das Erbe der fünfziger Jahre." *Neue Rundschau* 95, nos. 1/2 (1984): 163–69.

Büscher, Barbara. *Wirklichkeitstheater, Straßentheater, Freies Theater: Entstehung und Entwicklung freier Gruppen in der Bundesrepublik Deutschland, 1968–1976.* Frankfurt am Main: Lang, 1987.

Buselmeier, Michael. "Bedingungen des Straßentheaters." In *Straßentheater*, edited by Agnes Hüfer, 320–33. Frankfurt am Main: Suhrkamp, 1970.

———. "Gesellschaftliche Arbeit statt Kunst: Schluß der Diskussion." *Die Zeit* 5 (31 Jan. 1969): 11–12.

Camus, Albert. *Les Justes.* Paris: Gallimard, 1950.

Chambers, Ian. "A Strategy for Living: Black Music and White Subcultures." In *Resistance through Rituals: Youth Subcultures in Post-War Britain*, edited by Stuart Hall and Tony Jefferson, 157–66. London: Hutchinson, 1976.

Clarke, John, et al. "Subcultures, Cultures and Class: A Theoretical Overview." In *Resistance through Rituals: Youth Subcultures in Post-War Britain*, edited by Stuart Hall and Tony Jefferson, 9–74. London: Hutchinson, 1976.

Claußen, Bernhard. "Politisch-kulturelle Bildung im Circus?" In *Experiment: Politische Kultur: Berichte aus einem neuen gesellschaftlichen Alltag*, edited by Gerd Koch, 215–27. Frankfurt am Main: Extrabuch, 1985.

Cohn-Bendit, Daniel, and Reinhard Mohr. *1968: Die letzte Revolution, die noch nichts vom Ozonloch wußte.* Berlin: Wagenbach, 1988.

Cornel, Hajo. "Kultur." In *Handbuch der alternativen Kommunalpolitik*, edited by Wolfgang Pohl et al., 292–99. Bielefeld: AJT, 1985.

———. "Rahmenbedingungen für eine 'Kultur im Widerspruch' " and "Fortschreibung." In *Dem Struwelpeter durch die Haare gefahren: Auf dem Weg zu einer grünen Kulturpolitik*, edited by Die Grünen, 57–59. Bonn: Die Grünen, 1987.

Dahrendorf, Ralf. "Die Revolution, die nie stattfand: Abschied von 1968: Ein ironischer Streifzug durch die sechziger Jahre." *Die Zeit* 20 (13 May 1988): 3.

Danzmann, Gudrun. "Bericht über die fünfziger Jahre in der Schule." In *Fuffziger Jahre*, edited by Götz Eisenberg and Hans-Jürgen Linke, 203–20. Gießen: Focus, 1980.

Daum, Thomas. *Die 2. Kultur: Alternativliteratur in der Bundesrepublik.* Mainz: NewLit, 1981.

Deutschland im Herbst [*Germany in Autumn*]. Munich: Filmverlag der Autoren, 1978.

Dienstag, Matthis. "Provinz aus dem Kopf: Neue Nachrichten über die Metropolen-Spontis." In *Autonomie oder Ghetto? Kontroversen über die*

Alternativbewegung, edited by Wolfgang Kraushaar, 148–86. Frankfurt am Main: Neue Kritik, 1978.

Dietz, Gabriele, et al., eds. *Klamm, Heimlich und Freunde: Die siebziger Jahre.* Berlin: Elefanten, 1987.

Doehlemann, Martin. *Germanisten in Schule und Hochschule: Geltungsanspruch und soziale Wirklichkeit.* Munich: Carl Hanser, 1975.

Dokumentation: Alles über die Zeitung: Frankfurter Allgemeine Zeitung. 17th ed. Frankfurt am Main: Frankfurter Allgemeine Zeitung, 1981.

Döpfner, M. O. C., and Thomas Garms. *Neue deutsche Welle: Kunst oder Mode.* Frankfurt am Main: Ullstein, 1984.

Dröge, Franz. "Mescalero-Sprache und alternative Öffentlichkeit." In *Normalzustände: Politische Kulture in Deutschland*, edited by Eberhard Knödler-Bunte et al., 181–202. Berlin: Ästhetik & Kommunikation, 1978.

Dutschke, Rudi. "Die Widersprüche im Spätkapitalismus, die antiautoritären Studenten und ihr Verhältnis zur Dritten Welt." In *Rebellion der Studenten oder Die neue Opposition*, edited by Uwe Bergmann et al., 33–57. Reinbek: Rowohlt, 1968.

Dutschke, Rudi, Bernd Rabehl, and Christian Semler. "Ein Gespräch über die Zukunft mit Rudi Dutschke, Bernd Rabehl und Christian Semler." *Kursbuch* 14 (1968): 146–74.

Edwards, Jango. *Ich lebe Dich.* Basel: Sphinx, 1983.

Eisenberg, Götz, and Hans-Jürgen Linke, eds. *Fuffziger Jahre.* Gießen: Focus, 1980.

Eley, Geoff. "Nazism, Politics, and the Images of the Past." *Past and Present* 121 (1988): 171–208.

Elkins, Stephan. "The Politics of Mystical Ecology." *Telos* 82 (1989–90): 52–70.

Emig, Günter, et al. *Die Alternativpresse: Kontroversen, Polemiken, Dokumente.* Ellwangen: Emig, 1980.

Enzensberger, Hans Magnus. "Commonplaces on the Newest Literature." Translated by Michael Roloff. In *Critical Essays*, edited by Reinhold Grimm and Bruce Armstrong, 35–45. New York: Continuum, 1982.

———. *The Havana Inquiry.* Translated by Peter Mayer. New York: Holt, Rinehart & Winston, 1974.

———. "The Industrialization of the Mind." In *The Consciousness Industry: On Literature, Politics, and the Media*, 3–15. New York: Seabury, 1974. Reprint in *Dreamers of the Absolute: Essays on Ecology, Media and Power*, 7–19. London: Hutchinson, 1988.

———. *Der kurze Sommer der Anarchie: Buenaventura Durrutis Leben und Tod.* Frankfurt am Main: Suhrkamp, 1972.

Erhard, Ludwig. *Prosperity through Competition.* Translated by Edith Temple Roberts and John B. Wood. New York: Thames and Hudson, 1958.

Evans, Richard J. *In Hitler's Shadow: West German Historians and the Attempts to Escape from the Nazi Past.* New York: Pantheon, 1989.

———. "The New Nationalism and the Old History: Perspectives on the West German 'Historikerstreit.'" *Journal of Modern History* 59 (1987): 761–97.

Franck, Dieter, ed. *Die fünfziger Jahre: Als das Leben wieder anfing.* Munich: Piper, 1981.

Frankland, E. Gene, and Donald Schoonmaker. *Between Protest and Power: The Green Party in Germany.* Boulder CO: Westview, 1992.

Freud, Sigmund. "Civilization and Its Discontents." In *The Standard Edition of the Complete Psychological Works of Sigmund Freud,* vol. 21, translated by James Strachey, 177–204. London: Hogarth, 1972.

———. "Civilized Sexual Morality and Modern Nervous Illness." In *The Standard Edition of the Complete Psychological Works of Sigmund Freud,* vol. 9, translated by James Strachey, 57–146. London: Hogarth, 1951.

———. "Totem and Taboo." In *The Standard Edition of the Complete Psychological Works of Sigmund Freud,* vol. 13, translated by James Strachey, 1–162. London: Hogarth, 1955.

Fried, Erich. "Ja, aber . . . und . . . Der Warencharakter der Kunst ist kein Grund zur Verzweiflung." *Die Zeit* 3 (17 Jan. 1969): 13

Fröhner, Rolf. *Wie stark sind die Halbstarken? Beruf und Berufsnot: Politische, kulturelle und seelische Probleme der deutschen Jugend im Bundesgebiet und in Westberlin.* Bielefeld: Stackelberg, 1956.

Die Früchte der Revolte: Über die Veränderung der politischen Kultur durch die Studentenbewegung. Berlin: Wagenbach, 1988.

Geier Sturzflug. "Bruttosozialprodukt." *Heiße Zeiten.* Ariola, 1983. Lyrics reprinted in *Die Lage war noch nie so ernst: Eine Geschichte der BRD in ihrer Satire,* edited by Karl Hoche, 231. Königstein: Athenäum, 1984.

———. "Besuchen Sie Europa, solange es noch steht." *Heiße Zeiten.* Ariola, 1983.

Glaser, Hermann. "Das Exil fand nicht statt: Schulwirklichkeit im Deutschunterricht 1945–1965." In *10. Mai 1933: Bücherverbrennung in Deutschland und die Folgen,* edited by Ulrich Walberer, 260–84. Frankfurt am Main: Fischer, 1983.

———. *Die Kulturgeschichte der Bundesrepublik Deutschland.* 3 vol. 1986. Reprint. Frankfurt am Main: Fischer, 1990.

Glotz, Peter. "Jeder fünfte denkt etwa so wie der Mescalero: Berlins Wissenschaftssenator Peter Glotz über Sympathisanten und die Situation an der Hochschule." *Der Spiegel* 41 (1977): 49–63.

Goethe, Johann Wolfgang von. *Die Leiden des jungen Werthers.* Stuttgart: Reclam, 1984. *The Sufferings of Young Werther and Elective Affinities.* Translated and edited by Victor Lange. New York: Continuum, 1990.

Göttinger Mescalero, Ein. "Buback: Ein Nachruf." *Göttinger Nachrichten* 25 Apr. 1977: 10–12. Reprints in: *"Buback: Ein Nachruf": Eine Dokumentation.* Berlin: Das politische Buch, 1977. Peter Brückner. *Die Mescalero-Affäre: Ein Lehrstück für Aufklärung und politische Kultur,* 24–25. Hannover: n.p., [1977/78]. Peter Glotz. *Die Innenausstattung der Macht: Politisches Tagebuch, 1976–1978,* 169–73. Munich: Steinhausen, 1979. Karl Hoche, ed. *Die Lage war noch nie so ernst: Eine Geschichte der* BRD *in ihrer Satire,* 197–201. Königstein: Athenäum, 1984. Gabriele Dietz et al., eds. *Klamm, Heimlich & Freunde: Die siebziger Jahre,* 122–24. Berlin: Elefanten, 1987.

Gottschalch, Wilfried. "Gutachterliche Äußerung zum Beweiß dafür, daß . . ." In *Zwei Kulturen? Tunix, Mescalero und die Folgen,* edited by Dieter Hoffmann-Axthelm et al., 212–23. Berlin: Ästhetik & Kommunikation, 1978.

Gramsci, Antonio. *Selections from the Prison Notebooks.* Edited and translated by Quintin Hoare and Geoffrey Nowell Smith. New York: International, 1971.

Grube, Frank, and Gerhard Richter. *Die Gründerjahre der* BRD: *Deutschland zwischen 1945 und 1955.* Hamburg: Hoffmann & Campe, 1981.

Grünen, Die. *Bundesprogramm.* 2d ed. Bonn: Die Grünen, 1983. English translation. *Programme of the German Green Party.* 2d ed. Translated and edited by Jonathon Porrit. London: Heretic, 1985.

———. *Dem Struwelpeter durch die Haare gefahren: Auf dem Weg zu einer grünen Kulturpolitik.* Bonn: Die Grünen, 1987.

Gumpel, Liselotte. *"Concrete" Poetry from East and West Germany: The Language of Exemplarism and Experimentalism.* New Haven CT: Yale University Press, 1976.

Habermas, Jürgen. "Die Scheinrevolution und ihre Kinder: Sechs Thesen über Taktik, Ziele und Situationsanalyse der oppositionellen Jugend." In *Die Linke antwortet Jürgen Habermas,* 5–15. Frankfurt am Main: Europäische Verlagsanstalt, 1968.

———. *The Structural Transformation of the Public Sphere: An Inquiry into a Category of Bourgeois Society.* Translated by Thomas Burger and Frederick Lawrence. Cambridge MA: MIT Press, 1989.

Hahn, Ulla. *Literatur in der Aktion: Zur Entwicklung operativer Literatur-*

formen in der Bundesrepublik. Wiesbaden: Akademische Verlagsanstalt Athenaion, 1978.

Hamm, Peter. "Versäumte Solidarität: Eine Erwiderung auf Peter Handkes Aufsatz 'Totgeborene Sätze.'" *Die Zeit* 50 (13 Dec. 1968): 18.

Handke, Peter. "Für das Straßentheater gegen das Straßentheater." *Theater Heute* 7 (1968): 6–7.

———. *The Goalie's Anxiety at the Penalty Kick.* Translated by Michael Roloff. New York: Farrar, Straus & Giroux, 1972.

———. *A Moment of True Feeling.* Translated by Ralph Manheim. New York: Farrar, Straus & Giroux, 1977.

———. *Short Letter, Long Farewell.* Translated by Ralph Manheim. New York: Farrar, Straus & Giroux, 1974.

———. "Straßentheater und Theatertheater." *Theater Heute* 4 (1968): 4–7.

———. "Totgeborene Sätze." *Die Zeit* 49 (6 Dec. 1968): 17–18.

Hans, Jan, et al., eds. *Lyrik-Katalog Bundesrepublik: Gedichte: Biographien, Statements.* Munich: Goldmann, 1979.

Hansen, Klaus. "APO und Terrorismus: Eine Skizze der Zusammenhänge." *Frankfurter Hefte* 1 (1979): 11–22.

Hardach, Gerd. "Die Wirtschaft der fünfziger Jahre: Restauration und Wirtschaftwunder." In *Die fünfziger Jahre: Beiträge zur Politik und Kultur,* edited by Dieter Bänsch, 49–60. Tübingen: Gunter Narr, 1985.

Härlin, Benny. "Von Haus zu Haus: Berliner Bewegungsstudien." *Kursbuch* 65 (1981): 1–28.

Hartung, Harald. *Experimentelle Literatur und Konkrete Poesie.* Göttingen: Vandenhoeck & Ruprecht, 1975.

Hasenclever, Wolf-Dieter, and Connie Hasenclever. *Grüne Zeiten: Politik für eine lebenswerte Zukunft.* Munich: Kösel, 1982.

Häsing, Helga, et al., eds. *Narziß: Ein neuer Sozialisationstypus?* Bensheim: päd-extra Buchverlag, 1979.

Haug, Wolfgang Fritz. *Kritik der Warenästhetik.* Frankfurt am Main: Suhrkamp, 1971.

Hazel, Hazel, E. "Die alte und die neue Sensibilität: Erfahrungen mit dem Subjekt, das zwischen die Kulturen gefallen ist." In *Die Literatur nach dem Tod der Literatur: Bilanz der Politisierung,* edited by Hans Christoph Buch, 129–42. Reinbek: Rowohlt, 1975.

Hebdige, Dick. *Subculture: The Meaning of Style.* London: Methuen, 1979.

Heckelmann, Günther, and Lucas Heumann. "Herbert Marcuse und die Szene 1978: Studentenrevolte und Terror-Eskalation." *Die politische Meinung* 181 (1978): 54–69.

Hensel, Georg. "Don Carlitos, der Infantile von Spanien." *Frankfurter Allgemeine Zeitung* 1 Oct. 1979: 23.

———. "Fluchtwege des Theaters aus der Sprache: Beobachtungen beim 'Theater der Nationen' in Hamburg." *Frankfurter Allgemeine Zeitung* 12 May 1979: 23.

———. "Der Infant von Spanien und sein Vogel." *Frankfurter Allgemeine Zeitung* 6 Oct. 1979: 25.

Hermand, Jost. *Die Kultur der Bundesrepublik Deutschland, 1965–1985.* Munich: Nymphenburger, 1988.

———. *Kultur im Wiederaufbau: Die Bundesrepublik, 1945–1965.* Munich: Nymphenburger, 1986.

———. "Dem Struwelpeter durch die Haare gefahren: Anmerkungen zu einer kulturpolitischen Broschüre der Grünen." In *Im Wettlauf mit der Zeit: Anstöße zu einer ökologiebewußten Ästhetik,* 189–97. Berlin: Bohn, 1991.

Hermand, Jost, and Hubert Müller, eds. *Öko-Kunst? Zur Ästhetik der Grünen.* Hamburg: Argument, 1989.

Hillach, Ansgar. "Walter Benjamin: Korrektiv Kritischer Theorie oder revolutionäre Handhabe?" In *Literatur und Studentenbewegung,* edited by Martin Lüdke, 64–89. Lesen 6. Opladen: Westdeutscher Verlag, 1977.

Hiltl, Michael, ed. *Die Alternativbewegung: Ansprüche, Praxis, Perspektiven.* Special issue of *Ulcus Molle Sonder-Info* 4 (1981).

Hirsch, Joachim. *Der Sicherheitsstaat: Das 'Modell Deutschland,' seine Krise und die neuen sozialen Bewegungen.* Frankfurt am Main: Europäische Verlagsanstalt, 1980.

"Historikerstreit": Die Dokumentation der Kontroverse um die Einzigartigkeit der nationalsozialistischen Judenvernichtung. Munich: Piper, 1987.

Hochhuth, Rolf. *The Deputy.* Translated by Richard Winston and Clara Winston. New York: Grove, 1963.

Hoffmann-Axthelm, Dieter, et al., eds. *Zwei Kulturen? Tunix, Mescalero und die Folgen.* Berlin: Ästhetik & Kommunikation, 1978.

Hohendahl, Peter Uwe. *The Institution of Criticism.* Ithaca NY: Cornell University Press, 1982.

———. "Politisierung der Kunsttheorie: Zur ästhetischen Diskussion nach 1965." In *Deutsche Literatur in der Bundesrepublik seit 1965,* edited by Paul Michael Lützeler and Egon Schwarz, 282–99. Königstein: Athenäum, 1980.

Holler, Eckard. "Grüne Kulturpolitik und kulturelle Bewegung 'von unten.'" In *Öko-Kunst? Zur Ästhetik der Grünen,* edited by Jost Hermand and Hubert Müller, 55–70. Hamburg: Argument, 1989.

Holthusen, Hans Egon. *Sartre in Stammheim: Zwei Themen aus den Jahren der großen Turbulenz.* Stuttgart: Klett-Cotta, [1982].

Horkheimer, Max, and Theodor W. Adorno. *Dialectic of Enlightenment.* Translated by John Cumming. New York: Continuum, 1972.

Horx, Matthias. "Du bist, was du ißt: Sieg im Freßkrieg: Kleine Kulturgeschichte des jüngsten deutschen Küchenkampfes." *Frankfurter Rundschau* 18 July 1987: M 10.

———. *Das Ende der Alternativen, oder Die verlorene Unschuld der Radikalität.* 1985. Reprint. Munich: Goldmann, 1989.

Huber, Joseph. *Wer soll das alles ändern: Die Alternativen der Alternativbewegung.* Berlin: Rotbuch, 1980.

Hübner, Raoul. "Klau mich, oder Die Veränderung von Verkehrsformen: Anstöße der Studentenbewegung." In *Literatur und Studentenbewegung: Eine Zwischenbilanz,* edited by W. Martin Lüdke, 219–47. Opladen: Westdeutscher Verlag, 1977.

Hübsch, Hadayatullah. *Alternative Öffentlichkeit: Freiräume der Information und Kommunikation.* Frankfurt am Main: Fischer, 1980.

Hüfer, Agnes, ed. *Straßentheater.* Frankfurt am Main: Suhrkamp, 1970.

Huhn, Jens. "Die Stadtindianer auf dem Kriegspfad." In *Autonomie oder Ghetto? Kontroversen über die Alternativbewegung,* edited by Wolfgang Kraushaar, 129–47. Frankfurt am Main: Neue Kritik, 1978.

Hülsberg, Werner. *The German Greens: A Social and Political Profile.* London: Verso, 1988.

Huyssen, Andreas. *After the Great Divide: Modernism, Mass Culture, Postmodernism.* Bloomington: Indiana University Press, 1986.

———. "Das Versprechen der Natur: Alternative Naturkonzepte im 18. Jahrhundert." In *Natur und Natürlichkeit: Stationen des Grünen in der deutschen Literatur,* edited by Reinhold Grimm and Jost Hermand, 1–18. Königstein: Athenäum, 1981.

Jameson, Frederic. *Marxism and Form: Twentieth-Century Dialectical Theories of Literature.* Princeton NJ: Princeton University Press, 1971.

Juchler, Ingo. *Rebellische Subjektivität und Internationalismus: Der Einfluß Herbert Marcuses und der nationalen Befreiungsbewegungen in der sogenannten Dritten Welt auf die Studentenbewegung der Bundesrepublik Deutschland.* Marburg: Arbeiterbewegung & Gesellschaftswissenschaft, 1989.

Kafka, Franz. "Metamorphosis." In *Selected Stories of Franz Kafka,* translated by Willa and Edwin Muir, 20–90. New York: Random House, 1993.

Kändler, Klaus. "Das Straßentheater stellt sich vor." *Sinn und Form* 6 (1971): 1366–71.

Keitel, Evelyne. "Recent Literary Trends: *Verständigungstexte: Form Funktion, Wirkung.*" *German Quarterly* 56.3 (1983): 431–55.

Kessler, Dieter. *Untersuchungen zur Konkreten Dichtung: Vorformen— Theorie— Texte.* Meisenheim am Glan: Hain, 1976.

Kiesel, Helmut, and Paul Münch. *Gesellschaft und Literatur im 18. Jahrhundert: Voraussetzungen und Entstehung des literarischen Marktes in Deutschland.* Munich: Beck, 1977.

Koebner, Thomas, ed. *Tendenzen der deutschen Gegenwartsliteratur.* 2d ed. Stuttgart: Kröner, 1984.

Kolinsky, Eva, ed. *The Greens in West Germany: Organisation and Policy Making.* Oxford: Berg, 1989.

Kos, Wolfgang. "Landgemacht und handgemacht: Bemerkungen zur kulturellen Handschrift im alternativen Milieu." *Kunstforum International* 93 (1988): 126–234.

Kosta, Barbara. *Recasting Autobiography: Women's Counterfictions in Contemporary German Literature and Film.* Ithaca NY: Cornell University Press, 1994.

Kracauer, Siegfried. *Theory of Film: The Redemption of Physical Reality.* New York: Oxford University Press, 1960.

Kramer, Michael. *Pantomime und Clownerei: Geschichte der Clownerei von der Commedia dell' arte bis zu den Festivals of Fools.* 2d ed. Offenbach: Burckhardthaus-Laetare, 1986.

Kramer Ruoff, Karen. "/New Subjectivity/: Third Thoughts on a Literary Discourse." Ph.D. diss. Stanford University, 1983.

Kraushaar, Wolfgang. "Rockmusik als politischer Deckmantel?" In *Thema: Rock gegen Rechts: Musik als politisches Instrument,* edited by Bernd Leukert, 69–86. Frankfurt am Main: Fischer, 1984.

———. "Thesen zum Verhältnis von Altenativ- und Fluchtbewegung: Am Beispiel der frankfurter scene." In *Autonomie oder Ghetto? Kontroversen über die Alternativbewegung,* edited by Wolfgang Kraushaar, 8–67. Frankfurt am Main: Neue Kritik, 1978.

Krechel, Ursula. "Leben in Anführungszeichen: Das Authentische in der gegenwärtigen Literatur." *Literaturmagazin* 11 (1979): 80–107.

Kreuzer, Helmut. "Neue Subjektivität: Zur Literatur der siebziger Jahre in der Bundesrepublik." In *Deutsche Gegenwartsliteratur: Ausganspositionen und aktuelle Entwicklungen,* edited by Manfred Durzak, 77–106. Stuttgart: Reclam, 1981.

Krüger, Heinz-Hermann. "Exis habe ich keine gesehen: Auf der Suche nach einer jugendlichen Subkultur in den 50er Jahren." In *Die Elvis-Tolle, die hatte ich mir unauffällig wachsen lassen: Lebensgeschichten und jugendliche*

Alltagskultur in den fünfziger Jahren, edited by Heinz-Hermann Krüger, 129–51. Leverkusen: Leske & Budrich, 1985.

———. "Viel Lärm um Nichts? Jugendliche 'Existentialisten' in den 50er Jahren." In *Schock und Schöpfung: Jugendästhetik im 20. Jahrhundert,* edited by Deutscher Werkbund e.V. and Württembergischer Kunstverein, 263–74. Darmstadt: Luchterhand, 1986.

Kuckuck, Margareth. *Student und Klassenkampf: Studentenbewegung in der* BRD *seit 1967.* Hamburg: Association, 1974.

Kuhnert, Peter, and Ute Ackermann. "Jenseits von Lust und Liebe? Jugendsexualität in den 50er Jahren." In *Die Elvis-Tolle, die hatte ich mir unauffällig wachsen lassen: Lebensgeschichten und jugendliche Alltagskultur in den fünfziger Jahren,* edited by Heinz-Hermann Krüger, 43–81. Leverkusen: Leske & Budrich, 1985.

Lafargue, Paul. *Das Recht auf Faulheit.* n.p.: Sonne & Faulheit, 1980.

Lämmert, E., et al., eds. *Germanistik: Eine deutsche Wissenschaft.* Frankfurt am Main: Suhrkamp, 1967.

Langguth, Gerd. *The Green Factor in German Politics.* Boulder CO: Westview, 1984.

Leggewie, Claus. "1968: Ein Laboratorium der nachindustriellen Gesellschaft? Zur Tradition der antiautoritären Revolte seit den sechziger Jahren." *Aus Politik und Zeitgeschichte* B20/88 (13 May 1988): 3–15.

Lehnardt, Karl-Heinz, and Ludger Volmer. *Politik zwischen Kopf und Bauch: Zur Relevanz der Persönlichkeitsbildung in den politischen Konzepten der Studentenbewegung in der* BRD. Bochum: Druckladen, 1979.

Leineweber, Bernd, and Karl-Ludwig Schibel. "Die Alternativbewegung: Ein Beitrag zu ihrer gesellschaftlichen Bedeutung und politischen Tragweite, ihren Möglichkeiten und Grenzen." In *Autonomie oder Ghetto? Kontroversen über die Alternativbewegung,* edited by Wolfgang Kraushaar, 95–128. Frankfurt am Main: Neue Kritik, 1978.

Lethen, Helmut. "Zur materialistischen Kunsttheorie Benjamins." *Alternative: Zeitschrift für Literatur und Diskussion* 56/57 (Dec. 1967): 225–34.

Leukert, Bernd, ed. *Thema: Rock gegen Rechts: Musik als politisches Instrument.* Frankfurt am Main: Fischer, 1984.

Liebmann-Schaub, Uta. "Foucault, Alternative Presses, and Alternative Ideology in West Germany: A Report." *German Studies Review* 12.1 (Feb. 1989): 139–53.

Liessmann, Konrad Paul. "Natura Mortua: Über das Verhältnis von Ästhetik und Ökologie." *Kunstforum International* 93 (1988): 64–71.

Lindner, Rolf. "Jugendkultur: Stilisierte Widerstände." In *Immer diese Ju-*

gend! Ein zeitgeschichtliches Mosaik 1945 bis heute, edited by Deutsches Jugendinstitut, 14–24. Munich: Kösel, 1985.

Linstead, Michael. *Outer World and Inner World: Socialisation and Emancipation in the Works of Peter Handke, 1964–1981.* Frankfurt am Main: Lang, 1988.

Loukopoulos-Lepanto, Wassili. *Kunst für den Menschen, oder Für eine ökologische Kunst.* Freiburg: Hochschul, 1983.

Lübbe, Hermann. "Der Mythos der 'kritischen Generation': Ein Rückblick." *Aus Politik und Zeitgeschichte* B20/88 (13 May 1988): 17–25.

Lüdke, W. Martin. "Der Kreis, das Bewußtsein und das Ding: Aktuell motivierte Anmerkungen zu der vergangenen Diskussion um den Warencharakter der Kunst." In *Literatur und Studentenbewegung: Eine Zwischenbilanz*, edited by W. Martin Lüdke, 124–57. Opladen: Westdeutscher Verlag, 1977.

McCormick, Richard W. *Politics of the Self: Feminism and the Postmodern in West German Literature and Film.* Princeton NJ: Princeton University Press, 1991.

McGowan, Moray. "Neue Subjektivität." In *After the 'Death of Literature': West German Writing of the 1970s*, edited by Keith Bullivant, 53–68. Oxford: Berg, 1989.

Maier, Charles S. *The Unmasterable Past: History, Holocaust, and German National Identity.* Cambridge MA: Harvard University Press, 1988.

Marcuse, Herbert. *Eros and Civilization: A Philosophical Inquiry into Freud.* Boston: Beacon, 1955.

———. *An Essay on Liberation.* Boston: Beacon, 1969.

———. *One-Dimensional Man: Studies in the Ideology of Advanced Industrial Society.* Boston: Beacon, 1964.

———. "Repressive Tolerance." In *A Critique of Pure Tolerance*, edited by Robert E. Wolff et al., 81–117. Boston: Beacon, 1965.

Maren-Grisebach, Manon. *Die Philosophie der Grünen.* Munich: Günter Olzog, 1982.

Markovits, Andrei S., and Philip S. Gorski. *The German Left: Red, Green, and Beyond.* New York: Oxford University Press, 1993.

Meinel, Rüdiger. "Möglichkeiten eines sozialistischen Straßentheaters." In *Straßentheater*, edited by Agnes Hüfer, 306–12. Frankfurt am Main: Suhrkamp, 1970.

Michel, Karl Markus. "Ein Kranz für die Literatur: Fünf Variationen über eine These." *Kursbuch* 15 (1968): 169–86.

Micky. "Berlin, 1. Februar." In *Bohemien—Tramp—Sponti: Boheme und Al-*

ternativkultur, edited by Gerd Stein, 305–7. Frankfurt am Main: Fischer, 1982.

Mitchell, Tony. *Dario Fo, People's Court Jester.* London: Methuen, 1984.

Morsey, Rudolf. *Die Bundesrepublik Deutschland: Entstehung und Entwicklung bis 1969.* Munich: Oldenbourg, 1987.

Mosler, Peter. *Was wir wollten, was wir wurden: Studentenrevolte, zehn Jahre danach.* Reinbek: Rowohlt, 1977.

"Mueze." *Deutsches Wörterbuch.* Edited by Jacob and Wilhelm Grimm. Leipzig: Hirzel, 1885.

Mühlen, Bernt Ture von zur. "Straßentheater: Politische und ästhetische Kommunikation." In *Direkte Kommunikation und Massenkommunikation: Referate und Diskussionsprotokolle des 20. Deutschen Volkskunde-Kongresses in Weingarten,* edited by Hermann Bausinger and Elfriede Moser-Rath, 215–25. Tübingen: Gulde-Druck, 1976.

Müller, Heiner. *Gundling's Life Frederick of Prussia Lessing's Sleep Dream Scream.* In *Hamletmachine and Other Texts for the Stage,* translated by Carl Weber, 59–78. New York: Performing Arts Journal, 1984.

———. Hamletmachine. In *Hamletmachine and Other Texts for the Stage,* translated by Carl Weber, 49–58. New York: Performing Arts Journal, 1984.

Mündemann, Tobias. *Die 68er . . . und was aus ihnen geworden ist.* Munich: Heyne, 1988.

Müschen, Klaus. "Praktisch unübersichtlich, unübersichtlich praktisch." In *Alternativen zur alten Politik? Neue soziale Bewegungen in der Diskussion,* edited by Ulrike C. Wasmuht, 260–71. Darmstadt: Wissenschaftliche Buchgesellschaft, 1989.

"Mythos der 50er Jahre: Heimweh nach den falschen Fünfzigern." *Der Spiegel* 14 (3 Apr. 1978): 90–111.

"Natur." *Geschichtliche Grundbegriffe: Historisches Lexikon zur politisch-sozialen Sprache in Deutschland.* Vol. 4. Edited by Otto Brunner et al., 215–44. Stuttgart: Klett-Cotta, 1978.

Nettelbeck, Uwe. "Recht hat, wer zuletzt lacht." *Die Zeit* 2 (10 Jan. 1969): 11–12.

Noelle, Elisabeth, and Erich Peter Neumann, eds. *The Germans: Public Opinion Polls, 1947–1966.* Allensbach: Verlag für Demoskopie, 1967.

Offe, Claus. "Griff nach der Notbremse: Bewirken oder Bewahren: Der Aufstieg der Grünen bringt zwei Politikbegriffe ins Spiel, die einander widersprechen." In *Was sollen die Grünen im Parlament?* edited by Wolfgang Kraushaar, 85–92. Frankfurt am Main: Neue Kritik, 1983.

———. "New Social Movements: Challenging the Boundaries of Institutional Politics." *Social Research* 52.4 (1985): 817–68.

Peters, Butz. *RAF: Terrorismus in Deutschland.* Stuttgart: Deutsche Verlagsanstalt, 1991.

Plenzdorf, Ulrich. *The New Sufferings of Young W.* Translated by Kenneth P. Wilcox. New York: Ungar, 1979.

POFO. "Franz-Gans-Kampagne." In *Straßentheater,* edited by Agnes Hüfer, 279–82. Frankfurt am Main: Suhrkamp, 1970.

Poguntke, Thomas. "The Organization of a Participatory Party: The German Greens." *European Journal of Political Research* 15.6 (1987): 609–33.

Prospekt: Tageszeitung. n.p., 1978.

Raschke, Joachim. *Die Grünen: Wie sie wurden, was sie sind.* Köln: Bund, 1993.

―――. *Soziale Bewegungen: Ein historisch-systematischer Grundriß.* Frankfurt am Main: Campus, 1985.

―――. "Zum Begriff der sozialen Bewegung." In *Neue soziale Bewegungen in der Bundesrepublik Deutschland,* edited by Roland Roth and Dieter Rucht, 19–29. Frankfurt am Main: Campus, 1987.

Reiche, Reimut. "Sexuelle Revolution: Erinnerung an einen Mythos." In *Die Früchte der Revolte: Über die Veränderung der politischen Kultur durch die Studentenbewegung,* 45–72. Berlin: Wagenbach, 1988.

―――. "Verteidigung der 'neuen Sensibilität.'" In *Die Linke antwortet Jürgen Habermas,* 90–103. Frankfurt am Main: Europäische Verlagsanstalt, 1968.

Reichelt, Helmut, and Gert Schäfer. "Was heißt hier 'Ware?' Die Antwort des Karl Marx." *Die Zeit* 4 (24 Jan. 1969): 12.

Reich-Ranicki, Marcel. *Entgegnungen: Zur deutschen Literatur der siebziger Jahre.* Stuttgart: Deutsche Verlagsanstalt, 1979.

―――. "Rückkehr zur schönen Literatur: Eine Bilanz aus Anlaß der Frankfurter Buchmesse." *Frankfurter Allgemeine Zeitung* 8 Oct. 1975: 21.

―――. "Schriftsteller am stillen Herd." *Frankfurter Allgemeine Zeitung* 18 Oct. 1975: 1.

Rilke, Rainer Maria. *The Notebook of Malte Laurids Brigge.* Translated by Stephen Mitchell. New York: Random House, 1983.

Roberts, David. "Tendenzwenden: Die sechziger und siebziger Jahre in literatur-historischer Perspektive." In *Deutsche Vierteljahresschrift für Literaturwissenschaft und Geistesgeschichte* 56.2 (1982): 290–313.

Röder, Klaus. "Thesen zur Alternativkultur." In *Gegenkultur Heute: Die Alternativbewegung von Woodstock bis Tunix,* edited by J. Gehret, 152–60. Amsterdam: AZID, 1979.

Roth, Roland, and Dieter Rucht, eds. *Neue soziale Bewegungen in der Bundesrepublik Deutschland.* Frankfurt am Main: Campus, 1986.

Runge, Erika. *Bottroper Protokolle*. Frankfurt am Main: Suhrkamp, 1968.

Rutschky, Michael. *Erfahrungshunger: Ein Essay über die siebziger Jahre.* Cologne: Kiepenheuer & Witsch, 1980.

"Sachschaden: Häuserkampf und andere Kämpfe." *taz-Journal* 3 (1981).

Sandford, John. *The New German Cinema*. London: Wolff, 1980.

Sarkar, Saral. *Green-Alternative Politics in West Germany*. Vol. 1. *New Social Movements*. Tokyo: United Nations University Press, 1993.

Schäfer, Hermann. "Das Haus der Geschichte der Bundesrepublik Deutschland: Strukturgeschichtliche Darstellung im Museum." *Aus Politik und Zeitgeschichte* B2 (1988): 27–34.

Schäfer, W., ed. *Neue soziale Bewegungen: Konservativer Aufbruch im bunten Gewand*. Frankfurt am Main: Fischer, 1983.

Scharang, Michael. "Thesen zur Kulturrevolution." In *Zur Emanzipation der Kunst: Essays*, 26–54. Neuwied: Luchterhand, 1971.

———. "Zur Emanzipation der Kunst: Benjamins Konzeption einer materialistischen Ästhetik." *Ästhetik und Kommunikation: Beiträge zur politischen Erziehung* 1 (July 1970): 67–85.

Schechter, Joel. *Durov's Pig: Clowns, Politics, and Theater*. New York: Theater Communications Group, 1985.

"Schelm." *Deutsches Wörterbuch*. Edited by Jacob Grimm and Wilhelm Grimm. Leipzig: S. Hirze, 1893.

Schelsky, Helmut. *Die skeptische Generation: Eine Soziologie der Jugend*. 1957. Cologne: Eugen Diedrichs, 1963.

Schmid, Thomas. "Die Wirklichkeit des Traumes: Versuch über die Grenzen des autopoietischen Vermögens meiner Generation." In *Die Früchte der Revolte: Über die Veränderung der politischen Kultur durch die Studentenbewegung*, 7–33. Berlin: Wagenbach, 1988.

Schneider, Michael. "Von der alten Radikalität zur neuen Sensibilität." *Kursbuch* 49 (1977): 174–87.

Schneider, Peter. "Die Phantasie im Spätkapitalismus und die Kulturrevolution." *Kursbuch* 16 (1969): 1–37.

———. *Lenz*. Berlin: Rotbuch, 1973.

Schreiben oder Literatur. Special issue of *Literaturmagazin* 11 (1979).

Schreitmüller, Andreas. *Filme aus Filmen: Möglichkeiten des Episodenfilms*. Oberhausen: Laufen, 1983.

Schröder, C. J. "Drei Fallen grün-alternativer Kulturpolitik." *Kultur und Gesellschaft* 4 (1984): 5–6.

———. "Kunst als Klassenkampf, oder Kultur für Alle? Der Richtungsstreit in der grün-alternativen Kulturpolitik." *Grüner Basis-Dienst* 3 (1984): 23–27. Reprint in *Dem Struwelpeter durch die Haare gefahren: Auf dem Weg zu einer grünen Kulturpolitik*, edited by Die Grünen, 60–63. Bonn: Die Grünen, 1987.

Schröder, D., ed. *Terrorismus: Gewalt mit politischem Motiv*. Munich: List, 1986.

Schülein, Johann August. "Von der Studentenrevolte zur Tendenzwende oder Der Rückzug ins Private: Eine sozialpsychologische Analyse." *Kursbuch* 48 (1977): 101–17.

Schultz, Joachim, and Gerhard Köpf, eds. *Das Insel-Buch der Faulheit*. Frankfurt am Main: Insel, 1983.

Schütte, Johannes. *Revolte und Verweigerung: Zur Politik und Sozialpsychologie der Sponti-Bewegung*. Gießen: Focus, 1980.

Schwarzer, Alice. *So fing es an: Die neue Frauenbewegung*. Köln: Emma-Frauenverlags, 1981.

SDS-Gruppe "Kultur und Revolution." "Kunst als Ware der Bewußtseinsindustrie." *Die Zeit* 29 Nov. 1968: 12.

Seibold, Carsten, ed. *Die 68er: Das Fest der Rebellion*. Munich: Knaur, 1988.

Siepmann, E., ed. *Bikini: Die fünfziger Jahre: Kalter Krieg und Capri Sonne: Politik, Alltag, Opposition*. Berlin: Elefanten, 1981.

Simeon, Thomas. "Fetisch Objektivität: Die schillernden Wahrheiten der 'tageszeitung.'" In *Wie objektiv sind unsere Medien?* edited by Günter Bentele and Robert Ruoff, 276–89. Frankfurt am Main: Fischer, 1982.

Soden, Kristine von, ed. *Der große Unterschied: Die neue Frauenbewegung und die siebziger Jahre*. Berlin: Elefanten, 1988.

Sontheimer, Michael. "Rebellion ist gerechtfertigt: Bericht eines 'Post-68ers.'" *Aus Politik und Zeitgeschichte* B20/88 (13 May 1988): 36–46.

Das Sozialistische Straßentheater. "Kritik und Selbstkritik." In *Straßentheater*, edited by Agnes Hüfer, 285–305. Frankfurt am Main: Suhrkamp, 1970.

Spiegel-Spezial: Die wilden 68er: Die Spiegel-Serie über die Studentenrevolution. Hamburg: Spiegel, 1988.

Staiger, Emil. *Die Kunst der Interpretation: Studien zur deutschen Literaturgeschichte*. Zurich: Atlantis, 1955.

Stamm, Karl-Heinz. *Alternative Öffentlichkeit: Die Erfahrungsproduktion neuer sozialer Bewegungen*. Frankfurt am Main: Campus, 1988.

Stefan, Verena. *Shedding and Literally Dreaming*. New York: Feminist Press, 1994.

Stein, Gerd, ed. *Bohemien—Tramp—Sponti: Boheme und Alternativkultur*. Frankfurt am Main: Fischer, 1982.

Steinbeiß, Florian. *Deutsch-Folk: Auf der Suche nach der verlorenen Tradition*. Frankfurt am Main: Fischer, 1984.

Stephan, Peter M. "Das Gedicht in der Marktlücke: Abschließende Marginalien zur Diskussion über 'Neue Subjektivität' in der Lyrik." In *Lyrik-Katalog Bundesrepublik: Gedichte: Biographien: Statements*, 2d ed., edited by Jan Hans et al., 496–512. Munich: Goldmann, 1979.

Stölzl, Christoph, and Verena Tafel. "Das Deutsche Historische Museum in Berlin: Perspektiven und Ziele, Entstehung und gegenwärtiger Stand." *Aus Politik und Zeitgeschichte* B2 (1988): 17–26.

Stourac, Richard, and Kathleen McCreery. *Theater As a Weapon: Workers' Theater in the Soviet Union, Germany and Britain, 1917–1934.* London: Routledge and Kegan Paul, 1986.

Ströbele, Christian, and Udo Knapp. "Kunst und Kultur—das ist wie Senf und Schlagsahne." In *Dem Struwelpeter durch die Haare gefahren: Auf dem Weg zu einer grünen Kulturpolitik*, edited by Die Grünen, 30–33. Bonn: Die Grünen, 1987.

Struck, Karin. *Klassenliebe.* Frankfurt am Main: Suhrkamp, 1973.

"Theater und Revolte: Eine Debatte" *Theater Heute Jahresheft* (1968): 25–37.

Theobaldy, Jürgen. "Literaturkritik, astrologisch." In *Lyrik-Katalog Bundesrepublik: Gedichte: Biographien: Statements*, 2d ed., edited by Jan Hans et al., 463–67. Munich: Goldmann, 1979.

Tolmein, Oliver, and Detlef zum Winkel. *Tazsachen: Krallen zeigen—Pfötchen geben.* Hamburg: Konkret, 1989.

"The Travelling Musicians." In *Grimm's Fairy Tales*, 11–15. Harmondsworth: Penguin, 1982.

"Treffen in Tunix: Westberlin 27.–28.1.78." Tunix flyer. Reprints in: *Zwei Kulturen? Tunix, Mescalero und die Folgen*, edited by Dieter Hoffmann-Axthelm et al., 92–93. Berlin: Ästhetik & Kommunikation, 1978. *Bohemien—Tramp—Sponti: Boheme und Alternativkultur*, edited by Gerd Stein, 296–303. Frankfurt am Main: Fischer, 1982. Johannes Schütte, *Revolte und Verweigerung: Zur Politik und Sozialpsychologie der Sponti-Bewegung*, appendix, pp. xxiv–xxvi. Gießen: Focus, 1980 (text only).

Trotta, Margarete von. *Die Bleierne Zeit.* Munich: Filmverlag der Autoren, 1981. Released with English subtitles as *Marianne and Juliane.*

"Unheimlich klammheimlich: Das erste Interview mit dem Verantwortlichen und dem Autor des Buback-Nachrufs." *Konkret* 3 (1978): 12–16.

Wagner, Bernd. "Kulturpolitik und Politik des Kulturellen." In *Öko-Kunst? Zur Ästhetik der Grünen*, edited by Jost Hermand and Hubert Müller, 37–54. Hamburg: Argument, 1989.

———. "Von der Parteien Gunst getragen: Stichworte zur kulturpolitischen Situation." Reprint in *Dem Struwelpeter durch die Haare gefahren: Auf dem Weg zu einer grünen Kulturpolitik*, edited by Die Grünen, 8–30. Bonn: Die Grünen, 1987.

————. "Zwischen Klassenkampf und Lebensphilosophie: Zur Kulturdiskussion bei den Grünen." *Umbruch: Zeitschrift für Kultur* 4 (1985): 38–44. Reprint in *Dem Struwelpeter durch die Haare gefarhen: Auf dem Weg zu einer grünen Kulturpolitik*, edited by Die Grünen, 67–71. Bonn: Die Grünen, 1987.

Wählt Liste 8. Platform flier of the Bewegung Undogmatischer Frühling, Göttingen. Reprint in Johannes Schütte, *Revolte und Verweigerung: Zur Politik und Sozialpsychologie der Sponti-Bewegung*, Appendixes 4–9. Gießen: Focus, 1980.

Waldhubel, Thomas. "Sponti-Bewegung: Flucht in den Alltag?" *Das Argument* 113 (1979): 8–20.

Wannöffel, Manfred. "Auf politischem Gebiet kriegen Sie keine guten Antworten von mir: Aspekte zur politischen Sozialisation von Jugendlichen in den 50er Jahren." In *Die Elvis-Tolle, die hatte ich mir unauffällig wachsen lassen: Lebensgeschichten und jugendliche Alltagskultur in den fünfziger Jahren*, edited by Heinz-Hermann Krüger, 20–42. Leverkusen: Leske & Budrich, 1985.

Wasmund, Klaus. "Leitbilder und Aktionsformen Jugendlicher nach dem Zweiten Weltkrieg bis zu den 60er Jahren." In *Jugendprotest und Generationskonflikt in Europa im 20. Jahrhundert*, edited by Dieter Dove, 215–24. Bonn: Neue Gesellschaft, 1986.

Wasmuth, Ulrike C., ed. *Alternativen zur alten Politik? Neue soziale Bewegungen in der Diskussion*. Darmstadt: Wissenschaftliche Buchgesellschaft, 1989.

Watts, Meredith W., et al., eds. *Contemporary German Youth and Their Elders*. New York: Greenwood, 1989.

Wedekind, Frank. "Spring Awakening: A Children's Tragedy." In *Plays*, vol. 1, translated by Edward Bond and Elisabeth Bond-Pablé. London: Methuen, 1993.

Weinberger, Marie-Luise. *Aufbruch zu neuen Ufern: Grün-Alternative zwischen Anspruch und Wirklichkeit*. Bonn: Neue Gesellschaft, 1984.

Weiss, Peter. *Discourse on the Progress of the Prolonged War of Liberation in Viet Nam and the Events Leading Up to It As Illustration for the Necessity for Armed Resistance against Oppression and on the Attempts of the United States of America to Destroy the Foundations of Revolution*. Translated by Geoffrey Skelton. In *Two Plays by Peter Weiss*, 65–230. New York: Atheneum, 1970.

Weißler, Sabine. "Grüne Selbstverständlichkeiten: Zum Problem grün-alternativer Kulturprogramme." In *Dem Struwelpeter durch die Haare gefahren:*

Auf dem Weg zu einer grünen Kulturpolitik, edited by Die Grünen, 56–57. Bonn: Die Grünen, 1987.

Wellershoff, Dieter. "Puritaner, Konsumenten und die Kritik." *Die Zeit* 1 (3 Jan. 1969): 9–11.

Wensierski, Hans-Jürgen von. "Die Anderen nannten uns Halbstarke: Jugendsubkultur in den 50er Jahren." In *Die Elvis-Tolle, die hatte ich mir unauffällig wachsen lassen: Lebensgeschichten und jugendliche Alltagskultur in den fünfziger Jahren,* edited by Heinz-Hermann Krüger, 103–28. Leverkusen: Leske & Budrich, 1985.

Williams, Raymond. *The Sociology of Culture.* New York: Schocken, 1981.

Winter, Hans-Gerhard. "Von der Dokumentarliteratur zur 'neuen Subjektivität': Anmerkungen zur westdeutschen Literatur der siebziger Jahre." *Seminar: A Journal of Germanic Studies* 17 (1981): 95–113.

Wirsing, Sibylle. "Die Tragödie als Luxusartikel." *Frankfurter Allgemeine Zeitung* 28 Mar. 1979: 21.

Wolff, Frank. "Kultursterben: Bericht über den 1. Grün-Alternativen Bundeskongreß zur Kulturpolitik in Hamburg." *Pflasterstrand* 177 (1984): 54–56.

Wolf, Friedrich. "Cyankali." In *Das dramatische Werk* 2:169–345. Berlin: Aufbau, 1988.

Zahl, Peter Paul. *Die Glücklichen: Schelmenroman.* Berlin: Rotbuch, 1979.

Ziehe, Thomas. *Pubertät und Narzißmus: Sind Jugendliche entpolitisiert?* 4th ed. Frankfurt am Main: Europäische Verlagsanstalt, 1981.

Zimmer, Dieter E. "Die große Liquidierung." *Die Zeit* 49 (6 Dec. 1968): 18.

———. "Wo sind sie geblieben?" *Die Zeit* 24–26 (3–24 June 1977).

Zimmermann, Hans Dieter. "Die mangelhafte Subjektivität." In *Lyrik-Katalog Bundesrepublik: Gedichte: Biographien: Statements,* 2d ed., edited by Jan Hans et al., 468–78. Munich: Goldmann, 1979.

Zimmermann, Jörg. "Zur Geschichte des ästhetischen Naturbegriffs." In *Das Naturbild des Menschen,* edited by Jörg Zimmermann, 118–54. Munich: Fink, 1982.

Zorn, Fritz. *Mars.* Munich: Kindler, 1977.

INDEX

Index

Bruder-Bezzel, Almuth, 86
Bruttosozialprodukt, 9–11
Buback, Siegfried, 92
Buback Obituary, 6, 74, 92, 96–103, 133, 148; language of, 100, 149; public reception of, 96–97, 102–3; and violence, 98, 107
Büchner, Georg, 83
Bürgerinitiativen, 106
Büscher, Barbara, 49

Camus, Albert, 27
capitalism, 84–85, 114–15, 148
carnival, 145, 155–56
Carter, Jimmy, 10
Center for Contemporary Cultural Studies, 3, 216
circus, 145, 155, 157–59, 166, 171
citizens' initiatives, 106
civil disobedience, 107
class: and alternative culture, 69, 117–18, 150, 155–57, 210, 216; and *Faz*, 140; and Greens, 198, 204–5, 208; and New Subjectivity, 78–79; and student movement, 32–33, 67, 82–83, 174; and Tunix, 117–18; well-adjusted middle, 13, 15–16, 21, 23–24, 26–27, 29; working, 21, 23–24, 27, 117, 168
Clemenz, Manfred, 149
clown, 145, 159–60, 171–72; history of, 163; and *taz*, 160–61
Cohn-Bendit, Daniel, 37, 138
commodification/commercialization, 50–51, 58, 139–40, 155–56
consciousness industry, 51, 59, 154
Cornel, Hajo, 206
counterculture: definition of, 2–4; function of, 212–13, 217; influence, 217
Courage, 110
cultural politics, 144–48, 187
cultural revolution, 31, 43–49; and Adorno, 51; Chinese, 43–44; and Greens, 187
culture: definition of 2–5; from above/below, 150–53, 166; and Adenauer and Erhard agendas, 16, 18; bourgeois, 32, 39, 42–43,

49, 68, 89; CDU/CSU on, 201; Coca-Cola-Karajan, 153–55, 164–65, 199; commercialization of, 155-56; do-it-yourself/participatory, 8, 164–65, 178, 181, 198–99, 206, 211; Germanic (*völkisch*), 135, 164; high/low, 16, 51–52, 136, 139, 142–43, 154–57, 199, 204; neighborhood, 150–53; official, 150–53; of the people, 145, 153, 175–76; and politics in GDR, 15; second, 105, 129, 198
culture, alternative: definition of, 2–7; and community, 115–16, 118, 164, 211; dress code of, 212; ghettoization of, 69, 216; influence of, 215, 217; and irony, 116, 118, 213; periodization of, 128, 216; projects of, 68, 107–9, 118, 128, 150; self-perception of, 112, 150, 161; and SPD, 116; and student movement, 115–16, 118–19, 143, 148, 172–73, 177, 209–11, 215, 217; subgroups of, 108
culture industry: and alternative culture, 144, 156, 176–77, 210; and criticism, 135; and Greens, 199, 206; and literature, 62; and rock music, 167, 180–81; and student movement, 51–54, 57

Daum, Thomas, 107
de Gaulle, Charles, 45
democracy: grass-roots, 106, 107, 184–85; participatory, 106, 164, 185; representative, 14, 106, 164
desublimation, repressive, 40, 214–16
Deutscher Herbst, 120–21
Deutschland im Herbst, 72–73
Dialectic of Enlightenment, 50, 189–90
difference, 138–39, 166
dissent and style, 20–22
diversity: and alternative culture, 116, 142, 145–46, 215; and Greens, 198, 203, 206; and *taz*, 127
domination: structures of, 69, 76, 192, 204–5
Dröge, Franz, 100–103
Dutschke, Rudi, 47, 138

Index